Outcomes of Open Adopt

"This book helps to fill some gaps in research about the longer-term outcomes of children adopted from out-of-home care. It brings together the findings from a constructive jigsaw of research methods, based on what was possible to obtain for adoptive parents and the children from case file records, an online survey, and interviews with both the adoptees and adoptive parents. Its particular value is in the follow-up, on average 18 years, after the adoption, and the focus on permanence, belonging and the adoptees' contact and relationships with members of their birth family. It provides some important insights about the value and challenges of open adoption."
—Dr Judy Cashmore, Professor of Socio-Legal Research and Policy, *University of Sydney, Australia*

"Adoption has come to represent the best of what we do in establishing a family for life for a child who may not otherwise have had one. And in some respects, it represents the worst of what we do in severing a child from their family of origin. Adoption creates both a fundamental sense of hope for the future but can also create a profound sense of uncertainty, loss and grief. The reality and detail of these issues as they work out over time is set out in an inspiring and detailed way. We need to explore, reflect and learn from all that it tells us."
—Dr John Simmonds OBE, Director of Policy, Research and Development, *CoramBAAF, United Kingdom*

"The book is an important read for social work practitioners, therapists, child and family court judiciary and legal professionals, academics and students, specifically those interested or working in the areas of adoption, foster care, identity, child attachment and relationships and resilience, intervention and support following adversity. Although set within the context of the adoption policy in New South Wales it has international relevance. The book will no doubt be of importance for many years – potentially decades – due to the global importance and enduring nature of the topic."
—Julie Young, Research Fellow, *University of East Anglia, United Kingdom*

Harriet Ward • Lynne Moggach
Susan Tregeagle • Helen Trivedi

Outcomes of Open Adoption from Care

An Australian Contribution to an International Debate

palgrave
macmillan

Harriet Ward
The Rees Centre, Department of Education
University of Oxford
Oxford, UK

Susan Tregeagle
Barnardos Australia
Sydney, NSW, Australia

Lynne Moggach
Barnardos Australia
Sydney, NSW, Australia

Helen Trivedi
The Rees Centre, Department of Education
University of Oxford
Oxford, UK

ISBN 978-3-030-76431-9   ISBN 978-3-030-76429-6   (eBook)
https://doi.org/10.1007/978-3-030-76429-6

This Palgrave Macmillan imprint is published by the registered company Springer Nature Switzerland AG.
The registered company address is: Gewerbestrasse 11, 6330 Cham, Switzerland

Foreword

The story told in this book is set in Australia, but, like what happens when people's names are made anonymous, to some extent the story could refer to country X, meaning that the name matters little and that it could have happened almost anywhere. The story of birth parents overburdened with grievous problems and with neglectful or abusive behaviour towards their children; the need to remove children from these families to protect them from further adversity; the negative consequences of these experiences on all aspects of child development; the risks while in the care system, including placement instability; the children's feelings of loss and confusion; the long waiting times before decisions to ensure permanence are made; the search for new protective, committed and caring parents; the post-placement joys and difficulties for all concerned, are all familiar circumstances for those working in child protection in Australia and everywhere else.

However, the story told in the book has many singular aspects that in many ways could not have happened elsewhere. The singularity stems from the fact that the study reported herein occurs in places in Australia where all adoptions, by mandate of the law, have to be open, requiring regular face-to-face post-adoption contact between children and birth parents. The core of the book is the study carried out in the context of the Barnardos Find-a-Family programme with the aim of introducing empirical evidence into the nature and consequences of this legally mandated open adoption policy. If the initial characteristics of birth parents, children and adoptive parents in the Barnardos' sample are like those in many other places, it is the inclusion of the open adoption arrangements and their impact on all those concerned that makes the study singular.

The book is also singular for several other reasons. The authors make an effort to go beyond easy generalisations and simple analyses, as shown, for example, in the differentiation between different levels of adversity, vulnerability and needs in the studied sample. The same applies to diversity in the characteristics, motivations and resources of the adoptive parents. Another illustration is the fine-grained analysis of the relatively low number of adoptions that did not go well, some disrupted, some unstable or interrupted, with most children, nevertheless, keeping contact with and receiving support from the adoptive parents. Similarly, the authors consider the diversity of initial arrangements for open adoption and changes over time, with some contacts proving uncomplicated, while others were more troubled, the perspectives of birth parents, adopted children and adoptive parents being considered.

The book describes several journeys. There is a historical journey from past adoption policies and practices based on severed ties and secrecy to the current policies and practices of open adoption, a prerequisite of adoption orders in the unique legislation and practice in New South Wales and the Australian Capital Territory. This policy is reflected in the Barnardos programme's core principles of transparency, communicative openness and post-adoption contact with birth family members. Part of this historical journey is the radical change in the profile of contemporary adoptions, which do not involve babies who should have remained with their parents being voluntarily or forcibly relinquished because of social pressures or ill-conceived practices. Adoption now involves children of many different ages separated from their birth families after experiences of cumulative adversity, attempts to keep them in or restore them to their families, placement in alternative families and, finally, a Court order for adoption. The characteristics of these children when placed in new families and their subsequent development, described in detail in the book, can only be understood in the context of their severe initial adversity. These historical changes have not been limited to the adoptees. Children with early experiences of polyvictimisation and complex characteristics at placement could only have been adopted and become part of a new permanent family as a result of parallel changes in the motivations and capacities of adopters willing to sustain a permanent commitment to parenting them, at times in the midst of serious difficulties. There have also been historical changes in professional practices of preparation and continued post-placement support received from the adoption agencies.

Connecting all the chapters is the journey of the children from their early adversities to their adaptation later in life, with a follow-up spanning up to more than 30 years in some cases. Also described is the journey of the adoptive parents and their response to the needs of adoptees both during and after living together, even in those cases where the adoption did not go as well as expected. Being guided by the authors on this journey from start to finish is a fully rewarding reading experience.

There is also the journey into the open adoption model. As one adoptee interviewed for this study said, there are things that "look very good on paper". The book gives an insight into how open adoption works in practice: the barriers and facilitators of contacts, the difficulties of organising face-to-face meetings, the ambivalence and stress often associated with visits, the sometimes satisfying and sometimes painful experiences linked to contacts, the benefits and drawbacks of a way of practising adoption that is likely to expand in the future in many countries. Here are three of the many lessons on open adoption that readers will enjoy going into detail throughout the book: first, contacts are often difficult, but ultimately beneficial for most children, with favourable consequences in many respects, some of them less expected than others; second, the importance of tailoring the type and frequency of contacts to each child's needs; and third, the idea that open adoption is less about contact and more about relationships. This book will undoubtedly become a key reference in adoption research, as well as in the study and practice of open adoption.

Another value of the book to be highlighted is the authors' knowledge of contemporary adoption and child protection research. Their efforts to compare the results of the Barnardos' sample with those of other research in Australia and elsewhere, as well as with studies on Australian care leavers and the general population, are to be commended. These comparisons help to understand more accurately the progress and limitations of the sample studied. To this in-depth knowledge of contemporary adoption research, I would like to add the merit of a study that involves both quantitative and qualitative methods with survey, questionnaires and interviews skilfully used. Something that the reader will particularly appreciate is a presentation of the contents that follows the sequence that allows a better understanding of the results, as a simple glance at the table of contents confirms.

In the first lines of this book the authors acknowledge that adoption engenders strong feelings. This book provides some very relevant data that allow these feelings to be modulated. Its content proves that when undertaken within a rights and ethics framework that emphasises children's best interests, adoption responds to the complex long-term needs of those who started their life in circumstances of extreme initial adversity and with no possibility of returning safely to their birth or extended family. In this book, readers in Australia and country X will understand why, with what consequences and through what contemporary well-informed practices all this is possible.

University of Seville, Spain   Jesús Palacios

Acknowledgements

This book is based on the findings of a research study, funded by Barnardos Australia, that was designed to explore the outcomes of their programme of open adoption from out-of-home care. We are grateful to Louise Voigt (CEO, 1983–2015) and Deirdre Cheers (CEO from 2015) for finding funding for the project, for facilitating access to research participants and to data held on administrative systems, and for enabling the research to proceed without interference. The views expressed in this report are the authors' and not necessarily those of Barnardos.

The project greatly benefited from the wise counsel and expertise of our advisory group: Marc de Rosnay (Chair, University of Wollongong), Deirdre Cheers (Barnardos), Amy Conley Wright (University of Sydney), Melissa Kaltner (Family and Community Services, New South Wales), Lisa Vihtonen (Barnardos) and Fran Waugh (University of Sydney and Barnardos). We are grateful for the time they generously gave to this project.

We are particularly grateful for the advice and support of Julie Selwyn, Professor of Education and Adoption at the Rees Centre, University of Oxford, who acted as a consultant to the project and commented on early drafts of the manuscript, and Judy Cashmore, Professor of Socio-Legal Research and Policy at the University of Sydney, who produced a detailed academic review of the report of the project on which this book is based. We would like to thank them for the time and effort they put into this work.

The authors also wish to acknowledge the enormous contribution of Research Assistant Bethany Wilkinson, who undertook many of the interviews and managed the administration of the research. We acknowledge the contribution of social work students from Sydney, Newcastle and Boston Universities and social workers, Lizzie Blue, Dhamika Morrissey and Amanda Carter (who also assisted with the completion of questionnaires), for social media assistance and data collection.

We would also like to thank Dr Robert Urquhart for his assistance in finalising the production of the manuscript.

Most of all, we wish to acknowledge the generosity, honesty and openness of the many adoptees and adoptive parents who participated in this research. Without them, none of this would have been possible. Thank you.

Executive Summary

A full executive summary of the research report on which this book is based, including all key findings, is available from Barnardos Australia and can be downloaded at barnardos.org.au

Contents

List of Figures

List of Tables

1

Introduction: International Issues and Debates Concerning Adoption

Introduction

Adoption entails the permanent transfer of legal rights and responsibilities for a child from birth parents to adoptive parents. Inevitably, such a procedure can be controversial, for adoption has a profound and permanent impact on the lives of all the parties involved—the child, the birth parents and the adoptive parents, as well as grandparents, siblings and other relations on both sides. It also raises numerous ethical and philosophical questions concerning the appropriate role of the state within the family; the balance between parents' and children's rights; and the circumstances under which the blood tie can, or cannot, be broken.

However much an adoption may be in the best interests of a child, it will also entail feelings of grief: for birth parents, who mourn the loss of a child; for children who may lose contact not only with birth parents, but also with siblings and grandparents who were important to them; and sometimes for adoptive parents, especially if it reignites unresolved emotions concerning infertility (Neil, 2013; Thomas, 2013). It is therefore not surprising that the adoption debate engenders strong feelings

© The Author(s) 2022
H. Ward et al., *Outcomes of Open Adoption from Care*,
https://doi.org/10.1007/978-3-030-76429-6_1

and these can be exacerbated by media campaigns from individuals and pressure groups, supporting one or other side of the adoption triangle (see Albert, 2016; P., 2016).

Moreover, a series of scandals inform and colour the debate. There is no doubt that in many countries, adoption has been used to perpetrate gross and systematic injustices. In Spain in the 1940s (Richards, 2005) and Argentina in the 1970s (Lazzara, 2013), thousands of infants were removed from dissenting birth mothers and placed for adoption with loyalists as a means of punishing and quashing opposition to the regime. Adoption has also been used as a means of eradicating a culture or race that is perceived as alien: policies designed to eliminate Aboriginal culture in Australia through the forcible removal and adoption of the Stolen Generations have been widely publicised (Human Rights and Equal Opportunities Commission, 1997). In Switzerland, over a similar period, several hundred Yenish children were removed for a similar reason (Meier, 2008), and during the Second World War, thousands of Polish children were also separated from birth parents and placed for adoption with Aryan families for this purpose (Nicholas, 2005).

Adoption has also been used as a means of enforcing conformity to a social norm. Until the end of the twentieth century, in many countries, illegitimate children and their mothers were deliberately stigmatised, both by the law and by social conventions that ostracised those who engaged in extra-marital sexual relations and thereby undermined the sanctity of holy matrimony, for marriage was seen as essential to the stability of the family and, by extension, to the wider society. It was difficult for a single mother to earn enough to keep her child, or to live on state benefits if they were available, and many of those who had insufficient support from their wider families voluntarily relinquished their babies for adoption. Adoption was seen as a means of both enabling young women to dissociate themselves from an unfortunate past, of providing homes for infants who might otherwise have been destitute and of providing childless couples with a family—a solution to the problems of both illegitimacy and infertility in which all parties were thought to have gained (Keating, 2009). Had these infants remained with their birth parents, many of them would have lived lives blighted by poverty and stigma and some would have died (Hopkirk, 1949; Pinchbeck & Hewitt, 1973). There is also evidence that many of these adoptees grew up in loving families and achieved 'satisfactory wellbeing in adulthood' (Collinshaw et al., 1998; Maughan & Pickles, 1990). However, although many infants were voluntarily relinquished, subsequent enquiries have shown that some young women were coerced into giving up their babies against their wishes. Some mothers were tricked into believing the baby had died, or signed adoption papers without understanding the implications, and information about financial support that might have been available was systematically withheld. Inquiries undertaken in Australia (Kenny et al., 2012) and Ireland (Milotte, 2012) showed these 'forced adoptions' to have been systematic and widespread.

One of the defining features of adoption has been the secrecy with which it was surrounded. Babies placed for adoption in much of the twentieth century were given a new birth certificate and a new identity and records giving details of their birth families were sealed. The aim was to provide a new start in life, both for the child and for the birth mother, and the expectation was that they would have no further contact (Keating, 2009). The traumatic consequences of such policies for both birth parents and children have become increasingly apparent (Kenny et al., 2012; Triseliotis, 1973), and adoption has since become more transparent. Nevertheless, this tradition of secrecy may have provided a useful cover for implementing many of the policies and practices, discussed above, that contravene human rights and disregard ethical norms.

These issues are not confined to the past. Very similar concerns about widespread coercion, disregard for human rights, exploitation of parents and children and lack of transparency were raised over intercountry adoption practices in the late twentieth century and led to the development of the Hague Convention on Protection of Children and Cooperation in Respect of Intercountry Adoption in 1993. The Hague Convention is designed to 'protect children and their families against the risks of illegal, irregular, premature or ill-prepared adoptions abroad'. It specifies minimum standards both for countries of origin and for receiving countries. These are intended to 'ensure that intercountry adoptions take place in the best interest of the child and with respect for the child's fundamental rights', to protect birth families from undue pressure, to protect children from abduction, sale and trafficking, and to ensure that prospective adopters are eligible, suitable and adequately prepared. Although the child's rights are paramount, the Convention also 'respects and protects the rights of birth families and adoptive families' (HCCH, 2017; Phillips, 2013). At the time of writing, 103 countries have ratified the convention or have acceded to it. Nevertheless, although many thousands of children have clearly benefitted from international adoption (Baxter et al., 2015; Rutter et al., 2007; Sonuga-Barke et al., 2017), concerns about unethical and illegal practices, as well as substantial risks of child exploitation, persist (Goodno, 2015; Phillips, 2013).

The blatant injustices of past practices, together with evidence concerning the long-term impact of the lies, coercion and secrecy which have surrounded the families involved, as well as ongoing concerns about unethical and illegal practices, have created a context which sometimes makes it difficult to consider whether adoption might be appropriate for some children, if practised differently and in other circumstances. However, the public discourse on adoption sometimes overlooks the issue of child maltreatment (Ward & Brown, 2016). Evidence from empirical research (e.g. Brown et al., 2016; Davies & Ward, 2012; Radford et al., 2011) and official enquiries (e.g. Brandon et al., 2020; Lock, 2013; US Department of Health and Human Services, 2019) shows that some parents reject their children and others abuse and neglect them, and that family support and social work interventions are not always sufficient to ensure the safety of children within their homes. Where children cannot safely remain or be reunited with birth family members, there is a strong case to be made for adoption providing:

> a legitimate model for the alternative care of children, if undertaken within a rights and ethics framework that emphasises children's best interests, as set out in international conventions and national laws. (Palacios et al., 2019, pp.1–2)

This book focuses on domestic adoption within such a rights and ethics framework. Its purpose is to introduce more empirical evidence into what has become a highly emotive debate. The evidence we present enables us to explore the value of open adoption, as practised in Australia, as a route to permanence for abused and neglected children in out-of-home care who cannot safely return to their birth families. It sheds light on the question of whether adoption provides a better chance of permanence and more positive outcomes than long-term foster care for children whose previous experiences have been marked by extensive adversity. It also helps us to explore whether open adoption, entailing continuing regular face-to-face contact with birth family members, mandated by the courts as part of a legally enforceable adoption plan agreed by all parties, can avoid some of the detrimental consequences of past policies in which adoption was shrouded in secrecy and children frequently grew up with a conflicted sense of identity.

Domestic Adoptions from Care

For much of the twentieth century, in many Western societies, domestic adoption was primarily seen as a means of providing homes for the infants of single mothers who voluntarily relinquished them. However, improved contraception, greater access to abortion, de-stigmatisation of illegitimacy and improved financial and social support for single mothers, together with greater understanding of the adverse consequences of closed adoption, have all combined to reduce the numbers of infants who followed this pathway (Parker, 1999).

Around the time that infant relinquishments began to decline, concerns started to be raised about the failure of out-of-home care to provide abused and neglected children with permanent substitute homes (Parker et al., 1991). It also became apparent that a wider range of children in out-of-home care could be offered family-based, rather than residential, placements (Triseliotis, 1980). Adoption began to be seen as an integral part of the child protection system, with the potential to provide permanence for those children in care who could not return to birth families (Palacios et al., 2019). While infant relinquishments in the twentieth century proceeded, at least in theory, with the full knowledge and consent of birth parents, a high proportion of adoptions from care are made without parental consent. The non-consensual nature of much adoption from care is another reason why this is such a controversial issue.

Nevertheless, at least 50 countries, including all member states of the Council of Europe, the USA and Australia, have provisions for permitting adoption without consent for children who would otherwise be looked after by the state until they reach adulthood. The grounds for dispensing with parental consent include 'the child having formed a stable relationship with authorised carers' (Ross & Cashmore, 2016) and 'abandonment or lack of interest in the child; parental misconduct or deprivation of parental rights; and unjustifiable refusal of consent to adoption when this would be in the child's best interests' (Fenton-Glynn, 2015). While some states use a combination of these grounds for dispensing with parental consent, others will only do so on one of them; moreover, the thresholds for dispensing with consent, the weight given to parental views and involvement in decision-making, and the extent to which alternatives to adoption are preferred, differ between jurisdictions, with the result that a much higher proportion of children are adopted from care in some countries, particularly the UK and the USA, than in others.

It should be noted that adoption is only thought to be an appropriate option for children in out-of-home care for whom a decision has already been made to seek a permanent home away from birth parents or other members of their birth family. These are the children who cannot safely return home and who have no grandparents or other relatives who are able to look after them. They are likely to be few in number; in England, where policies to increase the numbers of adoptions from care have been pursued since the beginning of this century (Department of Health (UK), 2000), and courts exercise their power to dispense with parental consent to a greater extent than most other countries (Fenton-Glynn, 2015), they comprise 13% of all exits from care (Department for Education (UK), 2019). Children placed for adoption from care are also likely to have been seriously abused and/or neglected and their birth parents are unlikely to have been able to protect them from harm, or to change the circumstances which placed them at risk of further abuse within an appropriate timeframe; these are the most common reasons why they cannot go home (Brown et al., 2016; Selwyn, 2017; Ward et al., 2012). They are likely to be older than the infants who were previously relinquished for adoption and they are much more likely to be struggling with the consequences of early experiences of abuse and neglect. The change in the profile of children requiring adoption has significant implications for the recruitment, preparation and training and ongoing support of adoptive parents.

Characteristics and Vulnerabilities of Children Adopted from Care

The characteristics and needs of the population of children placed for adoption, their experiences while living with their birth parents and during the often lengthy period they spend in out-of-home care while decisions are made about their future, are likely to impact on the long-term outcomes of adoption.

Long-Term Consequences of Abuse and Neglect

Research from England shows that, before entry to care, about 71% of adopted children have been abused and/or neglected, about 35% have been actively rejected or abandoned, and about 20% have been sexually abused (Selwyn, 2017); an unknown number of adopted children in the UK have experienced significant neglect in utero, and 25% have foetal alcohol spectrum disorder (Adoption UK, 2020). There is a wealth of evidence indicating that abuse and neglect in early childhood can have long-term adverse consequences across all dimensions of children's development.

Early childhood development can be seen as a process of adapting to an environment in which, for a very young child, the important element is the primary caregiver (usually the birth mother). Abuse and neglect will affect the way in which the child attaches to their primary caregiver as they adapt to a hostile environment. This attachment relationship has an impact on the child's neurobiological, intellectual, emotional and social development in the key areas that form the building blocks for subsequent growth. Abuse and neglect can thus have an adverse impact throughout the life cycle, although not all children are equally affected (see Brown & Ward, 2012; Cicchetti, 2013; McCrory et al., 2010, 2011, 2012).

Adverse Childhood Experiences

Research on adverse childhood experiences (ACEs), which include all forms of abuse and neglect, and their consequences, has found a 'strong dose relationship between the breadth of exposure to abuse or household dysfunction during childhood and multiple risk factors for several of the leading causes of death in adulthood' (Felitti et al., 1998, p. 251). Studies have also shown specific relationships between adverse childhood experiences and illicit drug use (Dube et al., 2003); smoking in adolescence (Anda et al., 1999); suicide (Dube et al., 2001); and premature mortality (Brown et al., 2009). The initial study in this body of research (Felitti et al., 1998) explored the relationship between a range of health risk factors for disease conditions in adulthood and the following seven categories of adverse experiences in childhood:

- physical abuse
- sexual abuse
- psychological (emotional) abuse
- witnessing violence against their mother or stepmother
- exposure to substance misuse
- parental mental illness
- criminal behaviour in the household

When compared with adults who had been exposed to none of these adverse childhood experiences, those who had been exposed to four or more had 4–12 fold increased health risks for alcoholism, drug abuse, depression, and suicide attempt; a 2–4 fold increase in smoking, poor self-rated health, 50 or more sexual partners and sexually transmitted disease; and a 1.4–1.6 fold increase in physical inactivity and severe obesity. (Felitti et al., 1998, p. 245)

The number of categories also showed a graded relationship to several of the leading causes of death in adulthood, such as coronary heart disease, cancer, chronic lung disease, skeletal fractures and liver disease (ibid.). Early ACE studies used a seven-point scale. Later studies include three additional variables—emotional neglect, physical neglect and parental separation—resulting in a ten-point ACEs scale, now commonly used by a wide variety of agencies (see Harvard Center on the Developing Child, 2015).

Children in foster care, or adopted from care, have disproportionately higher ACE scores. In the USA, Turney and Wildeman (2017) found that these children are more likely than other disadvantaged children to have experienced 'parental divorce or separation, parental death, parental incarceration, parental abuse, violence exposure, household member mental illness, and household member substance abuse'.

Children who go on to be adopted are more likely to have been abused and neglected before they are separated from their birth parents than those who remain in care (Selwyn et al., 2014). Some will also have had poor experiences in out-of-home care (Selwyn et al., 2006). They are thus exceptionally vulnerable to adverse outcomes, including poor mental and physical health in adulthood. However, there is considerable evidence that adoption can act as a strong protective factor that strengthens the resilience of previously maltreated children and enables them to follow more normative developmental pathways (Rutter et al., 2007).

Parents' Problems

Adverse childhood experiences that are associated with poor health and wellbeing throughout the life cycle include a number of problems which impair parents' capacity to meet their children's needs and increase the likelihood of maltreatment. Parental alcohol or drug misuse, learning disability, mental ill health and intimate partner violence have been identified as factors likely to increase the risk of maltreatment, particularly when they occur in combination (see Cleaver et al., 2011, for further details). Parents with learning disabilities are able to provide nurturing homes for their children, given appropriate long-term support; however, their capacity to parent can be significantly impaired if there are co-existing problems such as intimate partner violence or substance misuse (Cleaver & Nicholson, 2007). Parents who are struggling with these problems will not necessarily maltreat their children; however, if there are no protective factors, such as a non-abusive partner or a supportive extended family, then abuse and neglect are more likely.

Some abusive or neglectful parents are able to overcome adversities sufficiently to provide adequately nurturing homes within an appropriate timescale; however, others are not (Brown et al., 2016; Hansen, 2012; Ward et al., 2014; Ward, Brown, et al., 2019). In families where children are being harmed, where there are multiple problems that increase the likelihood of continuing abuse, no mitigating protective factors and no evidence of parental capacity to change, there is a strong possibility that children's life chances will be seriously compromised unless they are placed away from home (Brown et al., 2016; Ward et al., 2012). The dilemma then facing the courts and child welfare professionals is at what point they need to seek permanence for a child outside the immediate birth family and how this can be achieved. The preferred option will be to place children with members of their extended family, but where this is not possible then long-term foster care or adoption are the alternatives.

Outcomes of Out-of-Home Care

There are long-standing and justifiable concerns about the outcomes of out-of-home care in many countries (see Fernandez et al., 2016; House of Commons Children Schools and Families Committee, 2009; Stein & Munro, 2008). Evidence of abuse and neglect of children in institutions and in foster care has been an endemic problem in most Western countries and the extent of past maltreatment has only relatively recently come to light (Fernandez et al., 2016; Utting, 1997). Nevertheless, research on the outcomes of care in the late twentieth and early twenty-first century in France (Dumaret & Coppel-Batsch, 1998), Norway (Moe & Slinning, 2001) and the UK (Forrester et al., 2009; Zhang & Selwyn, 2020) and some, though not all, studies from the USA (Horwitz et al., 2001; Taussig et al., 2001; but see also Lawrence et al., 2006, and Lloyd & Barth, 2011) show that placing children in care can have a positive impact on their welfare. Bromfield et al.'s (2005) review of 17 research studies on outcomes for children and young people in care in Australia found that although all the studies showed that their outcomes were less satisfactory than those of their peers:

several studies however noted that not all children in care fare badly and that, for the majority, foster care appears to be a positive experience with large proportions of the children displaying improved psychological adjustment while in care. (Bromfield et al., 2005, p.42)

However, there are continuing systemic problems. These include a lack of stability exemplified by frequent changes of placement and school; low aspirations associated with insufficient attention to education and the acquisition of skills; lack of therapeutic support to overcome the consequences of past adversities; and insufficient integration into a substitute family, leading to a lack of emotional security (Rahilly & Hendry, 2014).

Of particular concern is the lack of support given to care leavers as they make what are often 'compressed and accelerated transitions' from care to independence in early adulthood, frequently at a much younger age than their peers in the community (Cashmore & Paxman, 1996, 2007; Stein, 2004; Stein & Munro, 2008). A very high proportion of children and young people in out-of-home care have complex needs (Tarren-Sweeney & Hazell, 2006; Ward & Holmes, 2008). These are the young people who are the least equipped to cope with premature independence and the least likely to receive adequate support either to address their needs in care or to help them make a successful transition to adulthood on leaving (Munro et al., 2012). Their experiences are likely to underlie the poor developmental outcomes of care that show too many care leavers struggling with insufficient qualifications, unemployment, mental health problems and social exclusion: these remain a continuing cause of concern (Rahilly & Hendry, 2014; Stein & Munro, 2008).

Outcomes of Adoption from Care Versus Long-Term Foster Care

Stability

Research on children in out-of-home care in several Western societies shows that placement instability is a common issue (Rock et al., 2015). A study of the placements of 242 long-stay children in the English care system found that many children move placements frequently through-out their care careers:

> More than half (52%) of the placements made in the first twelve months of the children's care episodes lasted for six months or less, with a median of four months. In the second year, however, a similar pattern emerged, with 56% of new placements lasting for six months or less, and a median of three months. It was not until the third year after entry to care that there was some evidence of increased permanence, but even then 42% of place-ments made during this period lasted for six months or less, and the median had only increased to seven months. (Ward, 2009, p. 1115)

Some Australian studies have found that most children in care find stable and secure placements within 12 months of entry (Barber & Delfabbro, 2003; Tarren-Sweeney & Hazell, 2006), while others experi-ence ongoing and severe placement disruptions. Osborn and Delfabbro's (2006) study of children with high support needs in the Australian care system (about 15–20% of the care population) found that, on average, they had experienced 10.53 placements (sd = 7.80) during their time in care and 4.95 disruptions, and that there was a strong relationship between early trauma and abuse and subsequent placement instability.

As we have seen, children adopted from care are the group most likely to have experienced early trauma and abuse, and their care experiences are likely to have been comparable to those in the Osborn and Delfabbro (2006) study discussed above. There are no Australian studies of long-term disruption rates or premature homelessness post-adoption. However, Selwyn et al.'s (2014) seminal study of adoption disruptions in England found that, over a 12-year period, administrative data indicated that 3.2% placements disrupted (i.e. a legally adopted child left the home before their 18th birthday). Responses to a survey produced a higher figure, although this could have been biased towards completion by those who had had less positive experiences; in the authors' view: 'it is probably safe to conclude that the proportions of adoptions that disrupt post-order lies between 2% – 9%' (ibid., p. 275). This is markedly lower than the rate of foster home breakdowns found by Osborn and Delfabbro (2006) in Australia and also by Ward (2009) who found that in England and

Wales, 21% of foster placements end at the request of the carer and a further 8% at the request of the child. However, it should be noted that age at placement is closely related to disruption and this may account for some of the difference, as adopted children tend to be placed in 'permanent' homes at a younger age than those in foster care (Biehal et al., 2010). Moreover, self-reports from adoptees suggest that disruption statistics mask an underlying unhappiness for some children in placements that do persist (Thoburn, 2002), and about one in four adoptive parents describe major challenges and inadequate support in caring for a child with multiple and overlapping difficulties (Selwyn et al., 2014).

'Belonging' and the Transition to Adulthood

Some children in care are placed with long-term foster carers who are highly responsive to their needs and regard them as permanent members of their families; however, such placements are relatively rare, at least in the UK and Australia (Cashmore & Paxman, 1996, 2006; Skuse & Ward, 2003). For instance, Cashmore and Paxman's (2007) longitudinal study of Australian care leavers found that four to five years after formally leaving care at age 18, less than a third (29%) of their sample had regular and frequent contact with former foster carers, and only three were still living with them. Less than one in three (29%) had a positive sense of 'felt security', a 'sense of being loved and belonging and having their needs met while they were in care' (Cashmore & Paxman, 2006, p. 235).

Adoption from care has been found to provide greater stability, better integration into a substitute family and therefore greater 'felt security' than long-term foster care (Biehal et al., 2010; Thomas, 2013). In the UK, Triseliotis (2002) found that adoption gave children higher levels of emotional security, sense of belonging and wellbeing than those growing up in long-term foster care. A more recent research study of Australian adoptees found that:

> ...while it is clear that early adoption engenders a deep sense of belonging and acceptance, which contributes profoundly to healthy identity forma-

tion, it is not clear that long-term fostering reliably engenders these same feelings. (de Rosnay et al., 2015, p.2)

Adoption involves the 'permanent transfer of parental legal rights and responsibilities from the child's birth parent(s) to adoptive parent(s)', and most adoptive parents regard their children as not only legally but also psychologically theirs. This changed relationship means that most adoptive parents, like most birth parents, assume that they will continue to support their child until they are fully independent and, indeed, throughout their lives. There is little research on this issue. However, Selwyn et al. (2014) found that even when the placement had disrupted, the majority of adoptive parents continued to have a relationship with their child, and only 6 (17%) of 35 were estranged. It is this life-long commitment that distinguishes adoption from foster care, for in these circumstances, children are more likely to feel an enhanced sense of belonging.

Developmental Outcomes

It is difficult to compare the adult outcomes of children who have grown up in long-term foster care with those who have been adopted from care, because there are different thresholds for decisions concerning adoption, because adoptees are likely to have had different early life experiences from those who remain in care, and because much of the research focuses on adults who were placed as intercountry adoptees after spending time in institutional care as infants and toddlers. Nevertheless, there are indications from research undertaken in the USA and Sweden that children adopted from care do better academically than those who remain in foster homes (Barth & Lloyd, 2010; Vinnerljung & Hjern, 2011) and that they are also better able to support themselves as young adults (Vinnerljung & Hjern, 2011).

There is, however, evidence that children adopted from care show similar levels of emotional and behavioural difficulties to those experienced by children in foster care (Biehal et al., 2010). Although adopted children appear to access more support than other children (Keyes et al., 2008), there is, nevertheless, evidence that significant difficulties, including child to parent violence, may emerge during adolescence (Selwyn et al., 2014). Research on adoption disruptions in the UK (Selwyn et al., 2014) found that many families struggle when the adoptee reaches adolescence or at key transitions (e.g. changing school), indicating a need for long-term post-adoption support.

Transparency

While, on a number of criteria, children placed for adoption tend to experience better outcomes than those who remain in foster care, over the last 30 years or so it has become increasingly apparent that the secrecy that traditionally accompanied adoption was detrimental to children's welfare. Even where there has been little evidence of 'forced' adoptions and systematic malpractice, birth parents have to contend with enduring feelings of grief and loss (Ryburn, 1998); it is also now evident that adopted children have a deep psychological need to feel some connection with their birth families and to understand why they cannot live with them and that policies designed to withhold this information, or to hide unpalatable truths, have been extremely damaging to their construction of a robust sense of self (Triseliotis, 1973). More recent research indicates that although structural openness (mutual sharing of identifying information, plus some degree of contact between the parties) is important, communication openness (open, direct and non-defensive communication about adoption between adoptive parents and children) may be of greater significance to healthy development (Brodzinsky, 2006; de Rosnay et al., 2015). Greater understanding of the information and communication needs of adopted children has led to changes in policy so that adoption is becoming more open in many jurisdictions, including the USA, the UK and Australia.

While adoptees may find it easier to access information about their birth families and legislation may allow for some form of contact, regular face-to-face post-adoption contact between adoptees and birth family members is still relatively rare and remains a contentious issue. While many adoptees may benefit from continuing face-to-face contact, there are concerns that it may re-traumatise children who were previously maltreated, that it will destabilise the placement, or that it will discourage potential adoptive parents from coming forward (Dodgson, 2014; Ryburn, 1998). Research on post-adoption contact in England (Neil et al., 2015), Northern Ireland (MacDonald & McLoughlin, 2016), the USA (Grotevant et al., 2019) and Australia (de Rosnay et al., 2015) suggests that many of these fears are unfounded and that face-to-face contact can benefit all parties. De Rosnay et al.'s (2015) small study of mandatory face-to-face contact in Australia concluded that post-adoption contact is critical for identity formation; that adoptive parents play a key role in promoting and facilitating it; and that post-adoption contact stimulates communicative openness. However, it should not threaten children's sense of safety and security within their adoptive family. On the other hand, Neil et al. (2015) found that direct contact can also be disappointing and that it is not necessarily more advantageous than indirect 'letterbox' contact. However, they also found that indirect 'letterbox' contact can be marred by misunderstandings and poor communication, especially where adults have inadequate literacy skills. They concluded that all types of contact should be considered on a case-by-case basis and that support should be available to make sure that it is a positive experience for adopted children (Neil et al., 2015). In England and Wales, adoption legislation introduced in 2014 now specifically makes provision for relatives to apply to the courts for post-adoption contact. However, at the time of writing, only 33% of adoptees have at least one direct contact agreement in place (Adoption, 2020), and indirect letterbox contact more frequently remains the option preferred by both practitioners and the courts.

Adoption in Australia

In Australia, domestic adoption has been a particularly contentious issue for about 40 years. A number of blatantly unjust past policies have had an enduring impact on the nature of the debate: these include the reception of approximately 7000 British and Maltese 'orphans' sent as child migrants to Australia between 1912 and 1968, many of them under the pretext of adoption; the forced removal of at least 1 in 10 (and possibly as many as 1 in 3) indigenous children from their birth families and communities between 1910 and 1970; and the 'forced adoptions' of up to 250,000 babies relinquished by single mothers who were often coerced or deceived into doing so between 1950 and 1980. A series of parliamentary inquiries were conducted into these policies in the late twentieth and early twenty-first centuries (Australian Senate Community Affairs Reference Committee, 1999; Australian Senate Community Affairs Reference Committee, 2012; Human Rights and Equal Opportunities Commission, 1997) and resulted in formal national apologies in 2008, 2009 and 2013.

The backlash against these injustices has had two enduring consequences. First, the well-publicised evidence of past wrongs, including the maltreatment of thousands of children, has had a major impact on public perceptions of adoption in Australia, leading to a strong bias against domestic adoptions. Second, the backlash produced a strong adoption reform movement, in which many of those who suffered previous injustices have been heavily involved. Reformers agitated successfully for increased openness in adoption policy and practice. Between 1984 and 1994, changes to adoption legislation:

> removed provisions for secret and sealed adoptions, put in place avenues for adoptees and birth parents to access previously sealed birth and adoption records, and with some variation, moved to make future adoptions more "open" in terms of both information and contact. (Cuthbert et al., 2010, p. 431)

More recent changes have meant that parts of Australia (New South Wales and the Australian Capital Territory) are now unique in requiring regular face-to-face post-adoption contact between children and birth parents, mandated by legislation. However, little is known about the consequences of this policy.

Between 1994 and 2004, the number of domestic adoptions in Australia declined by 79% (Australian Institute of Health and Welfare, 2018). Cuthbert et al. (2010) argue that this was only partly due to negative perceptions of domestic adoption held by both the general public and child welfare professionals. In their view, another factor was adoptive parents' reluctance to embrace open adoption, which entails a continuing relationship between the child and birth family members. Intercountry adoption, which was far more likely to entail a clean break with the past, therefore became the preferred option for those seeking to become adoptive parents; in 2004–2005, 74% of all adoptions in Australia concerned children from other countries (Australian Institute of Health and Welfare, 2005).

However, more recently there has been a drive to increase openness in intercountry adoption, accompanied by significant changes in the profile of children for whom it is considered appropriate and reductions in the numbers available (Cuthbert et al., 2010; Selman, 2009); at the same time, arguments in favour of domestic adoption as one element in a spectrum of child protection services have gained greater traction (Cuthbert et al., 2010; Palacios et al., 2019). In Australia, while domestic adoption remains controversial, there appears to be more acknowledgement of its potential to provide greater stability and permanence for abused and neglected children in out-of-home care who cannot safely return to birth parents, and whose other relatives are not in a position to look after them as kinship carers. In New South Wales, the Child Protection Amendment Act 2014 prioritises adoption over long-term foster care for children who have been placed under the parental responsibility of the Minister, specifying:

> For children who cannot be returned home safely to their parent/s, the first option to be considered is a long-term guardianship arrangement with other family members or suitable persons in kinship or relative care. The next option to be considered is **adoption by non-relatives and other carers**, with parental responsibility to the Minister until a child turns 18 (generally meaning foster care with unknown persons) as the 'last resort'. (Ross & Cashmore, 2016, p. 54, our emphasis)

The Act also introduced provisions designed to speed up the adoption process and to facilitate adoptions by long-term carers (Ross & Cashmore, 2016). As a result, greater use has been made of adoption as a means of offering permanence for Australian children in out-of-home care, particularly in New South Wales. In 2018–2019, 310 children were adopted in Australia, 253 of whom were domestic adoptions. The largest group of domestic adoptions (211) were 'known' adoptions of children by a relative, step-parent or carer. The majority (67%) of 'known' adoptions were of children in out-of-home care who were adopted by their foster carers; almost all of them were from New South Wales (Australian Institute of Health and Welfare, 2019, p.29).

Barnardos Find-a-Family Programme

One of the most vigorous proponents of domestic adoption for children in out-of-home care in Australia has been the child protection charity, Barnardos Australia. Between 1986 and 2020, it has arranged adoptions through its Find-a-Family programme for 440 children in out-of-home care who could not return home, about a quarter of all domestic 'known child' adoptions conducted in New South Wales over the period. In line with Australian policy and specific legislation in New South Wales, all adoptions in the Barnardos programme have been 'open adoptions', with an expectation of face-to-face contact between birth parents and children. The programme has had an influential role in the debate on domestic adoption in Australia over the last 35 years (Australian House of Representatives, 2018). Full information concerning the programme and how it developed can be found in Ward, Moggach, et al., 2019, Chap. 2.

Key Features of the Find-a-Family Programme

Find-a-Family has specialised in the placement of very young and older age children who have been described as 'hard to place' due to their age, challenging behaviours and the size of their sibling group. All children referred have experienced significant abuse and neglect (or have been deemed at high risk of significant harm due to parental factors or in utero damage) and have been made the subjects of final orders from the Children's Court, placing them in out-of-home care until the age of 18 years. Many have experienced multiple placements in out-of-home care and have challenging behavioural and/or emotional disturbances.

While the programme has not specialised in finding placements for children with disabilities, many of those who enter it have had significant health conditions.

Over the 30 odd years that the programme has been in operation there have, inevitably, been a number of changes. The first 16 children were placed in traditional foster homes at a very young age before Barnardos became an adoption agency in 1985. They were later adopted by their foster carers. Their profile is somewhat different from that of the children who were placed from September 1985 as part of an adoption programme that focused, at least initially, on older 'hard to place' children. In 1991, the programme was expanded in order to provide legal, residential and psychological permanence (Brodzinsky & Livingston Smith, 2019) for a wider age range (children aged from 2 to 12 years), and in 2007, it was extended further to include infants as well. With the increasing focus on younger children from 1991 onwards, the project gradually withdrew its emphasis on primary-school-aged children with emotional or behavioural difficulties.

Open adoption is supported both by New South Wales legislation and by Barnardos' adoption policy, which has included transparency and regular post-adoption contact as core principles since its inception. The expectation is that all children placed for adoption will have regular ongoing face-to-face contact with their birth family members after an adoption order is made, with the frequency ranging from 2 to 12 times per year to include all family members. The purpose of contact is to support the child's overall development, by providing an opportunity for maintaining relationships between the parties involved and by facilitating children's knowledge of their birth family in order to strengthen their sense of identity. The adoptive family receive training and support to assist them in facilitating this contact.

Aboriginal and Torres Strait Islander Children

Barnardos does not accept or promote the referral of indigenous children for adoption. The history of Aboriginal children being removed from family, country and culture in Australia has far-reaching consequences for indigenous families and communities today, and the historical legacy and impact of child welfare is such that the lessons learned about culture, identity and belonging are now enshrined in legislation via the Aboriginal Child Placement Principle. The Aboriginal community does not consider adoption as an appropriate plan for their children, and Barnardos' practice and underpinning philosophy has been to refer these children to indigenous foster care agencies so that their cultural identity can be preserved. However, on very rare occasions a child has been identified, after placement, as Aboriginal.

Post-adoption Support

Post-adoption financial support has varied to reflect changes in State Government policy with regard to a post-adoption allowance. Throughout the years that Find-a-Family has been in operation, New South Wales has made some provision for adoptive parents to apply for a post-adoption allowance. The basis for eligibility was substantially increased in 2008, with the result that almost all children with NSW Children's Court orders who have been adopted since then have been eligible for a post-adoption allowance; the financial support available currently stands at a one-off transitional payment of A$3000 plus an annual payment of A$1500 until the child reaches 18 years. Barnardos has not been able to offer separate financial support to adoptive families, but has always offered emotional support, advocacy and referral assistance.

Open Adoption from Care Research Project

With the aim of introducing empirical evidence into the highly emotive debate on adoption, in 2014–2016, Barnardos attempted to trace all 210 children who had entered the Find-a-Family programme and had been made the subject of an adoption order by the Supreme Court between 1 July 1987 and 30 June 2013. These children and their adoptive parents formed the focus of a formal research programme; it was not possible to trace and follow up birth parents within the budget and timeframe. The research project had three objectives: to assess the long-term outcomes of adoption from care and explore what contributed to positive and negative life trajectories; to discover how open adoption had been experienced by both adoptive parents and adoptees; and to find out what the adoptees thought of their experiences. Full information concerning the design of the study and the methodology, the composition of the subsamples, ethical considerations and consents given and the analysis of the quantitative and qualitative data are given in Appendix 1. The following paragraphs are intended to provide the reader with sufficient information to understand how the study was conducted, and the nature of the data we were able to collect concerning the adoptees, their adoptive parents and their birth parents; these data form the basis for our exploration of the relationship between the needs, experiences and outcomes of the Barnardos adoptees discussed in the subsequent chapters.

Methodology

The study was undertaken in three stages:

- **Baseline data on full cohort:** administrative data concerning all 210 adoptees, their birth parents and their adoptive parents were collected from case files and other records presented to the courts at the time the adoption order was made; these baseline data covered demographics, children's early life experiences and their pathways through care.
- **Follow-up survey:** in 2016, attempts were made to trace all of these adoptees and their adoptive parents to invite them to complete an online survey. The survey was sent to 168 adoptees and 107 adoptive parents; 5 adoptees had died, 8 were too young (aged under eight) and 29 could not be traced. Core questions covered issues such as contact, life story work and views on adoption; age-specific questions covered educational progress, employment, relationships and accommodation. Participants were also asked to complete standardised measures including the Australian Child Wellbeing Project survey instruments (2014), the World Health Organisation Abbreviated Quality of Life Questionnaire (WHOQOL-BREF) (1996) (adoptees) and the Child

Behaviour Checklist (Achenbach & Rescorla, 2001) (adoptive parents); however, completion rates for these measures were poor, and there was much missing data. Few data items could be included in the quantitative analysis.

The survey produced responses concerning 93 adoptees: 47 from adoptees and their adoptive parents, 39 from adoptive parents alone and 7 from adoptees alone. These 93 adoptees form the **core follow-up sample.** It included 46 young women and 47 young men; 33 were aged under 18 at the time the survey was completed and 60 were aged 18 and over. In the course of attempting to recruit non-participants, minimal data were also collected on a further 31 adoptees, with the result that some follow-up information is available on 124 of the original cohort of 210 adoptees.

- **Interviews with adoptees and adoptive parents:** 20 adult adoptees and 21 adoptive parents were interviewed up to a year after they had completed the survey. The interviews included 17 dyads (adoptees and their adoptive parents), and three adoptees and four adoptive parents who were not related to each other. All dyads were interviewed separately. Altogether, interviews focused on 24 adoptees, 13 young men and 11 young women, all aged 18 or over: these form the **interview sample.** Interviews were semi-structured and covered issues such as expectations of adoption; relationships within the adoptive family; experiences of face-to-face contact; relationships with birth family members; transparency and communicative openness within the adoptive family and transitions to adulthood.

Potential Bias of Core Follow-Up Sample

The 93 adoptees in the core follow-up sample were compared on a number of key variables with the 117 adoptees for whom there were no follow-up data, in order to ascertain whether there was any significant sample bias. The two groups showed very similar profiles in terms of age, gender, type of abuse and number of adverse childhood experiences before entry to care, and number of placements in out-of-home care before entering their adoptive homes. The only statistically significant difference we found was that the adoptees in the core follow-up sample were, on average, 9.7 months older at the time maltreatment was first notified[1] than the adoptees who did not participate in the follow-up survey or interviews. Length of exposure to abuse and neglect has been identified as having a significant impact on outcomes for children placed away from home (Rousseau et al., 2015). Detailed findings from this analysis of potential bias are presented in Appendix 2.

Strengths and Weaknesses of the Research

This study was commissioned by Barnardos and much of the fieldwork was undertaken by Barnardos personnel or by students placed with them whilst completing their courses. Locating the research within the agency brought the advantage of access to data on the pre-adoption experience, introductions to adoptees and their families and involvement of trusted caseworkers to encourage participation. The close involvement of Barnardos staff is likely to be one reason why the response rate for the core follow-up sample is relatively high by the standards of adoption research, which has frequently encountered difficulties in engaging adoptive families, who may be striving to put the past behind them (Ward et al., 2012). For instance, the response rate from adoptive parents in the current study was 67% compared with 34% for a similar survey undertaken in the UK (Selwyn et al., 2014).

However, involvement of Barnardos staff also raised concerns about a potential conflict of interest and the difficulties the agency would encounter in attempting to avoid subjective interpretations of data. In order to increase objectivity, an academic researcher with no connection to Barnardos was appointed, first to advise the team, and later to lead the project, with support from an expert in the field and guidance from a local independent research advisory group. In addition, survey questionnaires were designed to be completed over time and online, without any face-to-face contact with the agency; these data were anonymised and

---

[1] m = 24.1 months (sd = 36.3) vs m = 14.4 months (sd = 23.6); t = –2.214, df = 145, p = 0.028.

retrieved directly by the university. All data management and quantitative and qualitative analysis were also undertaken externally, without significant involvement from Barnardos.

Theoretical Framework

The theoretical framework we developed to explore the hypothesis that open adoption would offer abused and neglected children in care a better chance of positive outcomes is drawn from a wide body of research on children's developmental trajectories and the factors which facilitate or impede optimal progress. It is based on a simple model of resilience that focuses on 'healthy versus maladaptive pathways of development in lives through time' (Masten, 2001) and identifies the risk factors that increase the likelihood of maladaptive development and the protective factors (or assets) that strengthen children's adaptive systems and shield them from the potential consequences of early adversity as they grow towards adulthood. The basic model is specifically informed by Masten's (2001, 2014) work on resilience, by Rutter et al.'s (2007, 2009) and Sonuga-Barke et al.'s (2017) studies of recovery-to-normal trajectories of development in children who face extensive early adversity and by Felitti et al.'s (1998), Anda et al.'s (1999) and Brown et al.'s (2009) work on adverse childhood experiences (ACEs) and their consequences. Most of the children had spent many years in out-of-home care before being placed for adoption, and the model also encompasses evidence from the Australian and international literature on the extent to which care promotes or inhibits children's healthy developmental pathways.

This basic theoretical framework was extended to reflect research on issues that are specific to the circumstances of children who are adopted from out-of-home care. One of these is the relationship between the child and the adoptive parents. The presence of competent and caring adults features strongly as a positive factor in the literature on resilience, and the growing relationship with the adoptive parents may act as a turning point in the developmental trajectories of many adoptive children. However, open adoption requires children (and adoptive parents) to maintain a relationship with birth parents and other relations as well as developing new relationships within the adoptive family. The literature on attachment has informed the authors' understanding of children's relationships with both birth parents and adoptive parents and the study identifies a need for more research on how adoptive parents become closely attached to their children.

Finally, because of the evidence discussed earlier in this chapter concerning the adverse impact of secrecy on children's wellbeing, and particularly their sense of self, the theoretical framework is also informed by the literature on identity formation. Some elements are drawn from the findings of studies of adopted children, such as Brodzinsky's (2006) work on structural and communicative openness and de Rosnay et al.'s (2015) study of identity formation in Australian adoptees. However, the theoretical framework also draws on research on identity formation in the wider population, such as Chandler et al.'s (2003) and Lalonde's (2006) studies on the significance of a sense of belonging and connectedness to the past in enabling young people to make the transition from adolescence to adulthood.

Conclusion

The remainder of this book makes use of this theoretical framework to explore the antecedents, experiences and life trajectories of the Barnardos adoptees. The data we collected also shed some light on the characteristics and experiences of the children's adoptive parents and birth parents and enabled us to identify factors which contributed to adoptees' positive and negative life trajectories within the context of their position at entry to their adoptive homes. The chapters in Part I focus on the characteristics and experiences of the adoptees, their birth parents and their adoptive parents at the time the children entered their adoptive homes; the chapters in Part II focus on the outcomes of the open adoption programme. The findings bring into sharp focus the extensive vulnerability of abused and neglected children in out-of-home care who cannot safely return to their birth families and for whom adoption offers a route to permanence. Within this context they help us to better understand the advantages and disadvantages of mandatory face-to-face post-adoption contact with birth family members, practised uniquely in New South Wales and the Australian Capital Territory and an evolving element of adoption policy in many other countries. Finally, the findings have numerous implications for the development of adoption policy and practice and for the recruitment and preparation of adoptive parents and the provision of post-adoption support for adoptees and their families.

Key Points

- The permanent transfer of parental rights and responsibilities for a child from birth parents to adoptive parents is a contentious issue, and public perceptions of adoption have been coloured by the discovery of systematic injustices in the past. The purpose of this book is to introduce more empirical evidence on adoption from care into an emotive debate.
- The book argues that there is a place for domestic adoption, practised within an appropriate rights and ethics framework, as an integral part of a child protection system, offering the possibility of permanence to abused and neglected children in out-of-home care who cannot safely return home.
- Children adopted from care are typically older than children adopted through other routes. They are also likely to have suffered significant levels of abuse and neglect and other adverse childhood experiences while living with birth parents and may well have experienced further adversities while in care. The changed profile of the population of adoptees has implications for the recruitment of adoptive parents.
- There is some evidence to indicate that adoption can offer greater stability and a greater sense of commitment and belonging than long-term foster care.
- Adoption also offers better support through the transition from adolescence to adulthood than long-term foster care; as a result, adoptees may be at less risk than care leavers of negative adult outcomes such as unemployment and homelessness.
- Openness in adoption, through communication and contact, can assist with healthy emotional development of children.

- Adoption in Australia has been contentious because of its past history concerning child migrants, forced removal of Aboriginal children and 'forced adoptions' of infants whose mothers were coerced into relinquishing them.
- As a result, there has been a reluctance to place children for adoption, but on the other hand, there has been a strong movement for adoption reform, leading to more openness in adoption policy and practice.
- Since 1985, Barnardos Australia has been finding adoptive homes for children in out-of-home care who cannot return to their birth families. The initial focus was on primary-school-aged children who were considered 'hard to place'; the programme later expanded to include vulnerable younger children. It is not considered appropriate for Aboriginal children, who are referred on to indigenous foster care agencies. All adoption placements have included face-to-face contact between the child and their birth family.
- In 2014–2016, Barnardos attempted to trace all 210 children who had entered the Find-a-Family programme and had been made the subject of an adoption order between 1 July 1987 and 30 June 2013. These children and their adoptive parents formed the focus of a research project.
- The study was undertaken in three stages: an analysis of file data and records presented to the courts of all 210 adoptees, their birth parents and adoptive parents at the time of the adoption order; an online survey sent to those adoptees (168) and adoptive parents (107) who could be traced; interviews with 20 adult adoptees and 21 adoptive parents.
- The following chapters explore the antecedents, experiences and trajectories of the Barnardos adoptees and examine the implications for the development of adoption policy and practice, especially with regard to ongoing face-to-face contact post-adoption.

References

Achenbach, T. M. & Rescorla, L. A. (2001). *Manual for the ASEBA school-age forms and profiles*. University of Vermont, Research Center for Children, Youth, and Families. https://aseba.org/wp-content/uploads/2019/02/schoo-lagecbcl.pdf. Accessed 6 Oct 2020.

Adoption UK. (2020). *Adoption barometer: A stocktake of adoption in the UK*. Adoption UK. https://www.adoptionuk.org/Handlers/Download.ashx? IDMF=c79a0e7d-1899-4b0f-ab96-783b4f678c9a. Accessed 2 Oct 2020.

Albert, E. (2016, November 16). "Les enfants volés d'Angleterre", Un scandale passé sous silence. *Le Monde*. https://www.lemonde.fr/televisions-radio/article/2016/11/15/au-royaume-uni-le-scandale-des-enfants-arraches-a-leur-famille_5031213_1655027.html. Accessed 6 Oct 2020.

Anda, R. F., Croft, J. B., Felitti, V. J., Nordenberg, D., Giles, W. H., Williamson, D. F., & Giovino, G. A. (1999). Adverse childhood experiences and smoking during adolescence and adulthood. *Journal of the American Medical Association, 282*, 1652–1658.

Australian Child Wellbeing Project. (2014). http://www.australianchildwellbeing.com.au/acwp-database. Accessed 6 Oct 2020.

Australian House of Representatives. (2018). *Breaking barriers: A national adoption framework for Australian children: Inquiry into local adoption*. Report of Standing Committee on Social Policy and Legal Affairs. https://apo.org.au/sites/default/files/resource-files/2018-11/apo-nid205826.pdf. Accessed 7 Dec 2020.

Australian Institute of Health and Welfare (AIHW). (2005). *Adoptions Australia 2004–05* (AIHW Cat. no. CSW 25). AIHW.

Australian Institute of Health and Welfare (AIHW). (2018). *Adoptions Australia 2017–18* (AIHW. Cat. no. CWS 66). AIHW.

Australian Institute of Health and Welfare (AIHW). (2019). *Adoptions Australia 2018–19* (Cat. no. CWS 71). AIHW.

Australian Senate Community Affairs Reference Committee. (1999). *The lost innocents: Righting the record – Report on child migration*. Parliament of Australia.

Australian Senate Community Affairs Reference Committee. (2012). *Commonwealth contribution to former forced adoption policies and practices*. Parliament of Australia.

Barber, J. G., & Delfabbro, P. H. (2003). Placement stability and the psychological well-being of children in foster care. *Research on Social Work Practice, 3*(4), 415–431.

Barth, R. P., & Lloyd, C. (2010). Five year developmental outcomes for young children remaining in foster care, returned home or adopted. In E. Fernandez & R. B. Barth (Eds.), *How does foster care work?: International evidence on outcomes*. Jessica Kingsley Publishers.

Baxter, C., Johnson, D., Miller, L., & Juffer, F. (2015). Review of medical issues, growth failure and recovery, and development of internationally adopted children. In R. Ballard, N. Goodno, R. Cochran, & J. Milbrandt (Eds.), *The intercountry adoption debate: Dialogues across disciplines* (pp. 109–156). Cambridge Scholars Publishing.

Biehal, N., Ellison, S., Baker, C., & Sinclair, I. (2010). *Belonging and permanence: Outcomes in long-term foster care and adoption.* BAAF.

Brandon, M., Belderson, P., Sorensen, P., Dickens, J., & Sidebotham, P. (2020). *Complexity and challenge: A triennial analysis of serious case reviews 2014–2017.* Department for Education.

Brodzinsky, D. (2006). Family structural openness and communication openness as predictors in the adjustment of adopted children. *Adoption Quarterly, 9*(4), 1–18.

Brodzinsky, D., & Livingston Smith, S. (2019). Commentary: Understanding research, policy, and practice issues in adoption instability. *Research on Social Work Practice, 29*(2), 185–194.

Bromfield, L., Higgins, D., Osborn, A., Panozzo, S., & Richardson, N. (2005). *Out-of-home care in Australia: Messages from research.* Australian Institute of Family Studies.

Brown, D. W., Anda, R. F., Tiemeier, H., Felitti, V. J., Edwards, V. J., Croft, J. B., & Giles, W. H. (2009). Adverse childhood experience and the risk of premature mortality. *American Journal of Preventive Medicine, 37*(5), 389.

Brown, R., & Ward, H. (2012). *Decision-making within a child's timeframe.* Childhood Wellbeing Research Centre & Department for Education. https://assets.publishing.service.gov.uk/government/uploads/system/uploads/attachment_data/file/200471/Decision-making_within_a_child_s_timeframe.pdf . Accessed 7 August 2021

Brown, R., Ward, H., Blackmore, J., Thomas, C., & Hyde-Dryden, G. (2016). *Eight-year-olds identified in infancy as at risk of harm: Report of a prospective longitudinal study. RR543.* Department for Education. https://assets.publishing.service.gov.uk/government/uploads/system/uploads/attachment_data/file/534376/Eight-year-olds_identified_in_infancy_as_at_risk_of_harm.pdf. Accessed 20 Oct 2020.

Cashmore, J., & Paxman, M. (1996). *Wards leaving care: A longitudinal study.* NSW Department of Community Services.

Cashmore, J., & Paxman, M. (2006). Predicting aftercare outcomes: The importance of 'felt' security. *Child and Family Social Work, 11*, 232–241.

Cashmore, J., & Paxman, M. (2007). *Wards leaving care: Four to five years on.* University of New South Wales.

Chandler, M., Lalonde, C., Sokol, B., & Hallett, D. (2003). Personal persistence, identity development and suicide: A study of native and non-native North American adolescents. *Monographs of the Society for Research in Child Development, 68*(2), Serial No. 273.

Cicchetti, D. (2013). Annual research review: Resilient functioning in maltreated children – Past, present and future perspectives. *Journal of Child Psychology and Psychiatry, 54*, 402–404.

Cleaver, H., & Nicholson, D. (2007). *Parental learning disability and children's needs: Family experiences and effective practice.* Jessica Kingsley Publishers.

Cleaver, H., Unell, I., & Aldgate, J. (2011). *Children's needs – Parenting capacity: Child abuse: Parental mental illness, learning disability, substance misuse and domestic violence* (2nd ed.). The Stationery Office.

Collinshaw, S., Maughan, B., & Pickles, A. (1998). Infant adoption: Psychosocial outcomes in adulthood. *Social Psychiatry & Psychiatric Epidemiology, 33*, 57–65.

Cuthbert, D., Spark, C., & Murphy, K. (2010). That was then but this is now. *Journal of Historical Sociology, 23*(3), 427–452.

Davies, C., & Ward, H. (2012). *Safeguarding children across services.* Jessica Kingsley Publishers.

de Rosnay, M., Luu, B., & Conley Wright, A. (2015). *I guess I was an accident at first, but then I was chosen: Young children's identity formation in the context of open adoption in New South Wales. An examination of optimal conditions for child wellbeing.* University of Sydney Institute of Open Adoption Studies.

Department for Education (UK). (2019). *Children looked after by local authorities in England (including adoption), year ending 31st March 2019.* London: Department for Education. https://www.gov.uk/government/statistics/children-looked-after-in-england-including-adoption-2018-to-2019. Accessed 12 Nov 2020.

Department of Health (UK). (2000). *Adoption: A new approach, White Paper (Cm 5017).* The Stationery Office.

Dodgson, L. (2014, November 11). Post-adoption contact: All change or more of the same? *Family Law Week.* https://www.familylawweek.co.uk/site.aspx?i=ed136606

Dube, S. R., Anda, R. F., Felitti, V. J., Chapman, D., Williamson, D. F., & Giles, W. H. (2001). Childhood abuse, household dysfunction and the risk of attempted suicide throughout the life span: Findings from adverse childhood experiences (ACE) study. *Journal of the American Medical Association, 286*, 3089–3096.

Dube, S. R., Felitti, V. J., Dong, M., Chapman, D. P., Giles, W. H., & Anda, R. F. (2003). Childhood abuse, neglect and household dysfunction and the risk of illicit drug use: The adverse childhood experience (ACE) study. *Pediatrics, 111*(3), 564–572.

Dumaret, A. C., & Coppel-Batsch, M. (1998). Effects in adulthood of separations and long-term foster care: A French research study. *Adoption & Fostering, 22*(1), 31–39.

Felitti, V. J., Anda, R. F., Nordenberg, D., Williamson, D. F., Spitz, A. M., Edwards, V., Koss, M. P., & Marks, J. S. (1998). Relationship of childhood abuse and household dysfunction to many of the leading causes of death in adults. The adverse childhood experiences (ACE) study. *American Journal of Preventive Medicine, 14*(4), 245–258.

Fenton-Glynn, C. (2015). *Adoption without consent: Report to the Peti Committee.* European Parliament: http://www.europarl.europa.eu/supporting-analyses. Accessed 20 Nov 2020.

Fernandez, E., Lee, J.-S., Blunden, H., McNaara, P., Kovacs, S., & Cornefert, P.-A. (2016). *No child should grow up like this: Identifying long term outcomes of Forgotten Australians, Child Migrants and the Stolen Generations.* University of New South Wales.

Forrester, D., Cocker, C., Goodman, K., Binnie, C., & Jensch, G. (2009). What is the impact of public care on children's welfare? A review of research findings and their policy implications. *Journal of Social Policy, 38*(3), 439–456.

Goodno, N. (2015). The Hague: An endless balancing act of preventing intercountry adoption abuses and finding permanent homes for orphans. In R. Ballard, N. Goodno, R. Cochran, & J. Milbrandt (Eds.), *The intercountry adoption debate: Dialogues across disciplines* (pp. 207–238). Cambridge Scholars Publishing.

Grotevant, H. D., Wrobel, G. M., Fiorenzo, L., Lo, A. Y. H., & McRoy, R. G. (2019). Trajectories of birth family contact in domestic adoptions. *Journal of Family Psychology, 33*(1), 54–63. https://doi.org/10.1037/fam0000449

Hansen, P. (2012). Rescission or variation of Children's Court orders: A study of Section 90 applications in New South Wales. *Children Australia, 37*, 69–75.

Harvard Center on the Developing Child. (2015). *Take the ACE quiz and learn what it does and doesn't mean.* https://developingchild.harvard.edu/media-coverage/take-the-ace-quiz-and-learn-what-it-does-and-doesnt-mean/. Accessed November 2020.

HCCH. (2017). *The 1993 Hague Convention on protection of children and co-operation in respect of intercountry adoption: Information brochure.* Hague Conference on Private International Law. https://assets.hcch.net/docs/994654cc-a296-4299-bd3c-f70d63a5862a.pdf. Accessed December 2020.

Hopkirk, M. (1949). *Nobody wanted Sam: The story of the unwelcomed child 1530–1948.* John Murray.

Horwitz, S. M., Balestracci, K. M. B., & Simms, M. D. (2001). Foster care placement improves children's functioning. *Archives of Paediatric and Adolescent Medicine, 155*(11), 1255–1260.

House of Commons Children, Schools and Families Committee. (2009). *Children, Schools and Families Committee – Third report: Looked-after children.* https://publications.parliament.uk/pa/cm200809/cmselect/cmchilsch/111/11102.htm. Accessed 6 Oct 2020.

Human Rights and Equal Opportunity Commission. (1997). *Bringing them home: Report of the National Inquiry into the separation of Aboriginal and Torres Strait Islander children from their families.* Commonwealth of Australia Human Rights and Equal Opportunity Commission.

Keating, J. (2009). *A child for keeps: A history of adoption in England 1918–1945.* Palgrave Macmillan.

Kenny, P., Higgins, D., Soloff, C., & Sweid, R. (2012). *Past adoption experiences: National research study on the service response to past adoption practices* (Research Report No. 21). Australian Institute of Family Studies.

Keyes, M. A., Sharma, A., & Elkins, I. J. (2008). The mental health of US adolescents adopted in infancy. *Archives of Pediatrics & Adolescent Medicine, 162*(5), 419–425.

Lalonde, C. (2006). Identity formation and cultural resilience in Aboriginal communities. In R. J. Flynn, P. Dudding, & J. G. Barber (Eds.), *Promoting resilience in child welfare* (pp. 52–71). University of Ottawa Press.

Lawrence, C. R., Carlson, E. A., & Egeland, B. (2006). The impact of foster care on development. *Development and Psychopathology, 18*(1), 57–76. https://doi.org/10.1017/S0954579406060044

Lazzara, M. J. (2013). Kidnapped memories: Argentina's stolen children tell their stories. *Journal of Human Rights, 12*(3), 319–332.

Lloyd, E. C., & Barth, R. P. (2011). Developmental outcomes after five years for foster children returned home, remaining in care, or adopted. *Children and Youth Services Review, 33*(8), 1383–1391.

Lock, R. (2013). *Serious case review re Daniel Pelka: Born 15th July 2007 died 3rd March 2012: Overview report.* Coventry Safeguarding Children Board.

MacDonald, M., & McLoughlin, P. (2016). Paramountcy, family rights and contested adoption: Does contact with birth relatives balance the scales? *Child Care in Practice, 22*(4), 401–407.

Masten, A. S. (2001). Ordinary magic. Resilience processes in development. *American Psychologist, 56*(3), 227–238.

Masten, A. S. (2014). *Ordinary magic: Resilience in development.* Guildford Press.

Maughan, B., & Pickles, A. (1990). Adopted and illegitimate children grown up. In L. Robins & M. Rutter (Eds.), *Straight and devious pathways from childhood to adulthood* (pp. 31–61). Cambridge University Press.

McCrory, E., De Brito, S., & Viding, E. (2010). Research review: The neurobiology and genetics of maltreatment and adversity. *Journal of Child Psychology and Psychiatry, 51*(10), 1079–1095.

McCrory, E., De Brito, S., & Viding, E. (2011). The impact of childhood maltreatment: A review of neurobiological and genetic factors. *Frontiers in Psychiatry, 2*(48). https://doi.org/10.3389/fpsyt.2011.00048/

McCrory, E., De Brito, S., & Viding, E. (2012). The link between child abuse and psychopathology: A review of neurobiological and genetic research. *Journal of the Royal Society of Medicine, 105*(4), 151–156.

Meier, T. (2008). The fight against the Swiss Yenish and the 'Children of the open road' campaign'. *Romani Studies 5, 18*(2), 101–121.

Milotte, M. (2012). *Banished babies: The secret history of Ireland's baby export business.* New Island Books.

Moe, V., & Slinning, K. (2001). Children prenatally exposed to substances: Gender-related differences in outcome from infancy to 3 years of age. *Infant Mental Health Journal, 22*(3), 334–350.

Munro, E. R., Lushey, C., National Care Advisory Service, Maskell-Graham, D., & Ward, H. with Holmes, L. (2012). *Evaluation of the staying put 18+ family placement programme: Final report. RR191.* Department for Education.

Neil, E. (2013). The mental distress of the birth relatives of adopted children: 'Disease' or 'unease'? Findings from a UK study. *Health and Social Care in the Community, 21*(2), 191–199.

Neil, E., Beek, M., & Ward, H. (2015). *Contact after adoption: A longitudinal study of post adoption contact arrangements.* Coram BAAF.

Nicholas, L. (2005). *Cruel world: The children of Europe in the Nazi web.* Knopf.

Osborn, A., & Delfabbro, P. H. (2006). Research Article 4: An analysis of the social background and placement history of children with multiple and complex needs in Australian out-of-home care. *Communities, Children and Families Australia, 1*(1), 33–42.

P., Sarah. (2016, December 29). England's Stolen Children: Another missed opportunity. *The Transparency Project.* https://www.transparencyproject. org.uk/englands-stolen-children-another-missed-opportunity/. Accessed 8 October 2020.

Palacios, J., Brodzinsky, D., Grotevant, H., Johnson, D., Juffer, F., Martinez-Morah, L., Muhamedrahimove, R., Selwyn, J., Simmonds, J., & Tarren-Sweeney, M. (2019). Adoption in the service of child protection: An international interdisciplinary perspective. *Psychology, Public Policy, and Law, 25*(2), 57–72.

Parker, R. (1999). *Adoption now: Messages from research.* Wiley.

Parker, R., Ward, H., Jackson, S., Aldgate, J., & Wedge, P. (1991). *Looking after children: Assessing outcomes in child care.* HMSO.

Phillips, C. (2013, July). International adoption: Controversies and criticisms. *The Chronicle: International Association of Youth and Family Judges and Magistrates,* pp. 73–78.

Pinchbeck, I., & Hewitt, M. (1973). *Children in English society.* Routledge and Kegan Paul.

Radford, L., Corral, S., Bradley, C., Fisher, H., et al. (2011). *The maltreatment and victimization of children in the UK: NSPCC Report on National survey of young people's, young adults' and caregivers experiences.* NSPCC.

Rahilly, T., & Hendry, E. (2014). *Promoting the wellbeing of children in care.* NSPCC.

Richards, M. (2005). Ideology and the psychology of war children in Franco's Spain 1936–1945. In K. Ericsson & E. Simonsen (Eds.), *Children of World War II: The hidden enemy legacy.* Bloomsbury.

Rock, S., Michelson, D., Thomson, S., & Day, C. (2015). Understanding foster placement instability for looked after children: A systematic review and narrative synthesis of quantitative and qualitative evidence. *The British Journal of Social Work, 45*(1), 177–203.

Ross, N., & Cashmore, J. (2016). Adoption reforms New South Wales style: A comparative look. *Australian Journal of Family Law, 30*(1), 51–75.

Rousseau, D., Roze, M., Duverger, P., Fanello, S., & Tanguy, M. (2015). *Étude sure le devenir à long terme des jeunes enfants placés à la Pouponnière Sociale Saint Exupéry entre 1994 et 2001. Rapport recherche St-Ex 2013–2014.* Unité de Psychiatrie de l'Enfant et de l'Adolescent du CHU d'Angers.

Rutter, M., Beckett, C., Castle, J., Colvert, E., Kreppner, J., Mehta, M., Stevens, S., & Sonuga-Barke, E. (2007). Effects of profound early institutional deprivation: An overview of findings from a UK longitudinal study of Romanian adoptees. *European Journal of Developmental Psychology, 4*(3), 332–350.

Rutter, M., Beckett, C., Castle, J., Kreppner, J., Stevens, S., & Sonuga-Barke, E. (2009). *Policy and practice implications from the English and Romanian adoptees (ERA) study: Forty five key questions*. BAAF.

Ryburn, M. (1998). In whose best interests? – Post adoption contact with the birth family. *Child and Family Law Quarterly, 10*(1), 53–70.

Selman, P. (2009). The rise and fall of intercountry adoption in the twenty-first century. *International Social Work, 52*(5), 575–594.

Selwyn, J. (2017). The adoption of looked after maltreated children in England: Challenges, opportunities and outcomes. *Developing Practice: The Child, Youth and Family Work Journal, 47*, 50–63.

Selwyn, J., Sturgess, W., Quinton, D., & Baxter, C. (2006). *Costs and outcomes of non-infant adoption*. BAAF.

Selwyn, J., Wijedasa, D., & Meakings, S. (2014). *Beyond the adoption order: Challenges, interventions and adoption disruptions, RR 336*. Department for Education.

Skuse, T., & Ward, H. (2003). *Outcomes for looked after children: Children's views, the importance of listening. Report to the Department of Health*. Loughborough University Centre for Child and Family Research.

Sonuga-Barke, E., Kennedy, M., Kumsta, R., Knights, N., Golm, D., Rutter, M., Maughan, B., Schlotz, W., & Kreppner, J. (2017). Child-to-adult neurodevelopmental and mental health trajectories after early life deprivation: The young adult follow-up of the longitudinal English and Romanian Adoptees study. *Lancet, 389*, 1539–1548.

Stein, M. (2004). *What works for young people leaving care?* Barnardo's.

Stein, M., & Munro, E. (2008). *Young people's transitions from care to adulthood: International research and practice*. Jessica Kingsley.

Tarren-Sweeney, M., & Hazell, P. (2006). The mental health of children in foster care and kinship care in New South Wales, Australia. *Journal of Paediatrics and Child Health, 42*, 89–97.

Taussig, H. N., Clyman, R. B., & Landsverk, J. (2001, July). Children who return home from foster care: A 6-year prospective study of behavioral health outcomes in adolescence. *Pediatrics, 108*(1) e10. https://doi.org/10.1542/peds.108.1.e10.

Thoburn, J. (2002). *Adoption and permanence for children who cannot live safely with birth parents or relatives: Quality Protects Research Briefing 5*. Department of Health.

Thomas, C. (2013). *Adoption for looked after children: Messages from research: An overview of the Adoption Research Initiative*. BAAF.

Triseliotis, J. (1973). *In search of origins: The experiences of adopted people.* Routledge and Kegan Paul.

Triseliotis, J. (1980). *New developments in foster care and adoption.* Routledge and Kegan Paul.

Triseliotis, J. (2002). Long-term foster care or adoption? The evidence examined. *Child and Family Social Work, 7,* 23–33.

Turney, K., & Wildeman, C. (2017). Adverse childhood experiences among children placed in and adopted from foster care: Evidence from a nationally representative survey. *Child Abuse & Neglect, 64,* 117–129.

U.S. Department of Health & Human Services, Administration for Children and Families, Administration on Children, Youth and Families, Children's Bureau. (2019). *Child maltreatment 2017.* https://www.acf.hhs.gov/cb/research-data-technology/statistics-research/child-maltreatment. Accessed November 2020.

Utting, W. (1997). *People like us: The report of the review of the safeguards for children living away from home.* HMSO.

Vinnerljung, B., & Hjern, A. (2011). Cognitive, educational and self-support outcomes of long-term foster care versus adoption: A Swedish national cohort study. *Children and Youth Services Review, 33,* 1902–1910.

Ward, H. (2009). Patterns of instability: Moves within the English care system: Their reasons, contexts and consequences. *Child and Youth Services Review, 31,* 1113–1118.

Ward, H., & Brown, R. (2016). Cumulative jeopardy when children are at risk of significant harm: A response to Bywaters. *Children and Youth Services Review, 61,* 222–229.

Ward, H., Brown, R., Blackmore, J., Hyde-Dryden, G., & Thomas, C. (2019). Identifying parents who show capacity to make and sustain positive changes when infants are at risk of significant harm. *Developing Practice, The Child, Youth and Family Work Journal, 54,* 47–61.

Ward, H., Brown, R., & Hyde-Dryden, G. (2014). *Assessing parental capacity to change when children are on the edge of care: An overview of current research evidence. RR369.* Centre for Child and Family Research, Loughborough University and Department for Education. https://assets.publishing.service.gov.uk/government/uploads/system/uploads/attachment_data/file/330332/RR369_Assessing_parental_capacity_to_change_Final.pdf. Accessed 30 Dec 2020.

Ward, H., Brown, R., & Westlake, D. (2012). *Safeguarding babies and very young children from abuse and neglect.* Jessica Kingsley Publishers.

Ward, H., & Holmes, L. (2008). Calculating the costs of local authority care for children with contrasting needs. *Child and Family Social Work, 13*(1), 80–90.

Ward, H., Moggach, L., Tregeagle, S., & Trivedi, H. (2019). *Outcomes of open adoption from out-of-home care in Australia. Report to funders.* Oxford University Rees Centre.

WHO. (1996). *WHOQUOL-BREF.* https://www.who.int/mental_health/media/en/76.pdf. Accessed 6 Oct 2020.

Zhang, M. F., & Selwyn, J. (2020). The subjective well-being of children and young people in out of home care: Psychometric analyses of the "Your Life, your Care" Survey. *Child Indicators Research, 13,* 1549–1572.

Part I

Birth Parents, Adoptive Parents and Children When They Entered Their Adoptive Homes

2

Issues Facing the Birth Parents and Their Implications for Open Adoption

Introduction

The most complex and difficult decisions that child welfare professionals have to make are those concerning the safety of children. Decisions about whether parents have sufficient capacity to change circumstances and behaviour patterns that pose a risk of significant harm to their child, or whether the problems they face are so severe that the child can only be adequately protected through removal, are often finely balanced. On the one hand, leaving a child in an abusive environment can have serious and sometimes life-changing consequences, yet on the other hand, unnecessary or premature removal not only contravenes ethical standards and human rights legislation, it too may also have long-term adverse consequences for both parent and child (Broadhurst et al., 2016; Brown & Ward, 2014; Brown et al., 2016; Neil et al., 2010). This chapter focuses on the adoptees' birth parents; it explores the complex problems with which they struggled. Many of these were known risk factors, such as substance misuse, mental health problems and domestic abuse, that reduce parents' capacity to provide nurturing homes for their children and jeopardise their long-term wellbeing. Professionals had to assess these and other factors in deciding whether or not the adoptees could safely

© The Author(s) 2022
H. Ward et al., *Outcomes of Open Adoption from Care*,
https://doi.org/10.1007/978-3-030-76429-6_2

remain living with their birth parents, or whether they needed to be placed in out-of-home care on a temporary or permanent basis.

Between 1 July 1987 and 30 June 2013, the courts made adoption orders for 210 children placed through the Barnardos Find-a-Family programme. The children had entered their adoptive homes between 12 February 1979 and 7 July 2011. The documents and reports held on the Barnardos files and electronic information system provide a wealth of information concerning the children's experiences, both while living with birth parents before being separated and then during the period between separation and final placement with the adoptive family. Nearly one in five (19%) of the children had had their fifth birthday before they left their birth parents' home, and nearly one in four (24%) were six years old or more before they entered their adoptive homes, so many of them could remember the time before they were adopted. The interviews with adult adoptees illuminate much of the information held on files.

It is worth exploring these data in some detail because they shed light on the extreme vulnerability of not only the adoptees, but also their birth parents at the time key decisions were made, thus clarifying the reasons why the children were first placed in out-of-home care and then referred to the Find-a-Family programme with a view to adoption.

They also point to the challenges Barnardos faced in introducing and maintaining a programme of open adoption, and the difficulties some adoptive parents were likely to have encountered in trying to meet the children's needs.

Birth Parents

Most (58%) of the 210 children in the full cohort entered Find-a-Family with at least one sibling; altogether they came from 142 birth families. Before entry to out-of-home care, almost all the children (205: 98%) had been primarily looked after by their birth mothers; only three children had had their father as their primary carer and two had been looked after by adoptive mothers, in placements made by other agencies that had disrupted before referral to the programme. Nothing is known about the birth families of these two children and the following paragraphs focus on the 140 families for whom data are available.

The majority of the birth mothers were Australian or New Zealanders (111: 79%) or European (21: 16%). Adoption is not considered appropriate for Aboriginal children (see Chap. 1) and none of the mothers were Aboriginal, although four were Maori or Pacific Islanders. The fathers were slightly more diverse: 83 (72%) were Australian or New Zealanders and 18 (16%) were European; however, four fathers were Asian, five were Maori or Pacific Islanders and three were found to be Aboriginal after the children's placement.

There is comprehensive information about all the 137 birth mothers who acted as primary carers and 120 (85%) of the fathers. Only 17 fathers were unknown.

Birth Parents' Relationships

Tables 2.1 and 2.2 show the birth parents' relationship status at the time the children were born compared with when they were placed for adoption. Almost three-quarters (98: 70%) of birth mothers were still in a relationship with the children's birth fathers at the time the children were born; only 31 (22%) of them were lone parents. However, by the time of the adoption, on average nine years later, 90% of the parents had split up. Only 14 (10%) of the mothers were still in a relationship with the birth father, about one in three (45: 32%) had moved on to a new partner, and another third (43: 31%) were now lone parents. Thirty (21%) of the fathers had also moved on to a new partner. Although as a group the parents were relatively young, a high proportion (16 (11%) of birth mothers and 11 (8%) of birth fathers) had already died. There was no information available concerning almost half (59: 42%) the birth fathers at the time their children entered their adoption placements, possibly because they had already lost touch.

Frequent changes in parental relationships are a common experience of children who are placed in out-of-home care (Wade et al., 2011; Ward et al., 2006) and are one of the reasons why maintaining contact was likely to be problematic for this cohort of children. The high proportion of parents who had changed partners may also reflect some of the risk factors that diminished their capacity to parent (discussed below) and which may well have also had an adverse impact on their capacity to form stable relationships.

Table 2.1 Birth mothers: relationship status at child's birth and at adoption (N = 140)

Birth mother's relationship status at adoption	Birth mother's relationship status at birth			
	Both parents together in a relationship	In a relationship with a different partner	Single	Total
Birth parents together in a relationship	14	0	0	14 (10%)
In a relationship with a different partner	27	5	13	45 (32%)
Single	27	3	13	43 (31%)
Deceased	15	1	0	16 (11%)
Relationship status unknown	15	2	5	22 (16%)
Total	98 (70%)	11 (8%)	31 (22%)	140

Table 2.2 Birth fathers: relationship status at child's birth and at adoption (N = 140)

Birth father's relationship status at adoption	Birth father's relationship status at birth					
	Both parents together in a relationship	In a relationship with a different partner	Single	Relationship status unknown	Missing/ father unknown	Total
Birth parents together in a relationship	14	0	0	0		14 (10%)
In a relationship with a different partner	24	0	1	5		30 (21%)
Single	20	0	4	2		26 (19%)
Deceased	10	0	0	1		11 (8%)
Relationship status unknown	30	3	5	4		42 (30%)
Missing (father unknown)					17	17 (12%)
Total	98 (70%)	3 (2%)	10 (7%)	12 (9%)	17 (12%)	140

Factors That Affected Parenting Capacity

There is now a well-established body of evidence that shows how a range of adverse factors can impact on parents' capacity to meet their children's needs (for overview, see Cleaver et al., 2011). Poverty, poor housing, a hostile environment and social isolation are all known to increase the challenge of parenting and make abuse and neglect more likely, although these are neither sufficient nor necessary factors in the occurrence of child maltreatment (Bywaters et al., 2016). Although we know that the vast majority of the birth parents faced these adversities, as is common to most child welfare agencies (see Bywaters, 2013), data were not routinely collected on these issues.

There is a known relationship between parenting capacity and parents' age, with very young parents being more likely to show abusive or neglectful parenting. Forty-two (20%) children were born to a birth mother who was younger than 20; 170 (81%) to one who was under 30. The median age of mothers at the time of the child's birth was 24, five years younger than the median age for Australian mothers in 1998, the date for the national statistical release closest to the midpoint of the sample time-frame (Australian Bureau of Statistics, 1998).

Parents' Previous Experiences

Factors such as experiences of abuse in one's own childhood or having a previous history of abusing another child are known to be associated with abusive and neglectful parenting (Hindley et al., 2006; White et al., 2015). As Table 2.3 shows, a high proportion of the birth mothers were known to have experienced these adversities and the prevalence is likely to be considerably higher, given that this information is often under-reported. Almost 1 in 3 mothers were known to have experienced abuse in their own childhoods (42: 31%) and 20 (15%) had been in care. Almost half of them (61: 45%) were known to statutory child welfare services before the birth of the child; in fact, 42 (29%) had already had at least one child permanently removed. Nine of these mothers had already been permanently separated from three children and three from four, displaying a pattern of repeated pregnancy and removal that is likely to have exacerbated other problems (Broadhurst et al., 2016; Neil, 2013).

Table 2.3 Past experiences: issues affecting parenting capacity of birth mothers (*N* = 137*)

Issues affecting parenting capacity	Frequency**	Per cent
Experience of abuse in own childhood	42	31
In care as a child	20	15
Imprisoned prior to birth of child	10	7
Known to statutory agency prior to birth	61	45
Child(ren) previously removed	42	29

*No information on three birth mothers
**Some birth mothers had more than one of these experiences

Table 2.4 Past experiences: issues affecting parenting capacity of birth fathers (*N* = 120*)

Issues affecting parenting capacity	Frequency**	Per cent
Experience of abuse in own childhood	10	8
In care as a child	8	7
Imprisoned prior to birth of child	26	22
Known to statutory agency prior to birth	35	30
Child(ren) previously removed	25	21

*No information on 20 birth fathers
**Some birth fathers had more than one of these experiences.

The birth fathers' past experiences are shown in Table 2.4. There is extensive missing data on these variables for the fathers, and it is impossible to tell whether no evidence means a specific factor was not present or there is no record of it being present. As a result, these data are undoubtedly an underestimate. Nevertheless, it is notable that at least 35 (30%) were also known to the statutory agency before the birth of the child and at least 25 (21%) had already experienced the removal of a child—for 13 men this had happened more than once. Twenty-six fathers (22%) were also known to have served a prison sentence before the birth of the child. We do not have information about the offences, but they are likely to be indicators of diminished parental capacity, particularly if they were in response to crimes against the person (White et al., 2015).

Birth Parents' Problems at Time of Adoption Order

Numerous studies have found that parental mental health problems, drug and alcohol abuse and domestic abuse may reduce parenting capacity and increase the risk that children will be abused or neglected; this is most likely if these problems occur in combination and there are no protective factors such as the presence of a supportive adult in the household (Cleaver et al., 2011; Hindley et al., 2006; White et al., 2015). For instance, depression or the effects of substance and alcohol abuse may mean that parents find it difficult to organise their day-to-day lives and buy food or pay the rent, and children may be neglected. Some mental health problems may cause parents to lose touch with reality and become emotionally unavailable to their children. Parents who are living in an abusive relationship may be unable to protect their children from a violent partner, or from witnessing or becoming affected by the tensions in the household. Parents who misuse alcohol or drugs may spend money needed for essentials on their addiction; they may find it difficult to control their anger and become physically abusive; their children may be unsupervised and exposed to other substance users and unsuitable adults who frequent the home (for further information, see Cleaver et al., 2011).

As Tables 2.5 and 2.6 demonstrate, the birth parents displayed a high prevalence of these problems at the time the adoption order was made. The data indicate that more than half of the birth mothers had problems with substance misuse (58%) and/or domestic abuse (51%) and that more than one in three (37%) had mental health problems. Moreover, although 49 (36%) birth mothers were struggling with just one of these adversities, 57 (42%) were dealing with two and 12 (9%) with all three in combination. The 19 birth mothers who showed no evidence of any of these problems were struggling with other issues.

Sixteen of the birth mothers were also known to have cognitive impairments. Parents with cognitive impairment can provide nurturing homes for their children if they have adequate long-term support, but the challenges they already face are exacerbated if mental health problems,

Table 2.5 Birth mothers: current issues affecting parenting capacity (*N* = 137*)

Issues affecting parenting capacity	Frequency	Per cent**
Mental ill health	50	37
Substance misuse	79	58
Domestic abuse	70	51
None of the above	19	14

*No information on 3 birth mothers
**Percentages add to more than 100 because of comorbidity

Table 2.6 Birth fathers: current issues affecting parenting capacity (*N* = 120*)

Issues affecting parenting capacity	Frequency	Per cent**
Mental ill health	50	37
Substance misuse	79	58
Domestic abuse	70	51
None of the above	19	14

*No information on 3 birth mothers
**Percentages add to more than 100 because of comorbidity

substance misuse and/or domestic abuse are also present (Cleaver & Nicholson, 2007; Cleaver et al., 2011). Four of these mothers appeared to have cognitive impairment as their major risk factor, but five of them were also struggling with domestic violence and five with combinations of substance misuse, domestic violence and mental ill health.

Table 2.6 shows the prevalence of these risk factors amongst the birth fathers. For the reasons given above, this is undoubtedly an underestimate. Nevertheless, the data do indicate that almost half of the fathers were known to be struggling with substance misuse. In the majority of these cases (44: 80%), substance misuse was also an issue for the birth mother.

Five of the birth fathers were also known to have cognitive impairments, three of them in combination with both mental ill health and substance misuse. Three of these men also had a partner who had a cognitive impairment.

Although there is evidence that some parents can overcome complex patterns of problems such as these and provide nurturing homes for their children (Ward et al., 2019), many are unable to do so within an appropriate timeframe for the child; those who do succeed in making significant changes to lifestyles that threaten their children's wellbeing often need long-term support to sustain hard-won progress (Brown et al., 2016; Ward et al., 2014). The case study of Susan demonstrates the complicated web of problems with which many birth parents struggled, and the issues professionals had to assess in making decisions concerning the children's long-term welfare.

Susan

Susan was 19 years old when she gave birth to her first child, Michael. At that time Susan was living with Tony, Michael's father.

Personal History

Susan was one of four children and described a happy childhood until she was eight years old when her mother committed suicide. Following this, Susan and her siblings were placed in a strict children's home for four years, where there was frequent physical punishment. In her early teens, Susan left school and returned to her father; however, she ran away shortly afterwards. She soon came to the attention of the police and was assessed at a juvenile centre, where she met Tony when she was 15 years old. By the time of Michael's birth, Susan was using heroin.

Michael

Michael had several visits to hospital during the first couple of months of his life as a result of gastric troubles. He was again taken to hospital when he was three months old with multiple new and old non-accidental fractures to his skull, femurs and tibia. As a result, Michael was placed in foster care and care proceedings commenced.

Michael was made the subject of a care order and moved between various family members and foster care until he was 18 months old. He was then restored to the care of Susan, who had recently separated from Tony. Michael remained in Susan's care for the next two years, occasionally also living with Tony. During this time, Susan continued to use heroin and frequently changed accommodation, often living in housing frequented by numerous adults. When Michael was three years old, the pre-school began to notice a deterioration in his physical presentation and he began to display sexualised behaviour; he was also picked up from pre-school by a succession of different adults to whom he was apparently unrelated. Susan eventually became homeless and was offered emergency accommodation. Finally, after Susan failed to collect him after an arranged stay with Tony, Michael was returned to foster care:

(continued)

(continued)

Why she (birth mother) gave me up, why could she not get her act together? Why bring me into this world, while you're doing all that shit? I feel tainted from birth and I often say to my (adoptive) mum, "I feel like I was doomed in the womb, before I even had a chance."

After Michael returned to foster care, Susan's drug use continued and her criminal activity eventually led to her being imprisoned. At the age of four, Michael was placed with his prospective adoptive parents.

I already had heaps of problems before they adopted me, so it was already embedded into me, because my mum was a drug addict and men coming over and shit happening....

Susan was in prison at the time of the adoption application, and initially contested it; however, she later gave her consent.

Consent to Adoption

Adoption from out-of-home care is a traumatic experience for most birth parents; feelings of grief and loss are often compounded by anger at an 'unfair, hostile and alienating process' and shame at what may be perceived as a confirmation of their poor parenting capacity (Neil et al., 2010). Susan was one of 52 (37%) birth mothers who initially withheld their consent to the adoption order. However about one in three birth mothers (49: 32%) gave active consent to the order, including the mothers of 17 (8%) children who entered the programme because their parents had voluntarily relinquished them. Some of these parents placed their children for adoption because they felt that they could not provide them with a nurturing home:

She had her list of what she felt [adoptee] should be getting as a child, how he should be looked after, the whole family situation, the education, all of that, but I always felt that possibly [stepfather] didn't want children, so, it was [adoptee] or [stepfather] and [adoptee] lost out from that point of view... and he said, "Well, my stepfather didn't want children, and I probably really didn't work for her". I wanted him to know that – and she probably did too, that she really did care about him, that she's made a decision based on what she thought was the right thing. (Adoptive parent of a young man, aged 8 when permanently placed)

Contested Adoptions

In New South Wales, an adoption order requires the consent of both the child's birth parents. Under the Adoption Act (New South Wales) 2000, children over the age of 12 must also give consent to their adoption and, if they have been in the care of the proposed adoptive parents for two years, only the child's consent is required. Fifty-eight (28%) of the Barnardos adoptees met this criterion, and the adoption order was made on the basis of their consent, although the parents of six of them contested it.

The parents of 34 (22%) children under the age of 12 gave consent to their adoption; a further 94 (62%) parents did not give consent but did not actively oppose the adoption. Parents of 24 younger children contested the adoption in court; in these cases, both parties were legally represented and had to provide evidence. The courts made adoption orders against parental wishes or without their consent mainly on the grounds that the child was in the care of authorised carers, had established a stable relationship with those carers and that it was in the child's best interest to be adopted by them.

Implications for Open Adoption

Chapter 1 has described Barnardos' policy on open adoption. The agency is committed to working to ensure that all adoptees have contact with significant members of their birth family; furthermore, the legislation in New South Wales requires a plan for open adoption for all children for whom adoption orders are made. For older children, Barnardos recommends contact with the primary birth parent on average four times a year; for children who come into care when they are very young or have a poor attachment to their birth family, the recommendation is for contact between two and four times a year. These policies have been in place throughout the timeframe of the study, although it should be noted that the Supreme Court is the final decision-maker in determining contact levels and does not necessarily follow recommendations from Barnardos or any other agency.

Contact is generally face-to-face (direct); however, there are a (very) few situations where it is restricted to social media or mail contact (indirect). This is in contrast with the experience in Britain, where the majority of contact is indirect, and children in only 5% of newly established adoptive families have direct contact with birth mothers, 2% with birth fathers and 15% with birth siblings (Adoption UK, 2020).

The problems the birth parents were facing give some indication of the challenges involved in implementing a policy of regular direct contact. Parents who were struggling with a violent relationship, substance misuse or mental health problems may well have found it difficult to manage the practicalities of contact—of arriving in the right place at the right time, even if, as was the policy, expenses were paid. There were also emotional hurdles, for contact was painful for birth parents who found that visits reawakened old wounds, or who struggled to accept that their child was becoming attached to another family.

There were so many times [birth mother] was awful to [adoptive mother]. She would say things to her that were really horrible.... As you can imagine, being a parent, you feel jealousy and you feel angry because you're incapable of giving your child what you need, but someone else is capable. So she was horrible to her. (Young woman, aged 10 when permanently placed, aged 21 when interviewed)

I know seeing [adoptee] was difficult for [birth mother], and I can imagine why, and it would've been very difficult I'd have imagined for [birth mother] to see [adoptee] drift away and form a relationship with us. I suppose it depends on whether [birth mother] would ultimately admit to herself that she couldn't look after [adoptee], and [adoptee] was in a better place. But I suspect that probably wasn't the case. So I just imagine it would've been torture for [birth mother]. (Adoptive parent of young woman, aged 6 when permanently placed)

A recent British study found that well over three years after the adoption, 67% of birth mothers and 56% of birth fathers were displaying clinical levels of distress (Neil, 2013). Such factors are likely to have resulted in contact arrangements being broken or becoming problematic in other ways, an issue that is explored further in Chap. 6.

I saw him every – once a month or something, there was a visit. But he wouldn't turn up for a lot of them, or he'd turn up with five minutes left of the meeting. (Young woman. aged 8 when permanently placed, aged 31 when interviewed)

If [birth mother] showed up just like – sometimes she'd show up just like you could tell she just wasn't with it that day. And then when she showed up like that, I just was like, oh, well, great. She's doing something again. (Young man, aged 2 when permanently placed, aged 19 when interviewed)

Moreover, there were also reasons why post-adoption contact was impossible, or extremely unlikely, for many of the children in the cohort. As we have already seen, around 10% of the birth parents had died before the adoption order was made; furthermore, 28 (23%) birth mothers and 75 (60%) birth fathers who were known to be alive had already lost contact with their children before the adoption placement. We do not know how strongly the statutory and voluntary agencies which had provided out-of-home care for the children before they were referred to the Barnardos programme promoted contact with birth parents, but research evidence indicates that the longer children remain separated from birth parents, the greater the likelihood that contact will end, particularly if it is not openly encouraged (Millham et al., 1986). More than half of the children (54%) had already spent over a year separated from their birth families before moving to Find-a-Family and being placed for adoption;[1] more than one in four had already been separated for two years or more before moving to their adoptive home. In some cases, contact may have been lost because it was not encouraged or facilitated. In others, birth parents may not have wished to have contact; this may have been the case for three children who had been classified as 'abandoned or rejected'

---

[1] The median number of months between entry to care and a Find-a-Family placement was 14 (mean = 22.72, sd = 24.984); the median number of months between entry to care and entry to the adoptive home was 16 (mean = 26.47, sd = 28.207).

before their birth parents lost touch. Finally, loss of contact before adoption may have been as a result of deliberate action by the agencies concerned, since contact may not always have been perceived as being in the child's best interests. Contact between children in out-of-home care and/ or adoptees and birth family members who have seriously abused them in the past can be detrimental to their wellbeing (Neil & Howe, 2004). As Chap. 3 shows, some of the children in the cohort had had traumatic experiences before separation and these may well have led to contact being curtailed when children entered out-of-home care: for instance, one child, who had been sexually abused by both parents and at least six other adults before separation at the age of five, had no contact with either birth parent by the time of the adoption.

Moreover, where contact had taken place in the period between separation and adoption, it was rarely frequent. Tables 2.7 and 2.8 show the levels of contact between birth parents and at least one of their children at the time of the adoption order.

Table 2.7 Birth mothers: contact at time of adoption order (N = 140)

Contact with children per year	n	Per cent*	Cumulative per cent*
0	28	23	23
1	4	3	26
2	34	28	54
3	5	4	59
4	38	31	90
6	6	5	95
7	2	2	97
8	1	1	98
Frequency unclear	1	1	99
Indirect contact only	2	1	100
Total	**121**	**100**	**100**
N/A Mother had died	16		
Missing	3		

*Percentages have been rounded

Table 2.8 Birth fathers: contact at time of adoption order (N = 140)

Contact with children per year	n	Per cent*	Cumulative per cent*
0	75	60	60
1	3	2	62
2	19	15	77
3	2	2	79
4	20	16	94
5	1	1	95
6	3	2	97
Frequency unclear	1	1	98
Indirect contact only	2	2	100
Total	126	100	100
N/A Father had died	11		
Missing	3		

*Percentages have been rounded

Although contact was mainly direct, as already indicated, almost a quarter of the birth mothers and over half the birth fathers no longer had contact with their children by this time. Additionally, only 52 (42%) birth mothers and 26 (21%) birth fathers saw their children more than twice a year; only 9 (8%) birth mothers and 4 (3%) birth fathers saw their children more than once every three months and no birth parents had contact at more than six weekly intervals. This low level of contact indicates that, for most parents, the arrangements may have seemed more about keeping in touch than maintaining a relationship. The experiences of Susan and her son, Michael, whose history has been presented earlier in this chapter, demonstrate the complexities of making and fulfilling contact arrangements when parents are struggling with interlocking problems, they have inadequate access to professional support and their children are permanently placed away from home.

Susan

Susan's Contact with Michael

Before the Adoption

Following Michael's re-entry to care when he was three, Susan had very sporadic and limited contact with him; social workers also found it difficult to locate or make contact with her.

After the Adoption

Throughout Michael's childhood, Susan was frequently imprisoned. During these times, she would make contact with Barnardos and contact between Susan and Michael was gradually re-established. However, Susan was not able to sustain this following her release from prison:

> We had a couple of visits while she was still inside. And then she was coming out, and then she had promised on her life that she would keep contact with (adoptee), and didn't even turn up for the first visit, which was a bit shattering for (adoptee), and made me very angry. (Adoptive mother)

> So, she just didn't want me, didn't want to see me, the drugs – Like she never really wanted me in the first place... (Michael)

Susan lost contact with Michael until he was in his late teenage years, when he searched for her and succeeded in re-establishing it. He went to stay with her for a period but this was not a positive experience for either and contact again ceased. Michael had had no contact with Susan for several years prior to her death from a chronic medical condition when he was in his 20s.

The purpose of contact is an issue that needs to be explored within the context of open adoption, as well as in other situations in which children are separated from birth parents (Iyer et al., 2020). The high proportion of birth parents who had no or minimal contact with their children before the adoption order is also a factor to be taken into account in assessing the success of Barnardos' attempts to implement open adoption.

Recent research demonstrates that open communication about adoption issues, both within and between the parties in the adoption triangle (adoptees, adoptive parents and birth parents) is of greater significance to the adjustment and long-term wellbeing of adopted children than contact *per se* (Brodzinsky, 2006; Kohler et al., 2002). Although contact obviously makes communication easier, it is not a *sine qua non* for successful adjustment. Some families have contact, but no communication about adoption-related issues and their children may find it harder to adjust to their situation than those who have no contact with birth families, but whose adoptive parents provide them with encouragement and opportunities to ask questions and discuss these subjects (Brodzinsky, 2006). Chapters in Part II of this book explore these issues further.

Changes over Time

The children entered their adoptive placements over a period lasting slightly more than 30 years (February 1979–July 2011), and during that time there were changes to admission criteria as the age range expanded to include more younger children (see Chap. 1 for further details). It seems likely that the birth parents also changed over this period. We have sorted the data collected at the time children were placed for adoption into time periods, mirroring the changes in policy: 1 February 1979–31 August 1985 (young children in long-term foster care); 1 September 1985–30 June 1991 (older primary-school-aged children with behavioural/emotional challenges); 1 July 1991–30 June 2007 (wider age range) and 1 July 2007–30 June 2013 (inclusion of infants).

Birth mothers' age at the time of the child's birth tended to increase as time passed. In the first time period, they were significantly younger (mean = 22.5 years old) than those in the two time periods covering July 1991 up to June 2013 (25 years and 26 years respectively).[2] Contact with birth parents also changed significantly between the different time periods. Those adopted between 1 July 1991 and 30 June 2007 (when the age range was increased to include younger children) had significantly more contact with birth parents at the time of the adoption order application than those adopted between 1 January 1979 and 31 August 1985 (children adopted by long-term foster carers).[3]

---

[2] $t(21.2) = -2.13$; $p = 0.45$, and $t(42.5) = -2.19$; $p = 0.034$.
[3] $\chi^2 = 8.54$; $df = 3$; $p = 0.036$.

Conclusion

The following chapter explores the children's experiences, both while living with their birth parents before separation and during the period between entering out-of-home care and reaching their final placement with adoptive parents. Significant levels of abuse and neglect experienced by the children while living with their birth parents were the major reasons for decisions to place them away from home. Maltreatment was commonly related to parental factors such as mental ill health, substance misuse and domestic violence, which carry a risk of adversely impacting on parenting capacity and parent/child relationships, especially if there are no protective factors present. These factors often occurred in combination, increasing the likelihood of maltreatment: the data presented in this chapter show that over half the birth mothers (69: 51%) were struggling with two or more of these factors at the time the adoption order was made.

Such adversities also had an impact on the extent to which contact between birth parents and children was feasible (and, in a few cases, advisable) after separation. Personal issues such as a parent's ability to arrive at the correct meeting place at the assigned time and emotional issues surrounding parents' disengagement from the family unit or the circumstances of the separation would have acted as obstacles to contact. The length of time that children had spent in out-of-home care and the frequency of contact during that period, together with the extent to which agencies promoted (or sometimes obstructed) a contact plan, would all have had an impact on the likelihood of birth parents and children keeping in touch, let alone maintaining some sort of relationship before the child was admitted to the Barnardos programme. The interviews with adult adoptees reveal that most parents did not succeed in extricating themselves from the complex web of adversities that had led to the removal of their child (see also Ward et al., 2019). The few who did manage to overcome their problems moved on to new partners with whom they had other children; they only rarely developed a stronger relationship with the child who had been adopted.

In assessing the effectiveness of the policy of open adoption, these antecedents need to be taken into account. At the heart of this policy is the expectation that contact with parents will continue after the adoption order has been made: the outcomes of this policy need to be understood within a context in which 60% of birth fathers and 23% of birth mothers had already lost contact with their children before this had happened.

Key Points

- There were 142 birth families, with 58% of the children entering Find-a-Family with at least one sibling. Almost all the children (205: 98%) had been primarily looked after by their birth mothers. There was comprehensive information on 140 birth mothers and on 120 (85%) of the birth fathers. Seventeen (12%) fathers were unknown.
- The majority of the birth mothers were Australian or New Zealanders (111: 79%) or European (21: 16%). Three birth fathers, but none of the birth mothers, were Aboriginal.
- When the children were born, most birth mothers (98: 70%) were still in a relationship with the birth father; only 14 (10%) were still in this relationship by the time the children were adopted.
- One in three (42: 31%) birth mothers are known to have experienced abuse in their own childhoods and 20 (15%) had been in care. Almost half of them (61: 45%) were known to statutory child welfare services before the birth of the child. Forty-two (29%) birth mothers had already experienced the permanent removal of at least one child; nine had already been permanently separated from three children and three from four.
- At least 35 (30%) birth fathers were also known to the statutory agency before the birth of the child and at least 25 (21%) had already experienced the removal of a child, 13 of them more than once. Extensive missing data on birth fathers suggests that these are under-estimates.
- At the time of the adoption order more than half the birth mothers had chronic problems including substance misuse (58%), domestic abuse (51%) and/or mental health problems (37%). Forty-nine (36%) were struggling with just one of these adversities; 57 (42%) were dealing with two and 12 (9%) with all three in combination. Only 19 birth mothers showed no evidence of any of these problems.

- At least 54 (45%) birth fathers were misusing substances; 28 (23%) were in abusive partnerships; and 12 (10%) had mental health problems. Missing data mean that this is undoubtedly an underestimate.
- In at least 44 (31%) birth families, both parents were misusing substances.
- Sixteen birth mothers and five birth fathers were also known to have cognitive impairments. Twelve of these birth mothers and three of these birth fathers were also struggling with mental ill health, domestic abuse and/or substance misuse. In three families, both birth parents had cognitive impairments.
- At the time of the adoption order, almost a quarter of the birth mothers (23%) and over half the birth fathers (60%) no longer had contact with their children. Only 52 (42%) birth mothers and 26 (21%) birth fathers saw their children more than twice a year; only 9 (8%) birth mothers and 4 (3%) birth fathers saw them more than once every three months. This is the context within which outcomes of open adoption policies should be evaluated.

References

Adoption UK. (2020). *Adoption barometer: A stocktake of adoption in the UK.* Adoption UK. https://www.adoptionuk.org/Handlers/Download.ashx?IDMF=c79a0e7d-1899-4b0f-ab96-783b4f678c9a. Accessed 2 Oct 2020.

Australian Bureau of Statistics. (1998). *Births Australia* 1998. https://www.ausstats.abs.gov.au/ausstats/subscriber.nsf/0/CA25687100069892CA256889000C79F4/$File/33010_1998.pdf. Accessed 10 Oct 2020.

Broadhurst, K. E., Alrough, B., Mason, C. S., Yeend, E., Kershaw, S., Shaw, M., & Harwin, J. (2016). Women and infants in care proceedings in England: New insights from research on recurrent care proceedings. *Family Law, 46*(2), 208–211.

Brodzinsky, D. (2006). Family structural openness and communication openness as predictors in the adjustment of adopted children. *Adoption Quarterly, 9*(4), 1–18.

Brown, R., & Ward, H. (2014). Cumulative jeopardy: How professional responses to evidence of abuse and neglect further Jeopardise children's life chances by being out of kilter with timeframes for early childhood development. *Children and Youth Services Review, 47*(3), 260–267.

Brown, R., Ward, H., Blackmore, J., Thomas, C., & Hyde-Dryden, G. (2016). *Eight-year-olds identified in infancy as at risk of harm: Report of a prospective longitudinal study. RR543.* Department for Education. https://assets.publishing.service.gov.uk/government/uploads/system/uploads/attachment_data/file/534376/Eight-year-olds_identified_in_infancy_as_at_risk_of_harm.pdf. Accessed 20 Oct 2020.

Bywaters, P. (2013). Inequalities in child welfare: Towards a new policy, research and action agenda. *British Journal of Social Work, 45*(1), 1–18.

Bywaters, P., Bunting, L., Davidson, G., Hanratty, J., Mason, W., McCartan, C., & Steils, N. (2016). *The relationship between poverty, child abuse and neglect: An evidence review.* Joseph Rowntree Foundation.

Cleaver, H., & Nicholson, D. (2007). *Parental learning disability and children's needs: Family experiences and effective practice.* Jessica Kingsley Publishers.

Cleaver, H., Unell, I., & Aldgate, J. (2011). *Children's needs – Parenting capacity: Child abuse: Parental mental illness, learning disability, substance misuse and domestic violence* (2nd ed.). The Stationery Office.

Hindley, N., Ramchandani, P. G., & Jones, D. P. H. (2006). Risk factors for recurrence of maltreatment: A systematic review. *Archives of Disease in Childhood, 91*(9), 744–752.

Iyer, P., Boddy, J., Hammelsbeck, R., & Lynch-Huggins, S. (2020). *Contact following placement in care, adoption, or special guardianship: Implications for children and young people's well-being. Evidence review.* Nuffield Family Justice Observatory.

Kohler, J. K., Grotevant, H. D., & McRoy, R. G. (2002). Adopted adolescents' preoccupation with adoption: The impact on adoptive family relationships. *Journal of Marriage and Family, 64,* 93–104. https://doi.org/10.1111/j.1741-3737.2002.00093.x. Accessed 19 Oct 2020.

Millham, S., Bullock, R., Hosie, K., & Haak, M. (1986). *Lost in care: The problems of maintaining links between children in care and their families.* Gower.

Neil, E. (2013). The mental distress of the birth relatives of adopted children: 'Disease' or 'unease'? Findings from a UK study. *Health and Social Care in the Community, 21*(2), 191–199.

Neil, E., Cossar, J., Lorgelly, P., & Young, J. (2010). *Helping birth families: Services, costs and outcomes.* BAAF.

Neil, E., & Howe, D. (2004). *Contact in adoption and permanent foster care.* BAAF.

Wade, J., Biehal, N., Farrelly, N., & Sinclair, I. (2011). *Caring for abused and neglected children: Making the right decisions for reunification or long-term care.* Jessica Kingsley Publishers.

Ward, H., Brown, R., Blackmore, J., Hyde-Dryden, G., & Thomas, C. (2019). Identifying parents who show capacity to make and sustain positive changes when infants are at risk of significant harm. *Developing Practice, The Child, Youth and Family Work Journal, 54*, 47–61.

Ward, H., Brown, R., & Hyde-Dryden, G. (2014). *Assessing parental capacity to change when children are on the edge of care: An overview of current research evidence. RR369.* Centre for Child and Family Research, Loughborough University and Department for Education. https://assets.publishing.service. gov.uk/government/uploads/system/uploads/attachment_data/file/330332/ RR369_Assessing_parental_capacity_to_change_Final.pdf.   Accessed 30 Dec 2020.

Ward, H., Munro, E. R., & Dearden, C. (2006). *Babies and young children in care: Life pathways, decision-making and practice.* Jessica Kingsley Publishers.

White, O. G., Hindley, N., & Jones, D. P. H. (2015). Risk factors for child maltreatment recurrence: An updated systematic review. *Medicine, Science and the Law, 55*(4), 259–277.

3

The Children

Introduction

Adoption from care is the final step in a complex decision-making process. The previous chapter has considered the intricate web of problems with which the birth parents struggled. In many families where parents are faced with similar problems, there are sufficient protective factors, such as supportive grandparents, a partner who does not misuse drugs or alcohol and/or skilled professional support, to ensure that children are not exposed to experiences that cause them significant harm, and they can safely remain at home (Hindley et al., 2006; White et al., 2015). The extent to which children are protected from the impact of parents' problems are therefore also factors that influence the decision-making process (Ward et al., 2012). Before the study began, professionals had decided that the Barnardos adoptees could not be sufficiently protected from harm if they lived with their birth

Much of this chapter was published in *Children and Youth Services Review* 96, January 2019, Tregeagle, S., Moggach, L., Trivedi, H. & Ward, H. 'Previous life experiences and the vulnerability of children adopted from out-of-home care: the impact of adverse childhood experiences and child welfare decision-making' pp. 55–63 Copyright Elsevier Ltd 2018. We are grateful to Elsevier for permission to reproduce text and tables here.

© The Author(s) 2022
H. Ward et al., *Outcomes of Open Adoption from Care*,
https://doi.org/10.1007/978-3-030-76429-6_3

parents or other family members and that it was in their best interests to seek permanence through adoption.

This chapter focuses on the children's characteristics and experiences, first while living at home with their birth parents, and then in the sometimes lengthy period they spent in out-of-home care between the initial separation from their parents and the final placement in their adoptive homes. The outcomes of open adoption from care cannot be adequately understood unless they are set within the context of these experiences, which will have shaped the children's developmental trajectories. The chapter specifically seeks to identify whether there were factors within their personal characteristics and experiences prior to the adoption placement that were likely to increase the likelihood of maladaptive development and impact on their long-term wellbeing.

The chapter draws on data held on the Barnardos files and electronic case management system, and on the documents presented to the courts at the time of the adoption order concerning all 210 adoptees. Some data from the Pathways of Care Longitudinal Study (POCLS) (Australian Institute of Family Studies et al., 2015; Hopkins et al., 2019; Smart, 2015) are also presented in order to explore whether, and in what ways, the Barnardos cohort differed in characteristics and experience from other groups of children and young people in out-of-home care in Australia.

Children's Characteristics

The cohort of 210 children placed for adoption included 108 boys and 102 girls. Of these, 89 (42%) entered the programme as single children (although an unknown number had siblings from whom they had previously been separated) and 121 (58%) were admitted as sibling groups of two (40), three (12) and five (1). As we shall see (Chap. 4), although one of the objectives of the programme was to place siblings together, this was not always possible.

Ethnicity

Table 3.1 shows the ethnicity of the adoptees. The majority (89%) were of Australian, New Zealand or European heritage, and there were five

Table 3.1 Adoptees: ethnicity (*N* = 210)

Ethnicity	Frequency	Per cent*
Australian/New Zealander	132	63
Australian/European	35	17
European	19	9
Australian/Maori/Pacific Islander	10	5
Aboriginal	5	2
Maori/Pacific Islander	3	1.5
Asian	3	1.5
Australian/Asian	2	1
Maori/European	1	0
Total	**210**	**100**

*Percentages have been rounded

children whose parents were Asian or Australian/Asian. Adoption is not considered culturally appropriate for Aboriginal and Torres Strait Islander children and it was Barnardos' policy to refer these children to indigenous-run programmes. One child was found to be Aboriginal after referral but before placement; at the request of the New South Wales State Government, Barnardos worked alongside the Government Department's Aboriginal team to recruit an appropriate Aboriginal placement. No other children were known to be Aboriginal at the time of placement but four were later discovered to have Aboriginal fathers. The cohort also included 14 children who had at least one parent who was a Maori or Pacific Islander.

Health Conditions and Disabilities Prior to Adoption

Although the Barnardos programme did not specialise in finding adoptive homes for children with health conditions or disabilities (see Chap. 1), such conditions were prevalent amongst the adopted children in the study.

According to the case papers, at the time the application for an adoption order was made, 121 (58%) of the adoptees had at least one diagnosed long-term health condition or a developmental delay; 62 (30%) had one condition; 30 (14%) had two; 25 (12%) had three or four and 4 (2%) children had a combination of five health conditions or disabilities.

Table 3.2 (p. 68) shows the prevalence and nature of the long-term health conditions and developmental delays affecting the Barnardos adoptees. The most common conditions affecting children's physical health were diseases of the respiratory system such as asthma and bronchitis, affecting 14 (6.7%) of the sample. There was also a high prevalence of congenital malformations, affecting 11 (5.2%) children, and sight (11: 5.2%) and hearing (8: 3.8%) problems.

Many of the physical health conditions may be related to children's previous experience of abuse and neglect. Some of this had occurred during the pregnancy: 13 children (6.2%) showed signs of neonatal abstinence syndrome or foetal alcohol disorder; 2 were infected with hepatitis C and another child was recorded as having a 'fragile skull, following a physical assault on her mother'. Other children had severe health conditions related to physical abuse they had experienced as infants, as Lisa's case study shows. Some, but not all, of the problems with teeth or oral hygiene, affecting three (1.4%) children, may also have been related to neglect and/or physical abuse.

Lisa

Before Entering Her Adoptive Home

Lisa was admitted to hospital at the age of eight weeks with convulsions and head injuries. She was intubated and put on a ventilator, with medical examination showing a complex fracture of the skull with bruising and swelling to both sides of the brain. She also had a retinal haemorrhage, old and recent fractures to many ribs, fractures to her legs and coccyx, bruising to her face and chest and was anaemic and malnourished.

Lisa's parents gave an explanation for the injuries; however, the medical team felt that this was inconsistent with Lisa's presentation. Lisa was discharged after three weeks into foster care.

(continued)

(continued)

Just the way that [birth mother] didn't look after me very well, all that stuff. But, she did mean well, but when she got sick, she didn't do very much. She's okay now, but back in the old days, she trusted on [birth father] to look after me and that was one of the worst things that ever happened.

Impact of Injuries

When Lisa was seven months old, she was placed with her prospective adoptive parents, who had been advised by medical specialists that she might never see, talk or walk. She made considerable progress after placement and became a happy, contented, alert and responsive child with an engaging smile. However, she continued to have significant medical problems:

Eyesight: Lisa required her right eye to be patched and had ongoing assessment for a squint. She required glasses and continued to wear these in adulthood.

Therapy: Lisa had significant gross motor delay and did not walk until she was three years old; she also had a significant delay in expressive language abilities. Lisa had daily exercises at home and saw a speech therapist, occupational therapist and physiotherapist on a fortnightly basis for much of her pre-school years.

...a long time ago when I used to be brain damaged, but I can't remember that far, but when I used to be thrown into a brick wall and things like that, and all that kind of stuff. It was one of the worst lives that I ever had before, before I started being adopted.

A high proportion of the children also displayed emotional and behavioural problems, as has been found in other studies of children and young people in out-of-home care (see Meltzer et al., 2003; Tarren-Sweeney & Hazell, 2006). Again, many of these problems were likely to be related to the children's previous experiences. Six children were showing evidence of affective disorders or anxiety-related problems, including one child who was described as 'detached, emotionally deprived and suffering from chronic emotional distress', and another who was thought to suffer from 'attachment issues, self-loathing, nightmares, suicidal tendencies, self-blaming and anger issues'.

Table 3.2 Health conditions and developmental delays (Barnardos sample N = 210; POCLS sample N = 1285)

Health conditions and developmental delays	Barnardos n*	Barnardos %**	POCLS n*	POCLS %**
Developmental delay – cognitive/language	45	21.4	151	11.8
Developmental delay – emotional/social/behavioural delay & behavioural & emotional disorders including ADHD	30	14.3	125	9.7
Developmental delay – physical/motor skills	16	7.6	67	5.2
Developmental delay – unspecified	28	13.3	Not Known	Not Known
Developmental disorders including autism/Asperger's	4	1.9	Not Known	Not Known
Affective disorders and anxiety related problems	6	2.9	69	5.4
Allergies	2	1	116	9.0
Asthma /bronchitis	14	6.7	178	13.9
Blood disorder	1	0.5	8	0.6
Born substance affected/neonatal abstinence syndrome/foetal alcohol spectrum disorder***	13	6.2	19	1.5
Cerebral palsy	1	0.5	9	0.7
Congenital malformations	11	5.2	Not Known	Not Known
Diabetes	0	0	2	0.2
Epilepsy	3	1.4	9	0.7
Problems with eyesight	11	5.2	131	10.2
Problems with hearing	8	3.8	72	5.6
Heart conditions or disease	5	2.4	35	2.7
Hepatitis C	2	1	Not Known	Not Known
Kidney condition or disease	1	0.5	8	0.6
Problems with teeth/oral hygiene	3	1.4	111	8.6
Other long-term physical condition	15	7.1	155	12.1
None of the above	89	42.4	713	55.5

*Some children had more than one health condition or disability
**Percentages have been rounded
*** Not directly comparable – POCLS data refer specifically to foetal alcohol spectrum disorder.

We assumed that because we took a child on that was not a baby, she had her experience, bad experience, the baggage she came with…. There was a death in her birth family and she knows it all, she knew about it, she was heavily affected… she was crying almost every night for a long time. The difficulty was that she was very unsettled… she had this feeling of guilt because she survived a violent family life when her little brother didn't. (Adoptive parent of young woman, aged 3 when permanently placed)

When she came to me, lived in a pillowcase, literally had a pillowcase over her head, and she used to walk round in a pillowcase. And when I asked her why, she said she was being an egg. And the psychologist said – used to think it's because if she can't see anyone, they can't see her. (Adoptive parent of young woman, aged 4 when permanently placed)

However, the most common mental health problems (as classified according to the ICD10) were developmental disorders and/or delays. Forty-five children (21% of the sample) were showing evidence of cognitive or language delay; 16 (8%) had delayed motor skills or physical development and 30 (14%) were displaying behavioural disorders and/or emotional, social or developmental delays, including 21 (10%) children who had been diagnosed as suffering from ADHD or ADD. Altogether one in three (77: 37%) of the adoptees were showing delayed development, often across several dimensions.

When I was found, I had the mental and physical abilities of a two-month-old when I was almost two years old, and that's something that would have continued down a very dark trajectory. (Young man, aged 1 when permanently placed, aged 25 when interviewed)

While these data reflect formal health assessments, the case files also recorded less formal evidence, indicating that 49% of the Barnardos children were displaying behavioural problems by the time they entered their adoptive homes. At least 86 (41%) of them had accessed mental health services before the adoption order was made.

Thirteen children aged between 3 and 13 had also been recorded as having engaged in criminal activity before entering their adoptive homes—we do not know in what ways the younger children had been involved. There was also evidence of educational disadvantage: 26 (30%)

of those children who were aged five or more at entry to their adoptive homes were recorded as having reading difficulties. Chapter 7 explores these issues in some depth for the adoptees who took part in the follow-up, using information they and their adoptive parents provided through the survey and interviews.

Additional Support Needs

The extent to which the children in the full cohort were likely to have required additional support due to their behaviour, health and disability needs is evidenced in the levels of funding they received from the New South Wales Government before the adoption order was made. While the systems and classifications varied during the study period, in general, there were four different levels: children who were supported at the basic care level presented with very few challenges beyond what is considered 'normal' for their relevant age group; Care+1 indicates that a child required considered and regular supervision; Care+2 that they required comprehensive and constant support; and Care+2+ that they presented with extraordinarily difficult behaviour and required intensive wrap-around support.

Table 3.3 shows the care levels at which the children had been assessed at the time of adoption. Of the 195 adoptees for whom these data were available, nearly two-thirds (121: 62%) were supported at the normal

Table 3.3 Care level presented at the time of adoption (*N* = 210)

Care level	Frequency	Per cent*	Cumulative per cent*
Care	121	62	62
Care+1	50	26	88
Care+2	11	6	94
Care+2+	13	7	100
Total	195	100	
Missing	15		

*Percentages have been rounded

care level; however, more than one in four (50: 26%) required constant supervision and one in seven (24: 13%) were supported at either the second highest (11: 6%) or the highest possible care level (13: 7%) when they entered their adoptive homes.

Comparisons with Other Populations

The data on health conditions and disabilities in the Barnardos adoptees can be compared with information on a representative sample of all Australian children collected between 2014 and 2015 through the National Health Survey (Australian Bureau of Statistics, 2015) and also with similar data collected on a current population of children in out-of-home care in New South Wales (POCLS, First Wave) (Australian Institute of Family Studies et al., 2015).[1] While these comparisons are intended to set the Barnardos' data within a context, it should be noted that they are not exact, as the data were collected by different means: Barnardos, by extracting data from case files using a pre-determined checklist; the National Health survey through personal interviews with adults in selected homes; and the POCLS study through questionnaires completed by foster carers. Moreover, the categorisation of health conditions, though based on the ICD10, differs slightly between each study.

Variations in health conditions between the samples may simply reflect differences in the children's ages at the time of assessment, as some conditions do not develop or become apparent in early childhood. The POCLS children were aged between 9 months and 18 years at data collection, as were 99% of the Barnardos sample; however, the National Health Survey reports on children aged 0–14. Moreover, as Table 3.4 shows, there were considerable differences in the age structure of the two samples of children in out-of-home care.

---

[1] The National Health Survey 2014–2015 collected data from a sample of 19,000 Australians, including nearly 5000 children and young people aged 0–17. The POCLS data includes carer responses for 1285 children aged 9 months to 17 years who entered out-of-home care for the first time in New South Wales between May 2010 and October 2011.

Table 3.4 Age at assessment: Barnardos (N = 210) and POCLS children (Wave One interview) (N = 1285)

	Barnardos		POCLS	
Age	Frequency	Per cent*	Frequency	Per cent*
9-35 months	15	7	567	44
3-5 years	40	19	265	21
6-11 years	96	47	329	26
12-17 years	55	27	124	10
Total	206	100	1285	100
Missing	4			

*Percentages have been rounded

The children in the POCLS sample were significantly[2] younger than those in the Barnardos cohort, with the largest age group (44%) being under three years old at the time of the assessment; in contrast, only 7% of the Barnardos children were under three when assessed, the largest number (96: 47%) were 6–11 years old. The Barnardos sample also had a higher proportion of teenagers (27% vs 10%).

Children in the POCLS sample were found to be reasonably similar to the rest of the Australian child population in terms of types and prevalence of the most common long-term conditions; however, rates of psycho-social disabilities were considerably higher in the POCLS sample than in the general population (Australian Institute of Family Studies et al., 2015; Australian Bureau of Statistics, 2015).

Table 3.2 (p. 68) displays the data on health conditions and disabilities from the Barnardos sample alongside similar data from the POCLS study. Data on some physical conditions that may be related to abuse or neglect in utero, such as neonatal abstinence syndrome and congenital malformations, are not available for the POCLS sample. However, where comparable data are available, they show considerable differences. The most common physical long-term health conditions for both samples (and

---

[2] X^2 = 125.56; df= 3; $p < 0.001$.

indeed for the general population) were respiratory problems, and particularly asthma; however, the prevalence appears to have been lower in the Barnardos sample (6.7% vs 15.9% (POCLS) and 20.9% (National Survey)). This could be due to under-reporting.

Both out-of-home care samples had higher rates of mental health and behavioural problems than the general population, where the prevalence was 8.9%. The Barnardos adoptees showed a slightly (but not significantly) higher prevalence of cognitive developmental delay than the POCLS children (21.4% vs 11.8%). This difference may reflect the higher proportion of children aged under three in the POCLS group, many of whom may have been too young for incipient developmental problems to become evident.

The POCLS group had a slightly higher rate of affective disorders and anxiety-related problems than the Barnardos children; however, the Barnardos adoptees showed a slightly (but not significantly) higher prevalence of behavioural and emotional disorders (14.3% vs 9.7%). Smart (2015) found that the POCLS group were beginning to show evidence of emotional and behavioural disorders from the age of three (see also Ward et al., 2012): in the Barnardos sample, 18% of 3–5-year-olds, 19% of the 6–11-year-olds and 14% of the 12–17-year-olds had been diagnosed as having an emotional or behavioural disorder by the time they were adopted; in the two younger age groups, the prevalence was higher than in the POCLS sample, where the comparable percentages were 12% (3–5-year-olds) and 15% (6–11-year-olds). There was a slightly higher rate of emotional and behavioural disorders amongst teenagers in the POCLS group (17% vs 14%); this could reflect late entry to care and therefore longer exposure to abuse for this age group. However the difference may also reflect variations in the methodology—the Barnardos data are based on a formal diagnosis, whereas the POCLS data come from caregiver reports. The Barnardos case files indicated that nearly half of the adoptees (49%) had a behavioural problem as reported by caregivers and others, including at least 80% of those aged six and over. If the informal case file data are closer to the POCLS assessments, then the Barnardos children had far higher levels of emotional and behavioural disturbance.

The Barnardos children were assessed at the time the application for an adoption order was made, often many months after they had been

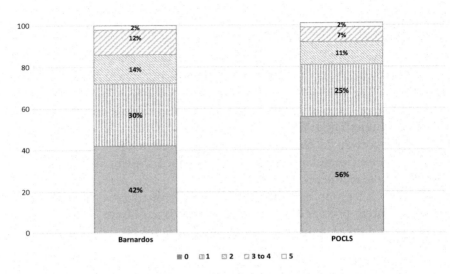

Fig. 3.1 Number of health conditions and developmental delays: Barnardos (*N* = 210) and POCLS (*N* = 1285) children compared

separated from their birth families. They did not have longer exposure to abuse than the POCLS children—in fact, more of them were separated before they were three (68% vs 55%). However early separation may have reflected high levels of abuse, as some of the case studies indicate. The higher prevalence of emotional and behavioural disorders amongst younger adoptees may reflect these experiences, which may also have been compounded by adverse experiences in out-of-home care before achieving permanence (see below).

Further evidence that the Barnardos children were more vulnerable in terms of physical and mental health than other children in out-of-home care is shown in Fig. 3.1, which displays the number of health conditions found in the two samples. A higher proportion of the Barnardos children had at least one health condition or disability (57.6% compared with 45.5% of the POCLS sample), and a higher proportion of them had two or more conditions (28% vs 20%). Such findings reflect the extreme vulnerability of children who are placed for adoption—these are, after all, the group of children in out-of-home care who are assessed as requiring permanent protection. It should also be remembered that, for many years, the Barnardos children were selected on the explicit criteria of being 'hard to place', often because of emotional or behavioural problems (see Chap. 1).

Children's Experiences Before Separation from Birth Families

Reasons for Separation

The primary reason recorded for the decision to remove over 90% of the children from their birth families was abuse or neglect. There were 20 children (10% of the cohort) for whom no evidence of maltreatment had been recorded. Over half (11/20: 55%) of these 20 children had been removed because an older child in the family had been abused and they were considered to be at high risk of harm. The other nine children for whom there was no evidence of maltreatment had been placed in out-of-home care because of concerns about their mother's mental health (three children) or because their parents had voluntarily relinquished them for adoption (four children), and two children were orphans, with no relatives to care for them.

Table 3.5 shows the children's experience of maltreatment before separation from their birth parents. Thirty-six (17%) had experienced one form of abuse, with the most frequently reported being neglect (23), followed by emotional abuse/psychological harm (11) and physical abuse (2). All other children had experienced composite patterns of abuse (polyvictimisation): 87 (42%) had experienced two forms of abuse, 44 (21%) children had experienced three forms and 23 (11%) had experienced all four. The combined data show that neglect and emotional abuse were the most common forms of maltreatment, experienced respectively by 164 (78%) and 151 (72%) of the sample; 72 (34%) children had experienced physical abuse and 47 (22%) had been sexually abused. This latter group may have been particularly vulnerable to poor outcomes, for children who have experienced sexual abuse are at particular risk of experiencing multiple placements in care, poor attachments to parent figures and disrupted adoptions (Smith & Howard, 1991; Nalavany et al., 2008).

Table 3.5 Experiences of abuse before separation (*N* = 210)

Abuse type experienced		Frequency	Per cent*
Single abuse type	No abuse	20	9
	Neglect	23	11
	Physical abuse	2	1
	Emotional abuse	11	5
Two abuse types	Neglect plus emotional abuse	73	35
	Neglect plus physical abuse	5	2
	Neglect plus sexual abuse	1	1
	Physical abuse plus emotional abuse	6	3
	Emotional abuse plus sexual abuse	2	1
Three abuse types	Neglect plus physical abuse plus sexual abuse	8	4
	Neglect plus physical abuse plus emotional abuse	23	11
	Neglect plus sexual abuse plus emotional abuse	8	4
	Physical abuse plus sexual abuse plus emotional abuse	5	2
Four abuse types	Neglect plus physical abuse plus sexual abuse plus emotional abuse	23	11
	Total	210	100

*Percentages have been rounded

In Chap. 1 we noted that the public discourse on adoption sometimes overlooks the issue of child maltreatment. It is therefore important to be aware of the extensive abuse experienced by the Barnardos adoptees before removal from home. The high proportion of adoptees who had experienced polyvictimisation indicates that these children were at very high risk of significant harm. We do not have detailed information concerning the exact nature of abuse experienced by all the Barnardos children, but we do know that the cohort included immobile infants who had received multiple fractures, toddlers whose physical and emotional needs were grossly neglected because of parental drug addiction, and children who had been loaned out to paedophiles in return for cash. The following reports from adoptive parents are not atypical:

His original reason for going into care was a choice of his mother's to let him go with two men – be taken away when he was a tiny, little two-year-old, and that he was very, very seriously abused and was hospitalised when he came back – they brought him back. They had him for 10 or 12 days or something, and he was hospitalised…

…So he's got a history of lots of physical abuse, emotional abuse and probably sexual abuse as well. (Adoptive parent of a young man, aged 6 when permanently placed)

As I understand it, by the time she was six weeks, she was already in hospital with multiple fractures. And then it was a very scattered sort of situation between various members of her birth family: her uncles and her grandfather and her mother and father… And there were about 12, 11, 13 moves before she went to [foster mother] when she was three and a half. (Adoptive parent of young woman, aged 4 when permanently placed)

Although there are no directly comparable data, it is likely that the experiences of the Barnardos adoptees were more severe than those of the POCLS cohort because the latter includes the whole range of children placed in out-of-home care. The vast majority of the Barnardos children were adopted because they could not safely return to birth parents; within five years of placement away from home, 26% of the POCLS children who had received final care and protection orders, and 81% of those who had not received a final order had been reunited, although almost one in four (22%) of the latter group had returned to out-of-home care (Hopkins et al., 2019).

Adverse Childhood Experiences

Chapter 1 has discussed some of the research on adverse childhood experiences (ACEs) that can have a long-term negative impact throughout the life trajectory. These include all forms of abuse and neglect, as well as growing up in a dysfunctional household; the two are interrelated (Felitti et al., 1998). Factors that are indicative of household dysfunction include parental substance misuse, mental health problems, domestic abuse and/

or criminal behaviour patterns. As Chap. 2 has shown, these factors were prevalent in many of the birth families: at least 112 (53%) children had lived with a mother or stepmother who was the victim of domestic abuse; 135 (64%) had lived in households in which there was substance misuse; 85 (41%) with a household member who had mental health problems and 50 (24%) had experienced the imprisonment of a birth parent. These are all known risk factors for the recurrent maltreatment of children (Hindley et al., 2006; Ward et al., 2014; White et al., 2015) and are likely to have contributed to the initial decision to place the child away from home.

The records of the Barnardos cohort include data on nine out of the ten ACEs identified as being related to adverse adult outcomes.[3] Table 3.6 shows the cohort compared with a normative Australian sample (7485 Australian adults interviewed at the outset of a longitudinal community study of psychological health in the Canberra region (Rosenman & Rodgers, 2004)).

First, the data provide strong evidence of the vulnerability of the Barnardos adoptees: before entering the Find-a-Family programme almost all (208: 99%) of them had had one or more adverse childhood experiences; just over two-thirds (145: 69%) had had four or more and 27 children (13% of the sample) had had seven or more. Moreover, these data are likely to be an underestimate, as information collected from case files depends on the quality of reporting and a lack of evidence concerning adverse factors does not necessarily mean they were not present.

Second, Felitti et al. (1998) found that exposure to four or more adverse childhood experiences significantly increased adult propensity to health risk factors and premature death (see Chap. 1 for further details). The data indicate that the Barnardos adoptees were markedly more likely to be subject to these increased risks than a normative population. Nearly 60% of the Australian population studied by Rosenman and Rodgers (2004) had not encountered any of the key adverse childhood experiences and less than one in five (17%) had encountered four or more.

---

[3] Physical abuse; sexual abuse; psychological (emotional) abuse; witnessing violence against their mother or stepmother; exposure to substance misuse; parental mental illness; criminal behaviour in the household; parental separation and neglect. The commonly used version of the ACE Questionnaire (see www.ncfjc.org) separates neglect into two categories: physical neglect and emotional neglect. The Barnardos data are not sufficiently detailed to allow for this.

Table 3.6 Prevalence of adverse childhood experiences: Barnardos adoptees (*N* = 210) and normative Australian sample (*N* = 7485)

ACE scores	Barnardos Adoptees Frequency	Barnardos Adoptees Per cent*	Barnardos Adoptees Cumulative per cent*	Normative sample (Rosenman & Rodgers, 2004) Per cent*	Normative sample (Rosenman & Rodgers, 2004) Cumulative per cent*
0	2	1	1	41	41
1	10	5	6	22	63
2	21	10	16	13	76
3	32	15	31	8	84
4	38	18	49	6	89
5	54	26	75	11 (5 or more)	100
6	26	12	87		
7	18	9	96		
8	6	3	99		
9	3	1	100		
Total	210	100			

*Percentages have been rounded

More than four times (69%) as many of the Barnardos adoptees had reached this critical threshold. These data, which demonstrate the extreme vulnerability of a relatively high proportion of the adoptees prior to placement with their adoptive parents, need to be taken into account when assessing the adoption outcomes.

Age at Notification

For many of the children, maltreatment was identified and notified at a very early age. As Table 3.7 shows, half of the cohort had been identified before they were six months old (102: 50%), 60% (123) before their

Table 3.7 Age at notification of abuse (*N* = 210)

Age	Frequency	Per cent*	Cumulative per cent*
Pre-birth	20	10	10
0-5 months	82	40	50
6–11 months	21	10	60
1 year	30	14	74
2 years	20	10	84
3–4 years	14	7	91
5 years and over	19	9	100
Total	206	100	
Missing	4		

*Percentages have been rounded

first birthday and nearly three-quarters (74%: 153) before they were two. In fact, 20 (10%) children had been identified before they were born. However, 19 (9%) children were not identified until after their fifth birthdays, including one child who was 11 and 3 children who were 12. Although some of these children may have lived in stable, nurturing homes before the abuse began, others may have been subject to chronic maltreatment for many years before action was taken (Brown et al., 2016).

Months Between Notification and Separation

Rousseau and colleagues (2015) monitored the development of 129 children who were placed in out-of-home care in France for 20 years and found that the length of time between notification and first placement had a more significant impact on children's long-term outcomes than the age at which they were separated. This finding is consonant with those of other studies which have found that the extensive mental health problems often displayed by older children in care are largely an artefact caused by

Table 3.8 Months between notification of abuse and separation from birth parents (*N* = 210)

Months	Frequency	Per cent*	Cumulative per cent*
Under 1 month	51	25	25
1-9 months	90	44	69
10-15 months	14	7	76
More than 15 months	50	24	100
Total	205	100	
Missing	5		

*Percentages have been rounded

late-placed children entering care with high levels of pre-existing disturbance (Tarren-Sweeney & Hazell, 2006; Ward & Holmes, 2008).

The French study found that children separated from birth parents within 10 months of notification of maltreatment had significantly better outcomes than those placed in out-of-home care more than 15 months after the authorities had been alerted. Table 3.8 shows the time in months between notification of abuse and first separation from birth parents of the 205 adoptees in the Barnardos cohort for whom data were available.

The mean length of time between notification and separation was 11.5 months (sd = 18), and just over half the adoptees were removed within 4 months of notification. Within this group were 51 adoptees (25%) who experienced less than a month's delay between the notification of abuse and separation from birth family, including 30 (15%) who were separated on the same day that the notification was received. More than two-thirds (141: 69%) of the children were separated within ten months of notification; the French study would indicate that these children were likely to have better outcomes than those for whom the gap between notification and separation was longer. Nearly one in four (50: 24%) of the children were separated more than 15 months after notification and were therefore likely to have less satisfactory outcomes. This group included 30 children, 15% of the cohort, who continued to remain with their birth parents for more than two years. One of the most difficult decisions a social worker has to make is whether to place a child in out-of-home care. With the benefit of hindsight, once a child has been placed for adoption, it may seem evident that the decision to separate took too long. However, the long time periods between notification and separation are likely to represent repeated attempts to support the parents in the hope that the situation will change and that the family can remain intact (Ward et al., 2012).

Age at Separation from Birth Families

Studies of children placed with adoptive parents following gross deprivation in Romanian orphanages have found that those who overcame the consequences of severe early deprivation were significantly more likely to do so if they were placed in a nurturing environment before they were six months old (Rutter et al., 2007; Sonuga-Barke et al., 2017). The extreme deprivation experienced by the Romanian adoptees was exceptional and care has to be taken in using these findings as comparators for other populations (Rutter et al., 2007). Nevertheless, there are several indications that the first 24 months of life are a sensitive period for childhood development, with the first 6 months perhaps being particularly crucial (Zeanah et al., 2011). Numerous studies have also found that children who are permanently separated from abusive families at an earlier age tend to have better outcomes than those who are separated later (see Rousseau et al., 2015; Tarren-Sweeney & Hazell, 2006; Ward et al., 2012).

Table 3.9 shows the ages at which the adoptees were first separated from their birth parents. A high proportion had indeed been separated within this sensitive period: 53 (25%) had been separated before they were six months old, including 13 (6%) who were separated within a month of their birth. More than one in three (77: 37%) had been separated before they were one, and over half (113: 54%) before they were 24 months old. On the other hand, more than one in ten of the children (22: 11%) were aged seven or older when removed from an abusive home.

Table 3.9 Age at first separation from birth parents (N = 210)

Age	Frequency	Per cent*	Cumulative per cent*
0–5 months	53	25	25
6–11 months	24	11	37
1 year	36	17	54
2 years	29	14	68
3–6 years	45	22	90
7 years and over	22	11	100
Total	**209**	**100**	
Missing	1		

*Percentages have been rounded

Months Between First Separation and Permanent Placement with Adoptive Parents

Selwyn, Wijedasa and Meakings (2014) found that children in England and Wales who spent more than 2 years in out-of-home care before entering their permanent placement with adoptive parents were significantly more likely to experience a disruption (i.e. leave their adoptive home before they were 18 years old). The mean length of time between first admission to care and admission to a permanent placement with an adoptive family was 27 months (sd = 28) for the Barnardos cohort. However, as Table 3.10 shows, there was a wide range of timeframes, with just over a third of the cohort reaching their permanent placement within a year (74: 35%), including nine children (4%) who were there within a month. Just over a third of the cohort (77: 36%) waited for more than two years. Twenty-eight children, 13% of the sample, waited for more than five years, including eight who did not reach their adoptive family

Table 3.10 Months between separation and permanence (*N* = 210)

Age	Frequency	Per cent*	Cumulative per cent*
Under 6 months	33	16	16
Six months to a year	41	20	35
Between 1 and 2 years	59	28	63
Between 2 and 5 years	49	23	87
Five years or more	28	13	100
Total	**210**	**100**	

*Percentages have been rounded

until more than eight years after they had first been placed away from home. During this often extended period, as we shall see, there were a number of factors that may have increased the children's vulnerability.

Age at Reaching Final Placement

There is considerable evidence concerning relationships between children's age at permanent placement and outcomes of adoption. Numerous studies have shown that the older children are at final placement, the greater the risk of adverse outcomes (Coakley & Berrick, 2008; Evan B. Donaldson Adoption Institute, 2004; Festinger, 2014). Van den Dries et al.'s (2009) meta-analysis of data from studies concerning attachment in adopted children found that those who were permanently placed with adoptive carers before their first birthdays were significantly more likely to form a secure attachment than those who were placed later. Zeanah et al.'s (2011) overview of evidence concerning sensitive periods of child development argued that:

> current studies show age-at-adoption cutoffs (after which deficiencies are reported) to be 6, 12, or 18 months (parent-rated behavior problems, security of attachment), 15 months (expressive and receptive language), 18 months (parent-reported executive functioning), and 24 months (IQ, security of attachment; EEG coherence). (Zeanah et al., 2011, p. 11)

Table 3.11 Age at entering adoptive home (*N* = 210)

Age	Frequency	Per cent*	Cumulative per cent*
Under 6 months	9	4	4
6–11 months	21	10	14
12–17 months	10	5	19
18–23 months	10	5	24
2–3 years	56	27	51
4–5 years	33	16	66
6–9 years	51	24	90
10 years and older	20	10	100
Total	**210**	**100**	

*Percentages have been rounded

Further research has identified another cut-off point, indicating that adoptive placements made after the child is four years old are significantly more likely to disrupt than those made earlier[4] (although the rate of disruption does not follow a linear progression) (Selwyn et al., 2014).

Table 3.11 shows the ages of the Barnardos adoptees when they entered their adoptive homes. Nine (4%) were permanently placed before they were six months old; 30 (14%) before their first birthdays; and 50 (24%) before they were two. However, just over three-quarters of this cohort (76%:160 children) were permanently placed outside the optimal timeframe for adoption placements, increasing the chances of less than satisfactory outcomes. Almost half the sample, 104 (49%) of the children, were aged four or older at the time they entered their adoptive homes and their placements would have been significantly more vulnerable to disruption than those placed earlier (Selwyn et al., 2014). This group includes 51 (24%) children who were between six and nine years old and 20 who were ten or older when permanently placed; 5 of them were teenagers.

---

[4] Although adoptive placements are more likely to disrupt after the child is four years old, disruptions do not increase incrementally each year. For instance, disruptions decrease for children adopted in their teens, possibly because they are more involved in the decision (Selwyn et al., 2014).

After they had reached their adoptive home, some children waited lengthy periods for an adoption order to be made. Although for young children, moving into the adoptive home will be the significant moment at which permanence is experienced, older children may be unable to feel that they belong to an adoptive family until their legal status is secure.

> He wanted to be adopted from the word go. "I want to be here, and I want to be here permanently".... as soon as he had his adoption papers, he was fine. It gave him strength. (Adoptive parent of young man, aged 2 when permanently placed)

There is some evidence to suggest that adoptions are significantly more likely to disrupt if the gap between entering the placement and the adoption order being made is longer than 12 months. This is possibly because long delays between placement and the adoption order may be indicative of adoptive parents' ambivalence or concerns about the placement (Selwyn et al., 2014). However, this evidence comes from a British study and it may not be so relevant in an Australian context, where there may be different reasons for delays. For instance, almost half of the Barnardos cohort (88: 42%) entered their adoptive home with a plan for long-term foster care, and it was sometimes years before adoption was considered as a long-term option. Moreover, some of the adult adoptees told the interviewer that they had asked for their adoption order to be delayed because they had not wanted to upset their birth parents.

> And they had all the paperwork ready and at the last point I said, "No. I don't want to go through this". It disappointed my [adoptive] mum and dad very much.... The reason why it stopped was because there was a major concern on my biological side – my biological mother's side. She disapproved the adoption process and that's something that I didn't want to hurt my mum about, so that's why I cancelled the adoption process, not to hurt her. (Young man, aged 9 when permanently placed, aged 40 when interviewed)

One of the Barnardos adoptees received their adoption order more than 25 years after the placement began, but this was an exception. It took between 6 months and 13.5 years from the time of placement for adoption orders to be issued for the other 209 adoptees in the cohort.

Ten (5%) of them had an adoption order within 12 months of being placed, 46 (22%) within 2 years and 144 (69%) within 5 years. The other 65 (31%) children waited between 5 and 13.5 years.

Children's Experiences Between First Separation from Birth Parents and Permanent Placement with an Adoptive Family

Not all the Barnardos adoptees had remained continuously separated from their birth parents after the initial admission to out-of-home care. Attempts had been made to reunite just under a third (68: 32%) of them. Fifty-eight (28%) of the cohort had experienced one failed restoration; seven (3%) had experienced two, and three children had been rehabilitated with their birth families and then returned to care on three occasions before being placed in permanent care with a view to adoption.

Failed restorations are known to be detrimental to children's wellbeing, particularly if they are repeated (Farmer et al., 2011). In addition, 23 (11%) children had experienced a failed kinship placement, including 9 who also had an unsuccessful attempt at reunification with birth parents. The majority of children whose kinship placements failed had been voluntarily relinquished to the statutory agency—only five were removed through court orders. Such experiences are likely to have enhanced the perceptions of rejection already held by these vulnerable children.

Most children were first placed in out-of-home care by the statutory agency and then referred to Barnardos. While they were looked after by the statutory agency, a substantial group of children had a relatively stable care experience. However, a number had experienced frequent changes of placements. As Table 3.12 shows, about half (106: 50%) the children had one placement prior to entering the Barnardos programme or moved there straight from their birth parents. However, just over a third (78: 37%) had between two and four previous placements and one in eight (26: 13%) had five or more, including ten children who had experienced at least ten previous placements. In this latter group was one child who had had 15, one who had had 17 and one who had had 22 previous placements in out-of-home care.

Table 3.12 Number of placements before entering the Barnardos programme (*N* = 210)

Number	Frequency	Per cent*	Cumulative per cent*
None	45	21	21
1	61	29	50
2–4	78	37	87
5–9	16	8	95
10 or more	10	5	100
Total	210	100	

*Percentages have been rounded

Not all children moved immediately to permanent Find-a-Family placements on entry to Barnardos. Altogether, 115 (55%) children experienced further moves within Barnardos before reaching their adoptive homes. Seventy-five of these children were placed in the Barnardos' Temporary Family Care programme prior to receiving a long-term care and protection order and then moving to Find-a-Family. Other moves occurred within the Find-a-Family programme. While 64 (30%) children had one additional placement within Barnardos before achieving permanence, 18 (9%) had three or more, including four children who had five additional placements and one child who had six.

A wealth of evidence shows that frequent changes of placement are detrimental to children's wellbeing, not least because of their adverse impact on children's ability to form secure attachments (e.g. Osborn & Delfabbro, 2006) and negative impact on mental health (Rubin et al., 2007). There is also evidence that a history of placement changes increases the likelihood of further disruptions, including disrupted adoptions. Selwyn et al. (2014) found that children who had experienced three or more placements before being placed with adoptive parents were 13 times more likely to experience a disruption. Table 3.13 shows the total number of placements experienced by the Barnardos children before entering their adoptive home. While 7 children (3%) moved straight to their adoptive parents, 103 (49%) had one or two interim placements and 100

Table 3.13 Total number of placements before entering adoptive home (*N* = 210)

Number	Frequency	Per cent*	Cumulative per cent*
0	7	3	3
1–2	103	49	52
3–5	70	33	86
6–10	20	9	95
More than 10	10	5	100
Total	210	100	

*Percentages have been rounded

(48%) had three or more. Thirty children had more than five interim placements and ten had more than ten.

> I kind of just remember little things like different houses. I just every now and again – when I was younger, I used to think – dream and stuff – like have memories of just all these different houses and like different – I couldn't really picture faces, but kind of blurred out faces sort of thing. And that's about it.
> I was scared whenever people came to the door just because I'd been through so many placements. (Young man, aged 3 when permanently placed, aged 19 when interviewed)

> So when he came to us, he had already been in nine different homes – some fostered, some homes for children – nine before he came to us.

> Well, it played with my anxieties – sometimes I didn't fit in, sometimes I would be going, "Okay, I can be friends with you, or I can hang around, but I know that I'm not going to stay here for long". So therefore, it's that, "Well I'm not going to be here for long so I can do whatever I want", whereas it played on emotions because you get the anxiety. You get the depression. You're not sticking with one group. You're just being shifted, so it's all of that, and there's no sense of belonging. (Adoptive parent and young man, aged 9 when permanently placed, aged 40 when interviewed)

Children who had experienced four or more placements before reaching their adoptive homes were significantly[5] more likely to be rated as

---

[5] X^2 = 15.005; *df* = 1; *p* = 0.000.

displaying emotional and behavioural problems than those who had moved less frequently.

Children's Vulnerability at Entry to Adoptive Homes

So far we have seen that a high proportion of the adoptees had suffered extensive and lengthy exposure to adverse childhood experiences before separation; about half the cohort also had repeated experiences of failed restoration and/or frequent moves in the months between separation and placement within a permanent family. For many children, it seems clear that pre-existing problems would have been exacerbated by harmful experiences within the care system. In addition to the data on placement instability, there is also evidence that 16 adoptees had made formal allegations of abuse while in care, though we do not know which placements were referred to in the complaints or how serious these allegations were. These harmful experiences, both before entering out-of-home care and in the period between separation from birth parents and permanent placement with adoptive carers, will have meant that many of the children were extremely vulnerable when they entered their adoptive homes.

Experiences of Loss

Furthermore, at this point many of the children would have been dealing with feelings of loss and confusion about their birth families. The vast majority (186: 89%) had already experienced their birth parents' separation and/or divorce. At least 21(10%) had already experienced the death of a birth mother and at least 16 (8%) the death of a birth father; 3 children had experienced the deaths of both parents. Only six of those children whose birth mothers had died had contact with their birth father. Forty-two (22%) of those children whose birth parents were alive had no contact with their birth mothers and 109 (56%) had no contact with their birth fathers by the time they were adopted; 52 (25%) children had no contact with either parent. Sixteen of these children had contact with a grandparent, 12 with other family members and 22 with a sibling. However, 13 children had no contact with any member of their birth family at the time the adoption order was made. This extensive experience of loss is likely to have impacted on the children's sense of identity as well as their emotional and behavioural development.

Changes over Time

To some extent the prevalence of vulnerability factors, such as those discussed above, changed over time and, specifically, as new legislation concerning adoption and permanence was implemented. In Chap. 1 we noted that policy and practice changed over the four time periods for this study: 1 January 1979–31 August 1985 (focus on young children in long-term foster care); 1 September 1985–30 June 1991 (older primary-school-aged children with behavioural/emotional challenges); 1 July 1991–30 June 2007 (wider age range) and 1 July 2007–30 June 2012 (inclusion of infants); and these are to some extent reflected in changes in the prevalence of some of the vulnerability factors. There were significant differences in the age at which children entered their adoptive homes.[6] Those who entered their adoption placements between September 1985 and June 1991 were older than those who entered within the other three time periods, reflecting the policy over this period to offer support to older primary-school-aged children with emotional or behavioural challenges. Those permanently placed in this time period tended to have had more previous placements (mean = 4.8) and be older at separation from their birth family (mean = 54 months) than children placed at other times. After being first placed in out-of-home care, they had also waited significantly longer before moving to a permanent placement than those in the two groups that focused on younger children.[7] This may reflect the vicious circle by which children's behavioural problems are exacerbated by a sense of insecurity and instability as they become older and harder to place.

---

[6] $F (3, 206) = 19.25$; $p < 0.001$.
[7] $F (3, 205) = 5.73$; $p = 0.001$.

Children who entered their adoptive homes between July 1991 and June 2007, when the policy changed to widen the age range to include younger children, were significantly more likely to have a behavioural problem than those permanently placed at other times.[8] These children were also more likely to have experienced more ACEs (mean = 4.7) than children who entered at other times. Children placed in this timeframe and in the previous one, when behavioural problems were most prevalent, were also significantly more likely to have been sexually abused while living with their birth parents than those who were permanently placed before September 1985 or after June 2007.[9]

Finally, those children who entered the Barnardos programme in the first phase of its adoption work waited on average longer for their adoption order than those who entered later (mean = 99.1 months). Almost all of them waited at least five years before the order was made. This reflects the specific nature of their placements, which had begun as long-term foster care and only later moved towards adoption. However, there was also considerable variance in the timeframes between adoptive placement and Supreme Court order within the other groups.[10]

Identifying Children with Different Levels of Vulnerability

The outcomes of the Barnardos Find-a-Family programme need to be understood within the context of the extensive evidence of adversity experienced by a high proportion of the cohort before they entered their adoptive homes. Before they were separated from their birth parents, 145 (69%) children had had four or more adverse childhood experiences, including 47 (22%) who had been sexually abused and 87 (41%) who had experienced polyvictimisation. Fifty (24%) children had remained for more than 15 months after notification of abuse with

---

[8] X^2 = 24.86; df = 3; $p < 0.001$.
[9] X^2 = 10.30; df = 3; $p = 0.016$.
[10] Range of months between permanence and adoption order for 1 January 1979–31 August 1985 = 102; 1 September 1985–30 June 1991 = 293; 1 July 1991–30 June 2007 = 135; and 1 July 2007–30 June 2012 = 33.

birth parents who could not meet their needs; 97 (46%) were more than two years old when first separated. Seventy-seven (36%) children waited for two or more years between separation and permanence, and during that period 10 (5%) children experienced two or more failed reunifications and 100 (48%) had three or more placements. By the time they were permanently placed, 102 (49%) children were reported to have behavioural problems and 24 (13%) of them had been assessed as requiring support at the two highest care levels. One hundred and four (49%) children had had their fourth birthdays before they entered their adoptive home, and 200 (96%) then waited more than 12 months before an adoption order was made. These 11 factors are all known to be significantly associated with poor outcomes in adulthood and/or disrupted adoption placements (Farmer et al., 2011; Felitti et al., 1998; Finkelhor et al., 2011; Nalavany et al., 2008; Osborn & Delfabbro, 2006; Rousseau et al., 2015; Selwyn et al., 2014; White, 2016); there is considerable overlap between them and many children experienced constellations of multiple risk factors.

Variations in the prevalence of these risk factors make it possible to distinguish between those children who were extremely vulnerable to adverse life trajectories and those whose life chances had been less severely compromised before they entered their adoptive homes; later chapters in this book will explore the relationship between children's vulnerability at the time of the adoption and their subsequent, adult outcomes. In order to facilitate comparisons, the children's experiences were categorised on each of the 11 risk factors identified above: **low risk** indicated that the child's experience in this area had not reached a level that other studies had shown to be significantly related to adverse outcomes (for instance, they had had less than four ACEs or they were less than two years old when first removed from their birth parents' care); **high risk** indicated that the child's experience had reached or surpassed the level which other studies have found to be significant; **extreme risk** indicated that the child's experience had reached at least twice this level (for further details, see Appendix 3). All the adoptees had encountered at least one experience which met the high-risk level and all but 17 of them (193: 91.9%) met the extreme risk level on at least one of these factors. Figure 3.2 shows the percentage of Low, High and Extreme occurrences amongst the sample, for the 11 risk factors.

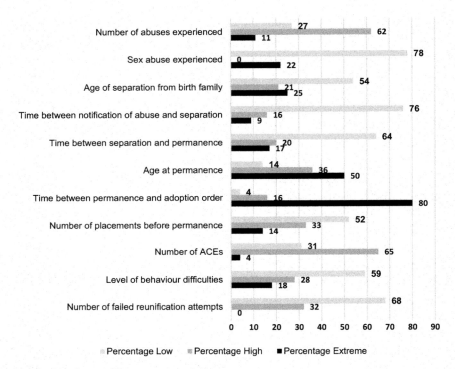

Fig. 3.2 Percentage* of Low, High and Extreme counts for each of the 11 significant risk factors that occur in the Barnardos sample (*N* = 210). *percentages have been rounded

Using these data, the adoptees were divided into two groups: the **'medium vulnerability group'** included 90 (43%) children who had been categorised as low on six or more of the 11 vulnerability factors (but high or very high on others) and the **'high vulnerability group'** included 120 (57%) children who had been categorised as high or very high on six or more of these factors. Within the medium vulnerability group is a sub-group of nine (4%) children who were categorised as low on nine or more of the variables and had no extreme scores: the **'low vulnerability sub-group'**. Within the high vulnerability group is a contrasting sub-group of 17 children who were categorised as at extreme risk of poor outcomes on six or more of the relevant factors: the **'extreme vulnerability sub-group'** (see Fig. 3.3).

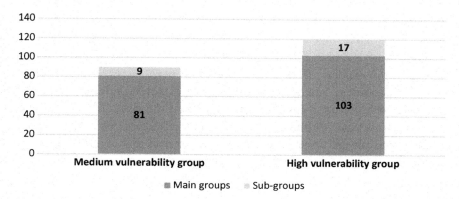

Fig. 3.3 Number of Barnardos adoptees in medium and high vulnerability groups, including extreme sub-groups (*N* = 210)

Conclusion

Identifying these risk factors and grouping the children according to levels of vulnerability gives us some indication of the likely risk of adverse outcome at the point when permanence was achieved. It is clear that, at the time they entered their adoptive homes, many of the children were at high risk of following negative life trajectories. They are likely to have been at greater risk than a normative care population, which includes children with a wider variation of experience and need. However, there is evidence from the research on Romanian orphans that supportive and sensitive substitute parenting can act as a strong protective factor and help many children who faced extensive early adversity move towards a more positive developmental trajectory (Rutter et al., 2007, 2009; Sonuga-Barke et al., 2017). Moreover:

> resilience does not come from rare and special qualities, but from the everyday magic of ordinary, normative human resources in the minds, brains and bodies of children, in their families and relationships and in their communities. (Masten, 2001, p. 235)

Subsequent chapters explore how far children's outcomes related to their previous experience; how far their adoptive parents were prepared for the challenges they presented; and whether the experience of adoption was part of the 'everyday magic' that could promote and strengthen their resilience.

Key Points

- There were 108 boys and 102 girls in the cohort, and the majority (89%) were of Australian, New Zealand or European heritage. Eighty-nine (42%) adoptees entered the programme as single children and 121 (58%) were admitted as sibling groups of two (40), three (12) and five (1).
- The Barnardos children showed a greater prevalence of health conditions and disabilities than other children in out-of-home care in New South Wales. At the time the application for an adoption order was made, 121 (58%) of the adoptees had at least one diagnosed long-term health condition or developmental delay; 62 (30%) had one condition; 30 (14%) had two; 29 (14%) had three or more. Some of these were related to the children's previous experiences of abuse and neglect.
- Developmental disorders and/or delays affected 77 (37%) adoptees. Forty-five children (21% of the cohort) showed evidence of cognitive or language delay and 30 (14%) had a diagnosed emotional or behavioural disorder.
- Over 90% of the adoptees had been removed from their parents' care because of serious, and often multiple, forms of abuse and neglect; there were maltreatment concerns for all but nine children.
- Most children had experienced composite patterns of maltreatment: 87 (42%) had experienced two forms of abuse; 44 (21%) had experienced three forms and 23 (11%) had experienced all four forms of abuse (neglect, emotional abuse, physical abuse and sexual abuse).
- Before entering the Barnardos programme, just over two-thirds (145: 69%) of the adoptees had had four or more adverse childhood experiences. The comparative figure for the general population in Australia is 17%.
- Children's experiences after notification of abuse may have increased their vulnerability: 50 (24%) remained for more than 15 months with birth parents who could not meet their needs; 96 (46%) were aged two or more when first separated; 77 (36%) waited for 2 or more years between separation and permanence;104 (49%) had had their fourth birthdays before they entered their adoptive home and 200 (95%) waited more than 12 months after placement before an adoption order was made. All these time points have been identified by other research as cut-off points beyond which the likelihood of adverse outcomes is increased.

- Instability in out-of-home care is also likely to have exacerbated children's vulnerability: before they entered their adoptive homes, 68 (32%) children had experienced failed reunifications and 100 (48%) had had three or more placements.
- Adverse childhood experiences before entry to care, compounded by harmful experiences in out-of-home care, as well as repeated exposure to grief and loss, are likely to have been factors underlying the high prevalence of emotional and behavioural difficulties displayed by the children. Case file reports indicated that nearly half (102: 49%) the adoptees had behavioural problems and 24 (13%) required support at the two highest care levels; 86 (41%) had accessed mental health services before the adoption order was made.
- The research team categorised the children according to the presence of 11 factors identified by other robust research studies as increasing the risk of adverse outcomes in adulthood. All the children in the sample had encountered at least one of these factors: 90 (43%) were categorised as at medium risk and 120 (57%) as at high risk of adverse outcomes. Combinations of risk factors were expected to correlate with adult outcomes.

References

Australian Bureau of Statistics. (2015). *National health survey first results 2014–2015.* https://www.ausstats.abs.gov.au/Ausstats/subscriber.nsf/0/CDA852A349B4CEE6CA257F150009FC53/. Accessed 20 Oct 2020.

Australian Institute of Family Studies, Chapin Hall Center for Children, University of Chicago & New South Wales Department of Family and Community Services. (2015). *Pathways of care longitudinal study: Outcomes of children and young people in out-of-home care in New South Wales, wave 1 baseline statistical report.* NSW Department of Family and Community Services.

Brown, R., Ward, H., Blackmore, J., Thomas, C., & Hyde-Dryden, G. (2016). *Eight-year-olds identified in infancy as at risk of harm: Report of a prospective longitudinal study. RR543.* London: Department for Education. https://assets.publishing.service.gov.uk/government/uploads/system/uploads/attachment_data/file/534376/Eight-year-olds_identified_in_infancy_as_at_risk_of_harm.pdf. Accessed 20 Oct 2020.

Coakley, J. F., & Berrick, J. D. (2008). In a rush to permanency: Preventing adoption disruption. Research review. *Child and Family Social Work, 13*, 101–112.

Evan B. Donaldson Adoption Institute. (2004). *What's working for children: A policy study of adoption stability and termination.* David and Lucile Packard Foundation.

Farmer, E., Sturgess, W., O'Neill, T., & Wijedasa, D. (2011). *Achieving successful returns from care: What makes reunification work?* BAAF.

Felitti, V. J., Anda, R. F., Nordenberg, D., Williamson, D. F., Spitz, A. M., Edwards, V., Koss, M. P., & Marks, J. S. (1998). Relationship of childhood abuse and household dysfunction to many of the leading causes of death in adults. The adverse childhood experiences (ACE) study. *American Journal of Preventive Medicine, 14*(4), 245–258.

Festinger, T. (2014). Adoption and disruption. In G. Mallon & P. Hess (Eds.), *Child welfare for the 21st century: A handbook of practices, policies and programs* (2nd ed.). Columbia University Press.

Finkelhor, D., Turner, H., Hamby, S., & Ormrod, R. (2011). Polyvictimization: Children's exposure to multiple types of violence, crime and abuse. *US Department of Justice Juvenile Justice Bulletin.* https://www.ncjrs.gov/pdf-files1/ojjdp/235504.pdf. Accessed 28 Nov 2020.

Hindley, N., Ramchandani, P. G., & Jones, D. P. H. (2006). Risk factors for recurrence of maltreatment: A systematic review. *Archives of Disease in Childhood, 91*(9), 744–752.

Hopkins, J., Watson, J., Paxman, M., Zhou, A., Butler, M., & Burke, S. (2019). *The experiences and wellbeing of children and young people in out-of-home care: The first five years (Wave 1-3). Pathways of Care Longitudinal Study: Outcomes of children and young people in out-of-home care. Research report 17.* Sydney: NSW Department of Family and Community Services.

Masten, A. (2001). Ordinary magic: Resilience processes in development. *American Psychologist, 56*(3), 227–238.

Meltzer, H., Gatward, R., Corbin, T., Goodman, R., & Ford, T. (2003). *The mental health of young people looked after by local authorities in England.* The Stationery Office.

Nalavany, B. A., Ryan, S. D., Howard, J. A., & Smith, S. L. (2008). Pre-adoptive child sexual abuse as a predictor of moves in care, adoption disruptions, and inconsistent adoptive parent commitment. *Child Abuse and Neglect, 32*(12), 1084–1088.

Osborn, A., & Delfabbro, P. H. (2006). Research article 4: An analysis of the social background and placement history of children with multiple and complex needs in Australian out-of-home care. *Communities, Children and Families Australia, 1*(1), 33–42.

Rosenman, S., & Rodgers, B. (2004). Childhood adversity in an Australian population. *Social Psychiatry and Psychiatric Epidemiology, 39*(9), 695–702.

Rousseau, D., Roze, M., Duverger, P., Fanello, S., & Tanguy, M. (2015). *Étude sur le devenir à long terme des jeunes enfants placés à la Pouponnière Sociale Saint Exupéry entre 1994 et 2001*. Rapport Recherche St-Ex 2013–2014. Unité de Psychiatrie de l'Enfant et de l'Adolescent du CHU d'Angers.

Rubin, D. M., O'Reilly, A. L. R., Luan, X. A., & Localio, R. (2007). The impact of placement stability on behavioral well-being for children in foster care. *Pediatrics, 119*(2), 336–344.

Rutter, M., Beckett, C., Castle, J., Colvert, E., Kreppner, J., Mehta, M., Stevens, S., & Sonuga-Barke, E. (2007). Effects of profound early institutional deprivation: An overview of findings from a UK longitudinal study of Romanian adoptees. *European Journal of Developmental Psychology, 4*(3), 332–350.

Rutter, M., Beckett, C., Castle, J., Kreppner, J., Stevens, S., & Sonuga-Barke, E. (2009). *Policy and practice implications from the English and Romanian adoptees (ERA) study: Forty-five key questions*. BAAF.

Selwyn, J., Wijedasa, D., & Meakings, S. (2014). *Beyond the adoption order: Challenges, interventions and adoption disruptions, RR 336*. London: Department for Education. https://assets.publishing.service.gov.uk/government/uploads/system/uploads/attachment_data/file/301889/Final_Report_-_3rd_April_2014v2.pdf. Accessed 30 Dec 2020.

Smart, D. (2015). Wellbeing of children and young people. In Australian Institute of Family Studies, Chapin Hall Center for Children University of Chicago, & New South Wales Department of Family and Community Services, *Pathways of Care Longitudinal Study: outcomes of children and young people in out-of-home care in NSW. Wave 1 Baseline statistical report* (pp. 81–124). N.S.W. Department of Family and Community Services.

Smith, S. L., & Howard, J. A. (1991). A comparative study of successful and disrupted adoptions. *Social Service Review, 65*(2), 248–265.

Sonuga-Barke, E. J. S., Kennedy, M., Kumsta, R., Knights, N., Golm, D., Rutter, M., Maughan, B., Schlotz, W., & Kreppner, J. (2017). Child-to-adult neurodevelopmental and mental health trajectories after early life deprivation: The young adult follow-up of the longitudinal English and Romanian adoptees study. *Lancet, 389*(10078), 1539–1548.

Tarren-Sweeney, M., & Hazell, P. (2006). The mental health of children in foster care and kinship care in New South Wales, Australia. *Journal of Paediatrics and Child Health, 42*, 89–97.

Van den Dries, L., Juffer, F., Van Ijzendoorn, M. H., & Bakermans-Kranenburg, M. J. (2009). Fostering security? A meta-analysis of attachment in adopted children. *Children and Youth Services Review, 31*(3), 410–421.

Ward, H., Brown, R., & Hyde-Dryden, G. (2014). *Assessing parental capacity to change when children are on the edge of care: An overview of current research evidence. RR369.* Centre for Child and Family Research, Loughborough University and Department for Education. https://assets.publishing.service.gov.uk/government/uploads/system/uploads/attachment_data/file/330332/RR369_Assessing_parental_capacity_to_change_Final.pdf.   Accessed 30 Dec 2020.

Ward, H., Brown, R., & Westlake, D. (2012). *Safeguarding babies and very young children from abuse and neglect.* Jessica Kingsley Publishers.

Ward, H., & Holmes, L. (2008). Calculating the costs of local authority care for children with contrasting needs. *Child and Family Social Work, 13*(1), 80–90.

White, K. R. (2016). Placement discontinuity for older children and adolescents who exit foster care through adoption or guardianship: A systematic review. *Child and Adolescent Social Work Journal, 33*(4), 377–394.

White, O. G., Hindley, N., & Jones, D. P. H. (2015). Risk factors for child maltreatment recurrence: An updated systematic review. *Medicine Science and the Law, 55*(4), 259–277.

Zeanah, C. H., Gunnar, M. R., McCall, R. B., Kreppner, J. M., & Fox, N. A. (2011). Sensitive periods. *Monographs of the Society for Research in Child Development, 76*(4), 147–162.

4

The Adoptive Parents

Introduction

Research on adoption has pointed to a number of issues that lead to adverse outcomes and increased stress in adoptive families. The factor most commonly associated with stress leading to disruption is the child's age at placement, with older children posing the greatest challenge (see Coakley & Berrick, 2008; Evan B. Donaldson Institute, 2008). This may be because age is related to other child-related stressors such as emotional or behavioural difficulties (Barth & Berry, 1988; Selwyn et al., 2006). Adoption of more than one child, including the simultaneous adoption of sibling groups, has also been found to increase parental stress (Bird et al., 2002; Sanchez-Sandoval & Palacios, 2012); this may be associated with other stressors such as being part of a blended family combining adoptive and biological children (Barth & Berry, 1988; Barth & Brooks, 1997) and conflict between adopted siblings and/or between adoptees and other children in the household (Selwyn et al., 2014). Parent-related factors that have been found to increase stress in adoptive families include parenting styles entailing less affection and communication (Palacios & Sanchez-Sandoval, 2006; Quinton et al., 1998); unrealistic expectations

© The Author(s) 2022
H. Ward et al., *Outcomes of Open Adoption from Care*,
https://doi.org/10.1007/978-3-030-76429-6_4

(Barth & Brooks, 1997; Barth & Miller, 2000); unresolved issues concerning infertility (Harris, 2013); and a lack of informal support including perceptions of less support for their decision to adopt, particularly felt by single parents and same-sex couples (Bird et al., 2002; Moyer & Goldberg, 2017). System-related factors include inadequate preparation or lack of transparency on the part of the adoption agency (Barth & Miller, 2000; Brodzinsky et al., 1998; Selwyn et al., 2014); inadequate financial support (Berry & Barth, 1990); and inadequate post-adoption psycho-therapeutic support (Selwyn et al., 2014).

We have already seen that child-related factors known to increase the risk of unsuccessful adoption were prevalent in the Barnardos cohort. The children had experienced numerous adversities before they were placed. Although not all of them were equally vulnerable, all had had at least one experience that was significantly related to poor outcomes in adulthood. All but 17 (193: 91%) met our extreme risk criterion of having had at least one experience that was at least twice the threshold at which adverse outcomes are significantly more likely. We know that a substantial proportion of children at high risk of negative life trajectories are sufficiently resilient to develop 'positive patterns of functioning following exposure to adversity' (Masten, 2006). Nevertheless, from what we know so far it must be clear that many of the adoptive parents would face considerable challenges in meeting the needs of children whose developmental chances had been severely compromised by early experiences of abuse and neglect and subsequently diminished by delayed decision-making and frequent moves before permanence was achieved. Adoptive parents may also have found it difficult to implement the policy of maintaining regular, ongoing face-to-face contact with birth parents. As Chap. 2 has shown, a number of birth parents had already lost touch before their children entered the Barnardos programme and many of the others were struggling with interlocking problems that would have made contact difficult.

Barnardos was well aware of the issues relating to adoptive strain and unstable placements. Throughout the period of the study, they provided comprehensive assessments of adoptive parents over six to eight sessions and core training over three days. Assessments included issues such as potential adopters' support from their wider family, their experiences of grief and loss concerning infertility and the possible impact on their biological family. The training encompassed issues such as the children's previous experiences of abuse and loss and the adoptive family's own expectations. Barnardos also provided practical and casework support to adoptive parents and children from the time the child entered the Find-a-Family programme until the order was made, often many years later (see Chap. 3). Nevertheless, some of the adoptive parents will have encountered greater strains than others and placements with them will have been at greater risk of instability, particularly if these parents were matched with children who had high levels of vulnerability.

The data collected from case files and court papers included information about the circumstances and motivation of the adoptive parents at the time of placement. Together with the information on birth parents and children, these data provide a context within which the outcomes for the adoptees in terms of both continuing relationships with birth family members, their relationships with adoptive parents and the stability of placements, and their long-term wellbeing can be better understood.

Adoptive Parents

The Find-a-Family programme found 138 adoptive homes for the 210 children in the sample. The vast majority (135: 98%) of primary carers were women; two of the three men who were primary carers were living in a same-sex partnership, the other was living in a heterosexual relationship where the traditional roles were reversed in that his wife worked full time while he acted as primary carer. Seven adoptive parents were single, so there were 131 secondary carers. The vast majority of these were men (128: 98%), but there were three women: two were living in female same-sex partnerships and the other was the partner in the couple where the traditional roles were reversed.

The majority of primary carers were Anglo-Australian or New Zealanders (101: 73%) or European (32: 23%). Two primary carers were Aboriginal; two others were Maori or Pacific Islanders. Secondary carers were very similar: 91 (69%) were Australian or New Zealanders and 35

(27%) were European. However, only one secondary carer was Aboriginal and none were Maori or Pacific Islanders.

Attempts were made to find adoptive parents who matched the children in ethnicity and culture. These were largely successful—179 (85%) of the children were considered to be satisfactorily matched, including all the Australian and Anglo/Australian children, as well as a number from other European countries: for instance, six Italian children were placed with at least one Italian adoptive parent and three Croatian children were adopted by a Croatian/Italian couple. However, children whose birth parents were Aboriginal or Maori were less well matched: it had only been possible to place one of the Aboriginal children and one of the Maori children with an adoptive parent of the same ethnicity and culture. The failure to match Aboriginal children appropriately was due to a lack of knowledge about their heritage at the time of placement and a reluctance to disrupt their established attachments to prospective adoptive parents with whom they had been permanently placed.

Age and Experience

In addition to the support provided by Barnardos, there were a number of factors that may have strengthened the capacity of the adoptive parents to meet the children's needs. First, the primary carers were significantly older than the birth mothers[1] and would have had more life experience. At the time the child was born, their median age was 34, ten years older than the median age of the birth mothers. At the time the children were placed in their adoptive homes, their median age was 39 and only five were under 30; six (4%) of the primary carers were aged 50 or more. Just under a third of the adoptive parents (30%) already had children of their own, and therefore had some experience of parenting, although this was not necessarily advantageous (Selwyn et al., 2006).

For many years Barnardos had a policy by which potential adoptive parents were first approved as permanent carers, with a view to adoption: we have seen (Chap. 3) that almost half (42%) of the children

---

[1] $t\,(272) = 12.859$; $p < 0.001$.

entered their adoptive homes with a plan for long-term foster care, and one in three (31%) had lived there for more than five years before the adoption order was made. In recent years, there has been an increase in numbers of adoptions in New South Wales of children in foster care, with these now comprising the majority of adoption orders. There is some evidence that adoptive placements with foster carers are less likely to disrupt (McRoy, 1999; Rosenthal et al., 1988), although some studies have shown conflicting results (Selwyn et al., 2014). However, the Barnardos programme offered both foster carers and the children intensive support until the order was made, and this may have acted as a powerful protective factor (Tregeagle et al., 2011). For example, families were visited by their allocated caseworker at weekly intervals during the initial period following placement, reducing gradually to a minimum of monthly visits; families were able to contact their worker at any time for support; regular respite care was provided when needed and case reviews were held every six months to consider the progress of the placement. Until the order was made, Barnardos also provided financial support for physical or psychological therapy that was required to assist the child's development.

Relationships

Some studies (e.g. McRoy, 1999) have identified the stability of the adoptive parents' relationship as a factor related to the success of an adoption, but the research findings on this are mixed (Palacios et al., 2019). Almost all the adoptive parents (131: 95%) had a partner with whom to share the challenges of parenting and nearly two-thirds (86: 62%) were in stable relationships that had lasted for ten years or more; however, not all partners proved to be as supportive as anticipated and some relationships were severely tested despite their longevity (see Chap. 8). The majority of the adoptive parents (127: 93%) were heterosexual couples; there were also four same-sex couples (two female and two male), reflecting a change in legislation and policy introduced in 2010, and seven lone parents (three single, two divorced and two widowed).

Informal Support

Data from the interviews indicate that, when they entered the placement, the adoptees were welcomed by members of the extended family, many of whom provided substantial support. There is no evidence from this study to support Moyer and Goldberg's (2017) finding that single parents and those living in a same-sex relationship receive less informal support. Although the interviews reflect the experiences of a very small subset of parents, the data suggest that at least some of the lone parents were very well supported:

They gave [adoptive mother] so much support for me. Because she's a single parent, so sometimes she would – actually, often for a while, she would have to go away for work. And my auntie – her sister lives a few doors down, right now. So I would just go there. I would go stay there and she would provide for me the exact same environment here: stability, routine. So I always had like a – yeah, and my grandparents would always come – if my auntie couldn't have me, my grandparents would just come here for the week or however long [adoptive mother] was gone for, and just look after me. They've always been supportive and so involved. (Young woman, aged 10 at permanent placement, aged 21 when interviewed)

As part of the assessment, adoptive parents were asked about their religious affiliation and observation. Although about half (73: 53%) of them had no close relationship with a religious community, just over one in four (37: 27%) attended a religious service weekly or fortnightly. Being a member of a religious community can be an important protective factor, providing extra support at times of stress, and some adoptive parents were able to draw on this resource.

We belong to a very little church because of its great points like community. And we had this – it's a really small church. So we were very much a part of it. So he was just welcomed in and was a big deal to everyone. And they would've been praying about him before he ever came as well, because we were a very integral part of that fellowship. (Adoptive parent of young man aged 9 at permanent placement)

Material Circumstances

The challenges the birth parents faced were exacerbated by factors such as inadequate housing and insufficient financial support (see Cleaver et al., 2011). Most adoptive parents had a number of material resources that buffered them from stressors such as these; for instance, most of them had the education and skills to enable them to earn a reasonable living. Table 4.1 shows the educational qualifications of the primary carers. Although 39 (28%) primary carers had no further or higher education, including 10 (7%) who had left or dropped out of school before completing Year 10 and obtaining basic qualifications, 59 (43%) had a trade certificate and 29 (21%) were educated to graduate or postgraduate level.

Although strong educational qualifications may enable primary carers to obtain well-paid employment, some studies have found that high achieving adoptive mothers can have unrealistic expectations, and this becomes a source of tension when adoptees fail to live up to them (Barth & Miller, 2000). There is some evidence of this from interviews with adult adoptees:

When I was at uni, if I got a pass it was like a fail. If I got a credit, it was always like I'd failed. If I got a distinction, that's all right. If I got a high distinction, okay, that's good. So if it wasn't a high distinction it was like – so there were very high expectations from her, but I think all of that came from a space of love. And there was also always this undertone of love... (Young man, aged 1 when permanently placed, aged 25 when interviewed)

Table 4.1 Primary carers: last year of school and education qualification ($N = 138$)

Last year of school	None	Trade Certificate	Diploma	Associate Diploma	Graduate	Post Graduate	Total
Year 8	3	2	0	0	0	0	**5**
Year 9	7	3	0	0	0	0	**10**
Year 10	19	34	5	1	2	1	**62**
Year 11	2	4	1	0	0	0	**7**
Year 12	8	16	4	0	18	8	**54**
Total	**39**	**59**	**10**	**1**	**20**	**9**	**138**

Table 4.2 Secondary carers: last year at school (*N* = 131)

School Year	Frequency	Per cent*	Cumulative per cent*
Year 6	1	1	1
Year 7	1	1	2
Year 8	4	3	5
Year 9	6	5	9
Year 10	51	40	48
Year 11	8	6	54
Year 12	59	45	99
Year 13	1	1	100
Total	131	100	

*Percentages have been rounded

The data on the education of secondary carers are less comprehensive. Table 4.2 shows their school careers. Twelve (9%) had left or dropped out of school before Year 10 and had therefore presumably left without obtaining qualifications. Just under half (59: 45%) had left after Year 10 or 11, presumably after sitting their School Certificate;[2] almost exactly the same number (60: 46%) had stayed on until Year 12 or 13 and presumably sat their Higher School Certificate. After leaving school, almost half of the 131 secondary carers (63: 48%) had gained a trade certificate and about one in four (34: 26%) had achieved a graduate or postgraduate degree. Six of those who had dropped out of school before Year 10 had later gained a trade certificate. There were also 25 secondary carers for whom no further or higher education data are available; the complementary data on the primary carers suggest that it is likely that the majority had no further qualifications, but it is not possible to distinguish them from those for whom these data were not collected.

---

[2] Discontinued in 2011, replaced by Record of School Achievement.

Employment

The majority of secondary carers (92%) were either self-employed or in full-time salaried employment. Table 4.3 shows the types of employment they were in. Two-thirds (80: 62%) were in managerial positions, such as running businesses or managing banks, or professional occupations, such as teaching, medicine or the law. There were 20 (15%) who were employed in technical work or trades, such as hairdressing or carpentry. Only four were unemployed and two more were retired.

The data from the survey and the interviews indicate that many of the primary carers gave up work or reduced their hours in order to focus on the adoptee's needs, although they may have regarded this as a temporary measure to help them settle into their new home. Almost half (57: 41%) of the primary carers were recorded as having no employment outside the home at the time the adoptee was placed with them; these include four

Table 4.3 Secondary carers: employment type* (*N* = 131)

Employment Type	Frequency	Per cent**	Cumulative per cent**
No employment***	6	5	5
Managerial	57	44	49
Professional	23	18	66
Technicians and Trade workers	20	15	82
Community and personal services workers	5	4	85
Clerical and administrative workers	3	2	88
Sales workers	2	2	89
Driver and machinery operator	8	6	95
Labourer	6	5	100
Total	**130**	**100**	
Missing	1		

*Australian and New Zealand Standard Classification of Occupations (ANZSCO (Australian Bureau of Statistics 2018)
**Percentages have been rounded
***Includes retirees

Table 4.4 Primary carers: employment type[*] (N = 138)

Employment Type	Frequency	Per cent[**]	Cumulative per cent[**]
No employment[***]	57	41	41
Manager	17	12	53
Professional	24	17	70
Technicians and trade workers	3	2	72
Community and personal services workers	3	2	74
Clerical and administrative workers	27	20	94
Sales workers	5	4	98
Driver and machinery operator	1	1	99
Labourer	1	1	100
Total	**138**	**100**	

[*]Australian and New Zealand Standard Classification of Occupations (ANZSCO (Australian Bureau of Statistics 2018)
[**]Percentages have been rounded
[***]Includes retirees

who were retired. The majority (45: 56%) of the primary carers who were working outside the home were in part-time or casual employment. However, 22 (16%) worked full time and 14 (10%) were self-employed. Table 4.4 shows their occupations: 27 (20%) were in administrative posts; 17 (12%) were in managerial positions and 24 (17%) were in professional occupations. Significantly fewer primary carers were in managerial or professional occupations than were secondary carers,[3] mirroring national patterns in occupational status by gender at the time the children were placed.

Although data on adoptive parents' income were collected at the time of the application, these cover a 30-year period and therefore cannot be meaningfully compared. We do know, however, that most adoptive parents had a regular income, although there were substantial variations across the sample. However, a small group of adoptive parents were reliant on pensions or benefits and may have been in relatively reduced material circumstances: three households were entirely dependent on

---

[3] $X^2 = 10.12$; $df = 1$; $p = 0.001$.

retirement pensions (one of them headed by a lone carer), and in three other households, the only declared income was workers' compensation or disability pension. Nevertheless, the majority (132: 96%), including those who were living on pensions, were living in owner-occupied homes. Although most of them had a mortgage, about a third of them (46: 35%) had paid it off and no longer had regular housing expenses. One other adoptive couple was living in free accommodation. Only five adoptive parents were living in rented accommodation.

Research evidence does not show a significant association between adoptive parents' material circumstances and adoption outcomes (Selwyn et al., 2006). Nevertheless, at the start of the placement, the majority of adoptive parents had sufficient material resources to cushion them from financial worries. They could also offer a significantly higher standard of living than the children had experienced with their birth parents. They also had considerable social capital, in the form of supportive friends and family and access to community resources.

Children in the Home

The Find-a-Family programme focused on finding permanent homes for children who were hard to place. This term covered both children who had extensive emotional and behavioural problems and those who were part of a large sibling group. Research studies that have focused on the adoption of sibling groups have produced mixed findings (see Palacios et al., 2019). However, it seems clear that sibling relationships between children who have experienced extensive maltreatment may not follow a normative pattern and may pose particular challenges for adoptive parents (Selwyn, 2019; Tasker & Wood, 2016).

Table 4.5 shows the number of children placed with each adoptive family. Just over half (78: 57%) had one child placed with them; however, over a third (47: 34%) had two, and 12 couples (9%) adopted three children. One couple adopted four children—three siblings and an unrelated child. Altogether there were 60 families who adopted two or more children through Find-a-Family; 11 adopted two or more children who were not related to each other and 49 adopted siblings.

Table 4.5 Number of children placed in each adoptive home (*N* = 138)

Number of children	Frequency	Per cent*	Cumulative per cent*
1	78	57	57
2	47	34	91
3	12	9	99
4	1	1	100
Total	138	100	

*Percentages have been rounded

Twenty-four (17%) of the adoptive families had biological children who had already left the home before the adoptee was placed there. However, about a third (47: 34%) already had at least one child living in the home when the adoptee arrived. These were mainly the adoptive parents' biological children, but eight parents had one or more foster children and one had a grandchild living with them. Twenty-two (16%) of the adoptive parents already had two or more children living in their homes at the time of the placement, including one couple who had four and another who had five. It has long been recognised that tensions can arise if adoptees or foster children are of a similar age to biological or other children already living in the household (Parker, 1966); however, age differences were not available in this study.

Jenny and Tom

Jenny and Tom were in their mid-40s when they applied to Barnardos to permanently care for a sibling group of primary-school-aged children. They were both born in England and had migrated to Australia shortly after their marriage 24 years ago. They had three children aged between 16 and 27 at the time of their application. Two of their children were still living in the family home at this time, as was Jenny's father.

Jenny and Tom lived in a rented five-bedroom house in a quiet suburban area in Sydney, which was in easy access to the local school, shops, parks and transport. Both Jenny and Tom worked full time, although Jenny intended to resign from her position should children be placed with them, so that she could be a full-time carer. Tom had been educated to the equiva-

(continued)

(continued)
lent of Year 12 in Australia and had stable employment as a qualified tradesperson; Jenny had been educated to the equivalent of Year 10 and was employed as an accounts clerk/co-ordinator.

Jenny and Tom felt that they had much to offer children who needed a home and, shortly after their application, a sibling group of three children was placed within the family. Jenny and Tom had support from their family, especially Jenny's father, and felt confident they could help the children feel more secure. However, the children who were placed with them came from a very traumatic background and Jenny and Tom found them challenging, especially around times of birth family contact, which triggered extremely difficult behaviours. However, Barnardos' workers provided support during contact visits:

> That was something that Barnados were very on to. Was the fact that they were never left alone. So if one of the kids had to go to the toilet and I was going with them, then another caseworker used to come in just to make sure that everything was – and if they were off the air then we used to have two caseworkers in there with us anyway.

There were also difficulties with the education system, as at least one child was in a learning difficulty class and another was diagnosed with ADHD; Jenny and Tom had to fight the school systems to allow for opportunities for each of the children.

> I had a fight with the school. I used to have a lot of fights with people. I had a fight with the school counsellor who told me she wouldn't amount to anything and she had to go to an all-girls school, and I said, "Well you don't know her very well do you?"

Jenny and Tom had regular, monthly separate respite care for each child and were reassured that ongoing financial support from the New South Wales Government would continue after an adoption order was made. Five years after the children were placed with them, they applied to adopt them, in order to make a lasting commitment to them. All three children gave their formal consent to their adoption.

One of these children said of her adoptive parents:

> It's affected me in a big way because it's taught me – even though I was like different to my brothers, they taught me how to be in a family environment. So I can do the best for my kids too. Like try and have the same goals and morals as what Mum and Dad did back then. They both

(continued)

(continued)

worked, they looked after us, they looked after the house, you know the structure of everything. I think it's helped me in my life because, before I went to them, structure was a very – it didn't exist.

You can talk to them about anything. I think kids need that. They need to know that even though you're their parents, you can also be their friends. But you're their enemies as well, in a sense. To have someone to go and talk to about anything, any problems, I think is great because it's taught me a lot to be able to.... But it's nice to be able to have that – how they've taught us morals and respect.

Sibling Groups

Table 4.6 shows the extent to which Barnardos succeeded in keeping sibling groups together. Eighty-six (41%) adoptees had no siblings (or no siblings referred to Find-a-Family). Sixty-six (53%) children were adopted in intact sibling groups of two: these include ten children who were initially placed alone but were later joined by a sibling after a split group was re-united, or after a new baby was born. Thirty children were adopted in intact sibling groups of three: these include six children in two families who were reunited or joined by a new baby in their adoptive placement. Reunification of a sibling group that had previously been split was not always successful:

Well, my idea was that they wanted me there, purely because I was me, and I was [birth sister's] brother, but realised that that wasn't the case. I never really lived with [birth sister].... Yeah, she's my sister on paper, but I hadn't had enough life with her to really – for that to matter. I think it looks good on paper. It looks very good on paper. You're with your sister, or half-sister, or it makes sense, but there is no sense if you didn't have a relationship with them anyway. (Young man, aged 10 when permanently placed, aged 40 when interviewed)

Twenty-eight children were in sibling groups that were split. These included 15 children from five families, who were all adopted. Seven of these children were placed separately apart from their siblings; however,

Table 4.6 Sibling placements (*N* = 210)

Sibling types	Frequency	Percentage (%)
Intact sibling groups of two (33 groups: 66 children)	66	53
Intact sibling groups of three (10 groups: 30 children)	30	24
Adopted with at least one sibling although split from others	18	15
Adopted alone, split from siblings	10	8
Total	**124**	**100**
No siblings	86	

the other eight were placed with at least one other sibling. There is some evidence from the interviews that, with support from adoptive parents, adoptees were able to continue a relationship with siblings who were adopted by other families.

> He (adoptee) contacts – he has social media contact with (birth sibling), that's the one that got removed from birth and adopted…. He has contact with him. They've had a sleepover at his house, and they have contact on social media with him. (Adoptive parent of young man, aged 2 when permanently placed)

Thirteen children were in sibling groups that were split when other children were not adopted because they returned to birth parents, remained in foster care or left the adoptive placement following a disruption before the order was made. Mostly, at least one sibling remained in the placement when others left: only three children in this group were adopted alone. Altogether 96 (77%) of the 124 children who were known to have siblings were placed together, 18 (15%) were split from one or more sibling but were adopted with others and only 10 (8%) were adopted alone.

Table 4.7 shows the number of children who were living in the adoptive homes after the adoptees and their siblings had arrived. The majority

Table 4.7 All children in household including adoptees (*N* = 138)

All children	Frequency	Per cent (%)*	Cumulative per cent (%)*
1	56	41	41
2	46	34	75
3	21	15	90
4	11	8	98
5	1	1	99
6	2	1	100
Total	137	100	
Missing	1	1	

*Percentages have been rounded

of adoptive parents looked after one or two children; however, about 10% had four or more, including one household with five children and two with six. The larger families were almost all composite families, including one or two adoptees plus foster children or biological children, and meeting their often disparate needs is likely to have been a complex and sometimes stressful task (Barth & Berry, 1988; Bird et al., 2002).

Motivation

Parents decide to adopt a child from out-of-home care for a number of complex reasons. Although infertility may be a significant driving factor, about one in four adoptive parents in the USA cite religious motivation as an important reason for their decision (Brooks & James, 2003). At the time of their application to Find-a-Family, adoptive parents were asked about their motivation for taking this step. Table 4.8 shows their responses.

Although the majority of parents applied to adopt because they were infertile (103: 75%), there was also a substantial proportion whose primary motivation was to help a child (27: 20%), a third of whom had no children themselves. Eight (6%) adoptive parents wanted primarily to expand their existing family, although there were six others who also

Table 4.8 Adoptive parents: motivation (*N* = 138)

Motivation	Frequency	Per cent*	Cumulative per cent*
Infertility/Same-sex couple**	103	75	75
Help a child***	27	20	95
Expand existing family	8	6	100
Total	138	100	

*Percentages have been rounded
**Three parents also indicated a desire to help a child or to expand their existing family.
***Six parents also indicated a desire to expand their existing family.

indicated that they wanted to help a child. Those adoptive parents who said their decision was influenced by their desire to help a child were not more likely to indicate a religious commitment than those whose primary motivating factor was infertility.

Conclusion

So far, we have seen that the adoptive parents had a number of strengths. Most of them had considerable personal, material and social capital on which they could draw. Most of them fostered the children before they adopted them, and in the often lengthy time before the order was made, they received considerable support from Barnardos. All but one family lived within an hour's drive of their local Find-a-Family office.

Nevertheless, they faced a number of challenges. Many of the children were 'hard to place' in terms of age and membership of a large sibling group with complex dynamics. A high proportion also showed emotional and behavioural difficulties that were likely to be related to their earlier adverse experiences; many had been harmed by the adults in their lives and may have been wary of making new relationships. The research on resilience (Masten, 2001, 2006) has identified a number of factors within the child, the family and the community that help children to develop the capacity to adapt and recover from such adversities. These include a number of benefits that the adoptive parents were able to offer, such as 'socio-economic advantages', belonging to 'a safe community' and the availability of other 'prosocial adults' within the family circle. However:

> A close relationship with a caring and competent adult is widely considered the most important and general protective factor for human development, particularly for younger children who are highly dependent on caregivers. (Masten, 2006, p. 6)

The extent to which the adoptive parents were able to develop such a relationship would be a key component in the outcome of the adoption.

The three chapters in this part of the book have each explored factors within the circumstances and experiences of different members of the adoption triangle—birth parents, adoptive parents and adoptees—that need to be taken into account when assessing the outcomes of open adoption. These include the complex web of adversities with which the birth parents struggled, the many adverse experiences that had impacted on the life trajectories of the children, and the strengths of the adoptive families, but also the challenges they faced.

The following chapters explore the children's subsequent experiences and outcomes within the context of their needs and early experience at the time the adoption order was made. The data collected through the follow-up survey and the interviews with adult adoptees and their adoptive parents enable us to examine how adoptive parents and children met the challenges we have identified so far. In assessing how the experience of adoption impacted on children's life trajectories we can attempt to identify those factors that were of particular significance, including the part played by the policy of open adoption.

Key Points

- The programme found 138 adoptive homes for the 210 children in the sample.
- Most of the children (179: 85%) appeared to be satisfactorily matched including all the Anglo/Australian children, as well as a number of

children from other European countries. However, a small number of Aboriginal and Maori children were less well matched in terms of ethnicity and culture.

- The adoptive parents had a number of personal, material and social resources that buffered them from some of the stresses of parenting. Many of these were not available to birth parents.
- Almost all the adoptive parents (131: 95%) had a partner with whom to share the challenges, and nearly two-thirds (86: 62%) had been in the relationship for ten years or more. Adoptive mothers were on average ten years older than the birth mothers.
- Just under half (41%) of the children had initially been fostered by their adoptive parents. In the long period before the adoption order was made, adoptive parents and children received substantial support from the agency.
- The majority of adoptive parents (132: 96%) were living in owner-occupied homes. Most (97: 74%) secondary carers had a trade certificate or a degree, and two-thirds (80: 62%) were in managerial positions.
- Almost all (135: 98%) the primary carers were women. Almost three-quarters (99: 72%) of them also had a further or higher education qualification. However, 57 (41%) were not working outside the home, and most others were in part-time or casual employment. Many had given up work or reduced their hours to look after the adoptee.
- Twenty-two (16%) of the adoptive parents already had two or more children living with them at the time of the placement. Just over half (78: 57%) of the families had one child placed with them; 47 (34%) had two children placed and 13 (10%) adopted three or more children. Fourteen (10%) of the adoptive families had four or more children living in the home.
- Siblings were mainly placed together. Of the 124 children with siblings, 96 (77%) were placed in intact groups of two or three and 28 (23%) were separated from at least one brother or sister. Only ten (8%) children with siblings were placed alone.
- The majority of adoptive parents applied to adopt because of their infertility (103: 75%), but there were 27 (20%) whose primary motivation was to help a child.

- While adoptive parents had considerable resources, they also faced a number of challenges. These included the children's emotional and behavioural difficulties and parenting several children with diverse needs.

References

Australian Bureau of Statistics. (2018, February). *Labour statistics: Concepts, sources and methods*. https://www.abs.gov.au/ausstats/abs@.nsf/Lookup/by%20Subject/6102.0.55.001~Feb%202018~Main%20Features~Classifications%20Used%20in%20Labour%20Statistics~15. Accessed 2 Dec 2020.

Barth, R., & Berry, M. (1988). *Adoption and disruption: Rates, risks and resources*. Aldine.

Barth, R., & Brooks, D. (1997). A longitudinal study of family structure and size and adoption outcomes. *Adoption Quarterly, 1*, 29–56.

Barth, R., & Miller, J. (2000). Building effective post-adoption services: What is the empirical foundation? *Family Relations, 49*(4), 447–455.

Berry, M., & Barth, R. P. (1990). A study of disrupted adoptive placements of adolescents. *Child Welfare, 69*, 209–225.

Bird, G., Peterson, R., & Miller, S. H. (2002). Factors associated with distress among support-seeking adoptive parents. *Family Relations, 51*, 215–220.

Brodzinsky, D. M., Smith, D. W., & Brodzinsky, A. B. (1998). *Children's adjustment to adoption: Developmental and clinical issues*. Sage.

Brooks, D., & James, S. (2003). Willingness to adopt black foster children: Implications for child welfare policy and recruitment of adoptive families. *Children and Youth Services Review, 25*(5-6), 463–489.

Cleaver, H., Unell, I., & Aldgate, J. (2011). *Children's needs – Parenting capacity: Child abuse: Parental mental illness, learning disability, substance misuse and domestic violence* (2nd ed.). The Stationery Office.

Coakley, J. F., & Berrick, J. D. (2008). Research review: In a rush to permanency: Preventing adoption disruption. *Child and Family Social Work, 13*, 101–112.

Evan B. Donaldson Institute. (2008). *Adoptive Parent Preparation Project: Meeting the mental health needs of adolescent children*. https://www.researchgate.net/profile/David_Brodzinsky/publication/271909970_ADOPTIVE_PARENT_PREPARATION_PROJECT_Phase_I_Meeting_the_Mental_Health_and_Developmental_Needs_Of_Adopted_Children_Policy_

Practice_Perspective/links/54d67dbd0cf2464758108cfd.   Accessed 21 Oct 2020

Harris, D. L. (2013). Infertility and intimacy: Life's layered losses. In B. DeFord & R. Gilbert (Eds.), *Living, loving and loss: The interplay of intimacy, sexuality and grief* (pp. 101–118). Baywood Publishing.

Masten, A. S. (2001). Ordinary magic; Resilience processes in development. *American Psychologist, 56*(3), 227–238.

Masten, A. S. (2006). Promoting resilience in development: A general framework for systems of care. In R. Flynn, P. Dudding, & J. Barber (Eds.), *Promoting resilience in child welfare* (pp. 3–17). University of Ottawa Press.

McRoy, R. G. (1999). *Special needs adoptions: Practice issues.* Garland.

Moyer, A. M., & Goldberg, A. E. (2017). 'We were not planning on this, but …': Adoptive parents' reactions and adaptations to unmet expectations. *Child and Family Social Work, 22,* 12–21.

Palacios, J., Brodzinsky, D., Grotevant, H., Johnson, D., Juffer, F., Martinez-Morah, L., Muhamedrahimove, R., Selwyn, J., Simmonds, J., & Tarren-Sweeney, M. (2019). Adoption in the service of child protection: An international interdisciplinary perspective. *Psychology, Public Policy and Law, 25*(2), 57–72.

Palacios, J., & Sanchez-Sandoval, Y. S. (2006). Stress in parents of adopted children. *International Journal of Behavioural Development, 30*(6), 481–487.

Parker, R. A. (1966). *Decision in child care: A study of prediction in fostering.* Allen and Unwin.

Quinton, D., Rushton, A., Dance, C., & Mayes, D. (1998). *Joining new families: A study of adoption and fostering in middle childhood.* Wiley.

Rosenthal, J. A., Schmidt, D., & Conner, J. (1988). Predictors of special needs adoption disruption: An exploratory study. *Children and Youth Services Review, 10,* 101–117.

Sanchez-Sandoval, Y. S., & Palacios, J. (2012). Stress in adoptive parents of adolescents. *Children and Youth Services Review, 34*(7), 1283–1289.

Selwyn, J. (2019). Sibling relationships in adoptive families that disrupted or were in crisis. *Research on Social Work Practice, 29*(2), 165–175.

Selwyn, J., Sturgess, W., Quinton, D., & Baxter, C. (2006). *Costs and outcomes of non-infant adoptions.* BAAF.

Selwyn, J., Wijedasa, D., & Meakings, S. (2014). *Beyond the adoption order: Challenges, interventions and adoption disruptions, RR 336.* Department for Education. https://assets.publishing.service.gov.uk/government/uploads/system/uploads/attachment_data/file/301889/Final_Report_-_3rd_April_2014v2.pdf. Accessed 30 Dec 2020.

Tasker, F., & Wood, S. (2016). The transition into adoptive parenthood: Adoption as a process of continued safe uncertainty when family scripts collide. *Clinical Child Psychology and Psychiatry, 21*(4), 520–535.

Tregeagle, S., Cox, E., O'Neil, C., & Humphreys, S. (2011). Worker time and the cost of stability. *Children and Youth Services Review, 33*, 1149–1158.

Part II

Outcomes of Open Adoption from Care

5

Permanence

Introduction

A wide body of research has identified a sense of 'stability', 'permanence' and 'belonging' as significant factors in the development of a child's ability to form the nurturing relationships that are essential to healthy development (for summary, see National Scientific Council on the Developing Child, 2004). The importance of promoting permanence for children in out-of-home care is reflected in child welfare legislation in England and Wales (Children Act 1989, Guidance and Regulations, Volume II), the USA (Adoption and Safe Families Act 1997) and much of Australia (Wise, 2017). There are, however, a number of ways in which the concept can be understood. Brodzinsky and Livingston Smith (2019) argue that 'permanence' has three components:

> *Legal permanence*, either with the child's biological parents or with other caregivers such as adoptive parents or guardians, affirms the authority and responsibility of these individuals to make all relevant decisions and to take all appropriate actions in raising a child. *Residential permanence*, often

© The Author(s) 2022
H. Ward et al., *Outcomes of Open Adoption from Care*,
https://doi.org/10.1007/978-3-030-76429-6_5

referred to as placement stability, emphasizes the importance of supporting continuity of care in a designated home. Finally, *psychological permanence*, often referred to as relational permanence, prioritizes maintaining children's connections to significant attachment figures and supports a felt sense of connection, continuity, nurturance, security, trust, and safety in relationships with caregivers. (Brodzinsky & Livingston Smith, 2019, p. 185; our emphasis)

All three aspects of permanence need to be achieved if children's long-term wellbeing is to be adequately supported.

Adoption is thought to offer the best chance of achieving permanence for children in out-of-home care who cannot safely return to birth parents. It provides the legislative support for creating permanent family links between adopted children and their adoptive parents (legal permanence), in a way that foster care does not. It may be more beneficial to vulnerable children than long-term foster care because it provides greater stability (residential permanence): research on the outcomes of adoption indicates that breakdown rates are lower than for other types of permanency arrangements (Selwyn et al., 2014). Adoption also appears to offer a more enduring relationship with carers (psychological permanence) (Biehal et al., 2010). The compressed and accelerated transitions to adulthood experienced by care leavers have been well documented (e.g. Stein & Munro, 2008): adoption placements are not time-limited in the way that foster placements are, and although there is little comparative research, there are indications that adoptees are more likely to receive ongoing support as they make the transition to independence (Selwyn et al., 2014). We would, therefore, expect the Barnardos adoptees to have achieved greater stability and more durable relationships when they moved to their adoptive homes in comparison with their own previous experience, as well as that of other children who remained in out-of-home care. An exploration of the data[1] collected through the survey, the

---

[1] The full follow-up sample includes 124 adoptees for whom at least minimal data were available in 2016. Of these, only minimal data are available for 31 adoptees; substantial data collected through responses to an online survey are available for 93 adoptees (the core follow-up sample); a subset of 20 adoptees and 21 adoptive parents in this latter group were also interviewed, providing qualitative data concerning 24 adoptees (the interview group). A flow chart, showing the numbers of adoptees included in each of the stages of data collection can be found in Appendix 1.

minimal follow-up with some of those who did not participate, and the interviews undertaken with about one in four of the core follow-up sample and/or their adoptive parents help us to understand the extent to which this objective was achieved.

Legal and Residential Permanence

The 124 adoptees for whom at least minimum follow-up data are available ranged in age from 5 to 44 years on 31 October 2016 (the cut-off point for responses to the survey). Figure 5.1 sets out the length of time since they were first placed with their adoptive families; the average length of time was 18 years, with a range of between 5 and 37 years.[2] The largest group (46 adoptees) had been placed more than 20 years previously, including three who were placed more than 30 years before follow-up.

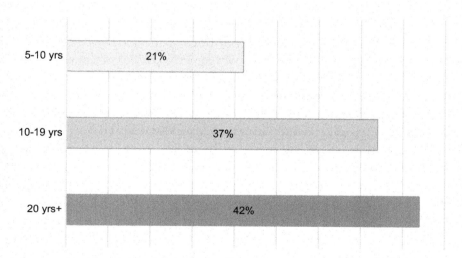

Fig. 5.1 Length of time in years since placed with adoptive family (full follow-up sample *N* = 124)

---

[2] sd = 8.8489.

Table 5.1 Number of adoptees living at home by age at follow-up (full follow-up sample *N* = 124)

Adoptee living at home?	Age 17 or under	Age 18 or over	Frequency (total)	Per cent
Yes	41	26	67	55
No	3	48	51	42
Died after leaving home	1	2	3	3
Total	**45**	**76**	**121**	**100**
Missing			3	

As Table 5.1 shows, the whereabouts of 121 (58%) of the adoptees were known at follow-up. Three adoptees whose parents responded to the survey had died in their teens. Over half (67/121: 55%) of the adoptees for whom we have follow-up information were still living with their adoptive parents. As would be expected, all but three of the adoptees aged under 18 years old were at home, but so too were 34% (26/76) of those aged 18 or over. This latter group included three adoptees who were in their 30s, one of whom was living in the family home with his spouse. The other two were sisters, living with the same adoptive parents; one of them had moderate learning disabilities and the other had a chronic health condition.

The 67 adoptees who were still at home had been living with their adoptive parents for an average of 13 years.[3] This is a strong indicator of residential permanence, particularly given the evidence about these young people's previous experience:

> *So when he came to us, he had already been in nine different homes – some fostered, some homes for children – nine before he came to us.* (Adoptive parent of young man, aged 9 when permanently placed)

---

[3] Range = 5–27 years; median = 12 years; sd = 6.1.

Well, I can't give you a number on how many homes I lived in before I moved here. (Young woman aged 10 when permanently placed, aged 21 when interviewed)

Thirteen (19%) of the adoptees who were still living at home had had four or more previous placements and 48 (72%) had experienced four or more adverse childhood experiences (ACEs). They include one adoptee who had been sexually abused by ten perpetrators including both birth parents, as well as experiencing seven other ACEs before being placed in out-of-home care at the age of five. She then had 12 different placements before entering her adoptive home at the age of nine. At the time of the survey she was 26 and had remained with her adoptive mother for 17 years.

Adoptees No Longer Living at Home

The majority of those adoptees who were no longer living at home (36/51: 72%) had moved away to study, to live independently or to be with a partner. They, too, had often experienced a lengthy period of stability in an adoptive home following an unstable care experience. For instance, one young woman, who had had eight previous placements in out-of-home care before entering her adoptive home at the age of eight, had remained there until she moved out to live independently when she was 26. In her view:

[adoption] will literally change your life, mostly for the better. Although there is a lot of emotional stress and confusion there is also a sense of stability in your life. You feel like you belong to someone and are part of a family, as though you are worth being cared for. (Young woman aged 8 when permanently placed, aged 35 when interviewed)

Research on leaving care in many Western societies shows that care leavers are often required to move from foster homes and residential units into independent living at a much earlier age than most of their peers would expect to leave the parental home (Stein & Munro, 2008). Cashmore and Paxman's (2007) study of *Wards Leaving Care* in the same Australian state (New South Wales), and over a timespan (1992–1998) that overlapped with the adoptees' experience, found that 83% (34/45) left their final placements to live independently between the ages of 18 and 19 years old. In comparison, the average age at which the adoptees had left home to live independently was 21[4]—two to three years later. Moreover, as we have seen, 26 of those aged 18 years or older (34% of adoptees in this age group) were still living at home. The average age of these young adults who had not left home was 22, indicating that the age at which the cohort as a whole would leave might be considerably older. Although we do not know the ages at which 23 (45%) adoptees left home, the data that are available do appear to show that most adoptees achieved greater residential permanence and had more extensive, long-term support as they made the transition to adulthood than they would have been likely to receive had they remained in long-term foster care.

Comparison with Normative Australian Population

There have been significant societal changes over the long timeframe of the study, and young people now leave home at a much older age than they did in the 1990s, when the first adoptees reached adulthood. Australian population data are categorised slightly differently from the *Wards Leaving Care* data. The population data indicate that in 2015 in Australia, 86% of women and 81% of men aged 18–21 and 48% of women and 60% of men aged 22–25 were still living in their parental home (Wilkins, 2017). Of the 20 adoptees aged 18–21, 13 (65%) were still living with their adoptive parents, as were 7/9 (78%) of those aged 22–25. The data are insufficient to provide reliable evidence but suggest that, while more adoptees than young people in the general population leave home in their teens, at least as many or more continue to live with their parents in their early twenties.

Disrupted, Interrupted and Unstable Placements

The data appear to indicate that the adoptees had a better chance of remaining in a stable home until they were ready to move on as independent adults in comparison with children in foster care. However, not all the

---

[4] Median = 20.5; sd = 4.46; range = 16–31 years.

Table 5.2 What was the main reason you left your adoptive parents on the last occasion? (Core follow-up sample *N* = 93)

Reason	Frequency	Per cent	Cumulative per cent
Study or work	4	8.9	8.9
Move into independent living or to live with partner	28	62.2	71.1
Conflict with adoptive family	5	11.1	82.2
Didn't like living in a family	2	4.4	86.7
Adoptive family issues e.g., illness, separation	2	4.4	91.1
Moved back to birth family	4	8.9	100
Total	**45**	**100**	
Still living with adoptive parents	48		

adoptive placements were stable: some of them ended prematurely and relationships between adoptees and adoptive parents did not always endure. Data that enable us to explore these issues further come from the smaller group of adoptees and adoptive parents who responded to the survey (the core follow-up sample) and the subset of this group who were interviewed. At the time of the survey, 48 (52%) of the 93 adoptees for whom we have responses were still living with their adoptive parents and 45 (48%) had left. Three of those who had left had since died. Table 5.2 shows the reasons why these 45 adoptees had left home. As with the full follow-up sample, the majority of adoptees in the core follow-up sample had left home to study or to live independently. However, 13 (29%) had left home for non-normative reasons: because of conflict with their adoptive family; because they had decided to move back to their birth families; or because of problems such as illness or divorce within their adoptive families.

Legal Permanence

Each year, about 4% of children in Britain return to care after an adoption order has been made (Triseliotis, 2002); in the USA, 1–10% of adopted children return to out-of-home care (Child Welfare Information

Gateway, 2012), and the rate of adoption dissolution (formal ending of the adoption) has been calculated at 2.2% (Smith, 2014). All of the 93 children in the Barnardos core follow-up sample achieved legal permanence in that there were no formal dissolutions; responses to the questionnaires also give no evidence that any adoptees returned to out-of-home care.[5] However, a number of placements disrupted.

Disruption Rate

Both the terminology and the definition as to what constitutes an adoption disruption (or 'displacement' (Rolock & White, 2016)) vary, making comparisons difficult (Palacios et al., 2019). The definition used by Selwyn et al. (2014) in their seminal study on this issue was: 'legally adopted children who left their families under the age of 18 years old' (p. 16). Responses to the survey give the ages at which 29 of the 45 adoptees who were no longer living with their adoptive families had moved out. At least 12 had left their parents' home before their eighteenth birthday (see Table 5.3).[6] These 12 placements would therefore have met this criterion. If this definition is used, the rate of disruption in the Barnardos study (at least 13% (12/93) premature endings) is substantially higher than the 3.2% over ten years found in Selwyn and colleagues' analysis of data on 37,335 adoptions made in England. However, that study covered all adoptions, while the Barnardos adoptees were relatively old at placement and many had been selected specifically because they were hard to place and therefore posed additional challenges (see Chap. 3). They were closer to the samples of older children adopted following troubled trajectories in out-of-home care in the UK, studied by Selwyn et al. (2006) and Rushton and Dance (2006). Selwyn et al. (2006) identified a disruption rate of 17%, but this included children whose placements broke down before the order was made, when disruptions are more common. Only 6% of their sample disrupted post order; however, the children were followed up for a shorter period than the Barnardos sample (6–11 years vs

---

[5] Barnardos staff are aware of discussions concerning potential returns to out-of-home care for two children in the core follow-up sample whose placements disrupted, but the outcomes are unknown; they are both known to have returned to live with birth family members.

[6] There are no data available on the ages at which 16 (36%) of the adoptees had left home.

Table 5.3 Age at leaving adoptive parents' home (core follow-up sample *N* = 93)

Age	Frequency	Per cent	Cumulative per cent
13	1	3.4	3.4
14	1	3.4	6.9
15	1	3.4	10.3
16	2	6.9	17.2
17	7	24.1	41.4
18	1	3.4	44.8
19	3	10.3	55.2
20	1	3.4	58.6
21	3	10.3	69
23	2	6.9	75.9
24	1	3.4	79.3
26	2	6.9	86.2
27	2	6.9	93.1
31	1	3.4	96.6
33	1	3.4	100
Total	**29**	**100**	
Still living with adoptive parents	48		
Missing	16		
Total	93		

3–29 years). Rushton and Dance (2006) undertook a prospective study of children placed for adoption from out-of-home care at 5–11 years old. They found a disruption rate of 23% and suggest that this is broadly in line with other studies of older children placed from care with non-relative adopters. However, it is not clear how many of these disruptions occurred after the order had been made. The Barnardos sample only included children who already had adoption orders; we do not know how many other children had adoptive placements that disrupted before the courts heard the application for an order.

Many studies have found that placements of older children are more likely to disrupt. Selwyn et al. (2014) found that disruptions are significantly more likely to occur if children are aged four or more when they enter their adoptive homes: 10 of the 12 Barnardos adoptees whose placements disrupted were aged over four at entry and 6 were aged eight or more, suggesting that age may also have been a factor for these children.

The Barnardos study also has the benefit of sufficiently fine-grained data to explore further why some placements apparently ended prematurely, the reason the adoptee left the adoptive home, and the extent to which the relationship appeared to be ruptured. These data make it possible to identify those placements which ended permanently before adulthood with an apparent breakdown of the relationship between the adoptee and adoptive parents (full-scale disruptions), and those which may have gone through, or have been going through, a period of turbulence during which the adoptee sometimes left the home, but later returned, or at least re-established a relationship (interrupted placements).

Table 5.4 shows the reasons why the 12 young people identified above left their adoptive homes before they were 18. Only one of them moved to live with another member of the adoptive family.

How many of these placements had genuinely broken down? Two adoptees had left their adoptive parents' home before they were 18, had no communication with their adoptive parents and received no ongoing support from them at the time of the study. These appear to be full-scale disruptions, with the relationship, as well as the living arrangements, having apparently terminated.

Two other adoptees who had left home early died when they were teenagers: one from a drug overdose and the other as a result of a car accident. It is unclear how far they had continued to be supported by their adoptive parents after they moved out. However, others, who had left as a result of conflict with their adoptive parents or to return to their birth parents, nevertheless continued to be in regular communication

Table 5.4 Reason for leaving home and age when last left (*N* = 12)

Main reason for last leaving home	Age when last left adoptive home (years)					Total
	13	14	15	16	17	
Move into independent living or to live with partner	0	0	0	1	4	5
Conflict with adoptive family	0	1	0	0	1	2
Didn't like living in a family	0	0	1	0	1	2
Moved back to birth family	1	0	0	1	1	3
Total	1	1	1	2	7	12

with their adoptive parents and/or to receive support from them, as did many of those who had moved at an early age to live independently. The extent to which the placements had disrupted appear to be on a continuum, ranging from one young woman, who had left home at the age of 16 to return to her birth family and now, 15 years later, never communicated with her adoptive family and received no support from them, to another who had left at 17 to live with a partner her adoptive parents disapproved of, briefly moved back to her birth parents and at the time of the survey, aged 32, communicated with her adoptive parents 'most days or at least once a week' and also relied on them emotionally.

Unstable and Interrupted Adoptions

Data collected from the core follow-up sample through the survey and subsequent interviews reveal an underlying pattern of instability in about a quarter of the adoptions that endured, as well as in those that ended prematurely. The survey asked whether the adoptee had ever run away or moved temporarily out of the adoptive home: 22 (26%) of the 85 adoptees for whom there were responses had run away or temporarily left home at least once and then returned; 9 (11%) of these young people were reported to have left multiple times. All 12 young people who had left the adoptive home before the age of 18 were reported to have left and returned on at least one previous occasion; 2 had done so more frequently. Three of those who had left before they were 18, and four of those who had left a few years later, were unsure whether they had permanently left home or whether they might yet return.

Temporary forays into independence are a well-established feature of transitions to adulthood in normative populations, as is conflict between adolescents and parents (Agllias, 2016). One of the issues that make the transition to adulthood more problematic for young people leaving foster care is that once they have left a placement, it may be much harder for them to return: beds may no longer be available in foster homes or residential units, and even if they have not been filled, resources to support a care leaver who tries to return may not be forthcoming (Munro et al., 2012; Stein & Munro, 2008). A small number of care leavers in the Cashmore and Paxman study expressed their hurt at the discovery that after they had left home, their former foster carers no longer appeared to be fully committed to them as family members (Cashmore & Paxman, 2007). The experiences of the Barnardos adoptees provide a very different picture. Not only, as we have already seen, was it relatively common for them to leave home and then return, but almost all those who had left continued to communicate with, and to receive support from, their adoptive parents.

Sarah

Before Entering Her Adoptive Home

Sarah was ten when she and her sisters were removed from their birth parents' home following evidence of sexual abuse by multiple perpetrators. They had three placements in out-of-home care before entering their adoptive home when Sarah was 12. At this time, Sarah was described as an angry child who was given to temper tantrums:

I used to chuck mentals. I used to break everything. I used to barricade myself in my room.

These tended to occur after contact with her birth mother, who had not accepted that her relationships with paedophiles had been harmful to her children, and they were now permanently placed away from her.

(continued)

(continued)
Progress During Adolescence

Sarah's behavioural problems began to diminish after she became settled in her adoptive placement. With intensive support from her adoptive parents, she was able to move into mainstream school and began to make academic progress. When she was 15, she finally felt able to call her adoptive parents Mum and Dad.

I started calling them Mum and Dad. I think when I started to realise that, oh, Jeez, you know, they're more like Mum and Dad to me than my real parents ever were in any way.

However, she became increasingly concerned about her younger siblings who had remained with her birth parents at continuing risk of harm and, at 15, she returned to her birth family in order to try to protect them. After one brief return to her adoptive parents, Sarah and her boyfriend moved 'permanently' to her birth family and settled near them. Although the placement had apparently broken down, Sarah's adoptive parents tried to make sure 'that if she wanted to come back the door was always open'.

As an Adult

Both Sarah and her adoptive parents were interviewed when she was 33. After a period during which there had been no communication, her adoptive parents had re-established contact when they were about to move to another state. At the time of the interview, Sarah was in close communication with her adoptive parents, telephoning them once or twice a week; she and her partner and children had recently spent a week's holiday with them. She spoke very positively about her relationship with them. From the adoptive parents' point of view, Sarah had never ceased to be one of the family: 'She's our daughter, you know. We try and support her.'

Psychological Permanence

Continuing Support from Adoptive Parents

Sarah's case study demonstrates how psychological permanence may be achieved, even if residential permanence does not persist. Most of the adoptees who had left home and whose adoptive parents were still alive reported that they communicated with them regularly, either 'most days or at least once a week' (14/41: 34%) or 'less than once a week but at least

Table 5.5 Type of support adoptive parents were giving to adoptees at time of the survey (*N* = 41)

Type of support offered	Frequency	Per cent*
Emotional support	29	70.7
Financial (any payments apart from gifts)	15	36.6
Practical help - washing, cooking	7	17.1
Childcare	4	9.8
Accommodation (away from adoptive family)	1	2.4
Other	6	14.6
None	6	14.6

*Percentages do not total 100 due to multiple responses from individual respondents

once a month' (10/41: 24%).[7] Many of these adoptees were now in their 30s or 40s, and at least 14 had left home more than ten years ago.[8] Only five adoptees (12%) reported never communicating with their adoptive parents and one (2%) was in touch less than once a year. In contrast, Cashmore and Paxman (2007) found that less than a third of state wards (12/41: 29%) had 'regular and frequent contact with their former carers' four to five years after they had left care.

Adoptive parents reported providing a wide range of continuing support to adopted adults who had left home, as is shown in Table 5.5.[9] The most commonly offered support was emotional (29/41: 71%), then financial (15/41: 37%), including one adoptee (aged 32) who also stated elsewhere that their main source of income was their adoptive parents. A handful of adoptive parents also offered practical support (7/41: 17%) and help with childcare (4/41: 10%). Only six adoptees received no form of continued support (6/41: 15%).

---

[7] Three of the 45 adoptees who had left home had died, and one other had experienced the deaths of both adoptive parents. Data on this variable are available for the remaining 41 adoptees who had left home.

[8] Range between 0 and 24 years; mean = 10; sd = 7.7.

[9] Data on this variable are available for the 41 adoptees who had left home, were still alive and whose adoptive parents had not died.

Failed and Fragile Relationships

At the time of the survey, three adoptees were no longer in communication with their adoptive families and received no ongoing support from them (or there was no evidence of support), and one received no support and was in contact less than once a year. These four adoptees appear to have had no ongoing relationship with their adoptive families. Four other adoptees claimed to have either no contact with their adoptive parents or no ongoing support from them. The relationship between them and their adoptive parents might be regarded as fragile. Adoption had not enabled these eight young people to achieve psychological permanence, although only four of them had left their adoptive homes before they were 18 and therefore failed to achieve residential permanence.

The number of failed or fragile adoptions is too small for much meaningful statistical analysis. However, age is likely to have been a factor in these outcomes: all eight of these adoptees were more than a year old before abuse was identified (mean age = 7 years 3 months);[10] six (75%) of them had had their second birthday before they were separated from their birth parents (mean age = 7 years 6 months);[11] and seven (88%) had had their fourth birthday before entering their adoptive homes (mean age = 8 years 4 months).[12] These timescales have all been identified as related to poor outcomes in adulthood (Rousseau et al., 2015; Selwyn et al., 2014; Zeanah et al., 2011). They also indicate considerably more delay than the timescales for the children in the follow-up group who did achieve psychological permanence, of whom 59% were identified before their first birthday (mean = 19 months),[13] 55% were separated from birth parents before they were two (mean = 2 years 8 months)[14] and 45% entered their adoptive homes before they were four (mean = 4 years 9 months).[15]

It is, however, also worth noting that this group of eight adoptees showed considerable diversity on a number of other key variables such as

---

[10] Range = 14–154 months; sd = 60.914.
[11] Range = 15–155 mths; sd = 59.096.
[12] Range = 39–172 mths; sd = 52.090.
[13] Range = 0–147 mths; sd = 29.184.
[14] Range = 0–150 mths; sd = 34.918.
[15] Range = 3–157 mths; sd = 43.455.

numbers of adverse childhood experiences, the types of abuse experienced, the extent of polyvictimisation and numbers of placements in out-of-home care. Five had been placed in our low vulnerability group (Chap. 3), suggesting that although this classification was based on research evidence concerning outcomes of adoption, it was a poor predictor of psychological permanence.

The group were also similar to the adoptees who achieved psychological permanence in terms of gender split, number of placements in out-of-home care and behavioural problems at entry to the placement. Considerably fewer of them had had contact with birth parents since entering their adoptive home (63% (5/8) vs 90% (71/79)), and it is possible that this may have made it easier to fantasise about their birth families and harder to commit to a new relationship with adoptive parents (see Chap. 6). The only other distinguishing feature was that the adoptive parents of seven (88%) of these children had reported that their primary motivation was infertility (as compared with 69% of adoptive parents of other children) and none had stated that they were motivated by a desire to help a child. Some of these parents may have been inappropriately matched with children with particularly challenging needs.

Comparisons with Normative Australian Population

Disruptions do occur in the general population and are not the exclusive experience of adoptive families. It is, therefore, worth considering how far the adoptees' experiences differed from those of the normative Australian population. The proportion of adoptees who had left home and who were in contact with their adoptive parents at least once a week (37%) was substantially lower than that of other Australians (57%) who took part in the Household, Income and Labour Dynamics (HILDA) survey, Wave 8, which asked specific questions on proximity to and contact with non-resident siblings and parents (Wilkins et al., 2011).

The HILDA survey also found that 4% of Australians had no contact with their parents or were in touch less than once a year; almost four times as many adoptees (15%) had lost contact or were only minimally in touch with their adoptive parents. The adoptees were therefore less likely to maintain very close relationships with their adoptive parents after they had left home and they were more likely to have become estranged from them. However, as we have seen, the relationship between adoptees and adoptive parents was almost twice as likely to persist after they had left home than that between care leavers and former foster carers.

Commitment of Adoptive Parents

Given the adoptees' experiences before entering their adoptive homes (Chap. 3), it is not surprising that, after they left home, they were less likely to have sustained a relationship with their adoptive parents than the normative population. Nevertheless, the extent to which adoptive parents were committed to their adopted children, even when the relationship became difficult, is noteworthy. One of the seven adoptees who had left home because of conflict with adoptive parents or because they 'did not like living in a family' had since died. Four of the others were still in contact at least once a month and three of them continued to receive financial and/or emotional support from adoptive parents, one of them while in prison. Two of the four adoptees who had returned to live with their birth parents were still in regular contact with their adoptive parents. Both were receiving support from them—one of them received 'accommodation, financial, emotional and practical support'. One other adoptee in this group had died.

It is also clear from the interviews that almost all adoptive parents regarded themselves as having made a life-long commitment that would be honoured, regardless of the challenges some of them faced in trying to provide a 'forever family' for children whose previous experiences had often been intensely damaging. Adoptive parents continued to show extensive parental commitment to adoptees who had become drug addicts or prostitutes, who had developed schizophrenia and were unlikely ever to be fully independent, or who had walked out on them and then reappeared, sometimes after years of silence.

Never give up…. When you make the commitment, it's got to be for life.
(Adoptive parent of a young woman, aged 6 when permanently placed)

Once he was with us as a forever family, we couldn't give up on him but it led us to nearly destruct ourselves!! (Adoptive parent of a young man, aged 10 when permanently placed)

Integration into the Adoptive Family

Adoption is qualitatively different from foster care in that the adoptee becomes not only psychologically, but also legally, a member of their new family. A number of studies of adoption (e.g. de Rosnay et al., 2015; Triseliotis, 1973) have found that the change in legal status is valued by adopted children because it marks the point at which they fully belong to their adoptive family and is therefore of symbolic importance. We have already seen that the adoptive parents were fully committed to their role as parents for life. Data collected through the survey and the interviews shed further light on the relationship between adoptive parents and adoptees; the evidence also indicates how far they perceived themselves as belonging to one another as members of the same family unit.

Belonging

It was clear that most adoptive parents regarded the children as family members. They talked of them as 'my son' or 'my daughter', and some emphasised that they saw no distinction between their adopted children and their birth children:

But I wouldn't want that word [adoption] to define her role in the family. Her role is that she's our daughter. And in a sense, why does that need to be distinguished between her and [birth children], right? So we wouldn't ever – I would never say, "This is [name], our adopted daughter". (Adoptive parent of a young woman, aged 6 when permanently placed)

All the adoptees had the opportunity to change their surname to that of their adoptive parents, and many did so before the order was made. Moreover, some adoptive parents made additional efforts to ensure that their adoptees felt fully integrated into their families. One adoptee was given the middle names of the adoptive parents' birth children; another took the adoptive mother's sister's name as her middle name and another helped choose the names of the adoptive parents' baby, born after she was placed with them. Tellingly, one of the few young people whose adoption failed bitterly regretted changing his name.

Most adoptees also regarded themselves as members of their adoptive families. They referred to their adoptive parents as 'Mum' and 'Dad' and their birth children as their brothers and sisters. Some adoptees objected when birth parents expected to have their genetic relationship acknowledged, as in this example:

> If anything, the bit that really annoys me at the moment is since Dad, [adoptive father], passed away, I feel like he [birth father] is playing – he's more trying to play the role of the dad and there are little references to, particularly from my grandmother, she refers to [birth father] as, "Your Dad", and I just ignore it, and let it slide. However, I never acknowledge it, and that irks me a bit. (Young man, aged 2 when permanently placed, aged 41 when interviewed)

Again, it is significant that the only adoptees who continued to refer to their birth parents as 'Mum' and 'Dad' were those with fragile or disrupted placements.

Given the extent to which most adoptees felt integrated into their adoptive families, it is, therefore, perhaps unsurprising that the majority of those who responded to the survey (45/54: 83%) considered that their adoptive family had been the greatest influence in their lives (see Table 5.6).

Those interviewed were also asked how often they talked, or thought about, the adoption nowadays. The majority of adoptive parents (18/21: 86%) 'never' or 'hardly ever' thought about it. The same was true of the adoptees, although slightly more of them (6/20: 30%) thought about adoption 'sometimes, frequently or all the time'. This last point is further supported by the evidence from the 17 interviews with dyads (interviews with adoptee and their adoptive parent, held separately). This shows that while their experience was generally congruent, adoption tended to be more of a live issue for adoptees than for their adoptive parents.

Table 5.6 Who do you think has been the greatest influence on who you are today, how you feel about yourself and how you see the world?* (Core follow-up sample *N* = 54)

Greatest influence	Frequency	Per cent	Cumulative per cent
My adoptive family	45	83.3	83.3
Both my adoptive family and birth family	5	9.3	92.6
Other people, e.g., friends	4	7.4	100
My birth family	0	0	
Total	54	100	

*All adoptees who responded to the survey were asked this question (*N* = 54).

Table 5.7 How did/do you fit in with your adoptive family?* (Core follow-up sample *N* = 46)

Did you fit in with your adoptive family when you first moved in?	How do you fit in with your adoptive family now?			
	I fit in really well	I fit in OK	I don't feel I fit in	Total
I fitted in really well	17	1	2	20
I fitted in OK	7	2	2	11
I didn't feel I fitted in	1	3	1	5
I can't remember	5	2	0	7
Total	30	8	5	43
Missing				3

*All adoptees aged 12 and over who responded to the survey were asked this question (*N* = 46).

Although some of them still thought about being adopted, almost all adoptees felt that they were genuinely part of their adoptive families. Table 5.7 shows how they felt they fitted in when they first arrived compared with how they fitted in at the time of the survey.[16] Almost half of those

---

[16] As already indicated, the distance between these two time points varies in the sample between 5 and more than 30 years.

who answered this question indicated that they felt they fitted in well at first with their adoptive family (20/43: 47%); this had increased to over two-thirds by the time of the survey (30/43: 70%). Only five (12%) adoptees indicated that they did not fit in at the time of the survey, one of whom had never felt he belonged, and four whose sense of being part of the family deteriorated over time. All but one of these adoptees were aged 4 or more when they entered their adoptive homes; one was 14, and the others were aged between 3 and 10. Two of them were in the group of eight adoptees discussed above, whose relationship with their adoptive parents appeared to be fragile and who appeared not to have achieved psychological permanence.

Adoptees were also asked whether their relationship with their adoptive family had changed since they were adopted.[17] Four (10%) thought it had deteriorated, but all the others thought that it had improved (25/39: 64%) or stayed the same (10/39: 26%).

Finally, adoptees were asked whether social workers had made a good match between them and their adoptive families (see Table 5.8). The two who disagreed both felt that they did not fit in with their adoptive families, that the relationship had deteriorated as they had grown older and that adoption might not have been the right decision for them. All other adoptees who were asked thought that adoption had always (30/43: 70%) or mostly (11/43: 26%) been the right decision for them.[18]

Table 5.8 Do you think social workers made a good match between you and your adoptive family? (Core follow-up sample *N* = 44)*

	Frequency	Per cent	Cumulative per cent
Yes, always	30	69.8	69.8
Yes, mostly	11	25.6	95.3
No, probably not	1	2.3	97.7
No, definitely not	1	2.3	100
Total	**43**	**100**	
Missing	1		

*All adoptees aged 14 and over who responded to the survey were asked this question (N = 44)

---

[17] This question was asked of all adoptees aged 12 and over (N = 46), 39 responded.
[18] This question was asked of all adoptees aged 14 and over (N = 43).

Adoptees' perceptions of psychological permanence were, perhaps unsurprisingly, related to their perceptions of sensitive parenting. While about three-quarters of the adult adoptees thought that their adoptive parents 'always' or 'often' praised them for doing well; helped if they had a problem; spent time just talking to them; listened to them; gave them presents; and helped them feel part of the family, about one in four felt that this had only 'sometimes', or 'never' been the case. When their responses to these questions were combined into a composite variable,[19] 57% (21/37) adoptees appeared 'always' to have experienced sensitive parenting, 38% (14/37) 'sometimes' or 'often', and 5% (2/37) 'never'. Adoptees who had 'always' experienced sensitive parenting were significantly more likely to regard themselves as fitting in well[20] and to think that social workers had made a good match between them and their adoptive families.[21]

Conclusion

There is substantial evidence to show that achieving legal, residential and psychological permanence (Brodzinsky & Livingston Smith, 2019) provides a positive context within which vulnerable children are most likely to achieve successful outcomes in adulthood. The 93 Barnardos adoptees in the core follow-up sample all achieved legal permanence through their adoption orders, none of which were subsequently dissolved. The evidence from the study shows that the majority also achieved residential permanence: 56% of them were still living with their adoptive parents on average 13 years after they had been placed with them; the average age for leaving home was 21 years and the majority (72%) left for normative reasons (to study or to live independently or with a partner). Although at least 12 adoptions (13%) had broken down according to the definition utilised by other adoption research, and a number of others were unstable, the evidence suggests that the majority of adoptees had also achieved

---

[19] For further details see Appendix 1.

[20] $X^2 = 6.311$; $df = 1$; $p = 0.12$

[21] $X^2 = 15.442$; $df = 1$; $p < 0.001$

a degree of psychological permanence, shown in the extent to which they appeared to be integrated into their adoptive families and continued to communicate with them and receive support from adoptive parents after they had left home. On the measure utilised by this study, only eight (8/93: 9%) adoptees appeared to be poorly integrated, with no enduring relationship, or only a minimal relationship with their adoptive parents. When we come to consider the extent to which the adoptees had achieved satisfactory wellbeing in adulthood, attention will be given to the ways in which this sense of permanence had served to strengthen their resilience and mitigate the extensive vulnerability they had shown at entry to the placement.

Key Points

- On 31 October 2016 (the cut-off point for the follow-up period), the adoptees ranged in age from 5 to 44 years: more than one in three (37%) had been placed more than 20 years before.
- The whereabouts of 121 (58%) of the adoptees were known at follow-up. All but three of those who were under 18 were still living with their adoptive parents, as were 34% (26/76) of those who had reached adulthood.
- The 67 adoptees who were still at home had been living with their adoptive parents for an average of 13 years. Given their previous experiences, the findings show strong evidence of residential permanence post-adoption.
- The average age at which the adoptees had left home to live independently was 21, two to three years older than the care leavers followed by Cashmore and Paxman (2007).
- All the 93 Barnardos adoptees in the core follow-up sample achieved legal permanence: there were no dissolutions and no child returned to out-of-home care.
- Data concerning the core follow-up sample indicate that 13 (29%) of those who had left home had done so for non-normative reasons
- Twelve adoptees left their adoptive placements after the adoption order had been made but before they were 18 years old, indicating a

disruption rate of 13% (12/93). Selwyn et al.'s (2006) comparable study of late adopted children found a 6% post-order disruption rate, but within a shorter timeframe.

- About a quarter (26%) of the adoptions showed an underlying fragility in that the adoptees had run away or temporarily left home at least once and then returned; 11% of adoptees had left multiple times. However, being able to return home after leaving was a factor that distinguished adoptees from care leavers.
- Almost all adoptive parents continued to offer emotional, financial or practical support to adoptees who had left home. Even after a disruption, most adoptees continued to have a relationship with their adoptive parents. Only eight adoptees appear not to have achieved psychological permanence in that they had no contact with their adoptive parents and/or received no continuing support from them.
- In comparison with young people in the general population, the adoptees were four times as likely to have lost contact or be only minimally in touch with their parents. However, the relationship was almost twice as likely to persist as that between care leavers and foster carers.
- Adoptive parents regarded the adoptees as fully integrated members of their families, as did most adoptees. Most rarely thought about the adoption.
- Over two-thirds (70%) of the adoptees thought that they fitted in well with their adoptive families. Four (10%) reported that their relationship with their adoptive family had deteriorated since they were adopted, whereas all the others thought that it had improved (64%) or stayed the same (26%).
- Two adoptees thought that social workers had not made a good match between them and their adoptive parents. All others 'always' or 'mostly' thought that adoption had been the right decision for them.

References

Agllias, K. (2016). Disconnection and decision-making: Adult children explain their reasons for estranging from parents. *Australian Social Work, 69*(1), 92–104.

Biehal, N., Ellison, S., Baker, C., & Sinclair, I. (2010). *Belonging and permanence: Long-term outcomes in foster care and adoption*. BAAF.

Brodzinsky, D., & Livingston Smith, S. (2019). Understanding research, policy, and practice issues in adoption instability. *Research on Social Work Practice, 29*(2), 185–194.

Cashmore, J., & Paxman, M. (2007). *Wards leaving care: Four to five years on*. University of New South Wales.

de Rosnay, M., Luu, B., & Conley Wright, A. (2015). *I guess I was an accident at first, but then I was chosen: Young children's identity formation in the context of open adoption in New South Wales. An examination of optimal conditions for child wellbeing*. University of Sydney Institute of Open Adoption Studies.

Gateway, C. W. I. (2012). *Adoption disruption and dissolution*. U.S. Department of Health and Human Services, Children's Bureau.

Munro, E. R., Lushey, C., National Care Advisory Service, Maskell-Graham, D., Ward, H., & with Holmes, L. (2012). *Evaluation of the Staying Put 18+ family placement programme: Final report. DFE: RR191*. Department for Education.

National Scientific Council on the Developing Child. (2004). *Young children develop in an environment of relationships* (Working Paper No. 1). http://www.developingchild.net. Accessed 17 Nov 2020.

Palacios, J., Rolock, N., Selwyn, J., & Barbosa-Ducharne, M. (2019). Adoption breakdown: Concept, research, and implications. *Research on Social Work Practice, 29*(2), 130–142.

Rolock, N., & White, K. R. (2016). Post-permanency discontinuity: A longitudinal examination of outcomes for foster youth after adoption or guardianship. *Children and Youth Services Review, 70*, 419–427.

Rousseau, D., Roze, M., Duverger, P., Fanello, S., & Tanguy, M. (2015). *Etude sure le devenir à long terme des jeunes enfants placès à la Pouponnière Sociale Saint Exupéry entre 1994 et 2001. Rapport recherche St-Ex 2013–2014*. Unité de Psychiatrie de l'Enfant et de l'Adolescent du CHU d'Angers.

Rushton, A., & Dance, C. (2006). The adoption of children from public care: A prospective study of outcome in adolescence. *Journal of the American Academy of Child and Adolescent Psychiatry, 45*(7), 877–883.

Selwyn, J., Sturgess, W., Quinton, D., & Baxter, C. (2006). *Costs and outcomes of non-infant adoptions*. BAAF.

Selwyn, J., Wijedasa, D., & Meakings, S. (2014). *Beyond the adoption order: Challenges, interventions and adoption disruptions, RR 336*. Department for Education. https://assets.publishing.service.gov.uk/government/uploads/system/uploads/attachment_data/file/301889/Final_Report_-_3rd_April_2014v2.pdf. Accessed 30 Dec 2020.

Smith, S. L. (2014). *Keeping the promise. The case for adoption support and preservation*. Donaldson Adoption Institute.

Stein, M., & Munro, E. (2008). *Young people's transitions from care to adulthood: International research and practice*. Jessica Kingsley.

Triseliotis, J. (1973). *In search of origins: The experiences of adopted people*. Routledge and Kegan Paul.

Triseliotis, J. (2002). Long-term foster care or adoption? The evidence examined. *Child & Family Social Work, 7*, 23–33.

Wilkins, R. (2017). *The household, income and labour dynamics in Australia survey: Selected findings from waves 1 to 15: The 12th annual statistical report of the HILDA survey*. Melbourne Institute: Applied Economic & Social Research, The University of Melbourne.

Wilkins, R., Warren, D., Hahn, M., & Houng, B. (2011). *Families, incomes and jobs, volume 6: A statistical report on waves 1 to 8 of the household, income and labour dynamics in Australia survey*. Melbourne Institute: Applied Economic & Social Research, The University of Melbourne.

Wise, S. (2017). *Developments to strengthen systems for child protection across Australia* (CFCA Paper No. 44). Child Family Community Australia Information Exchange, Australian Institute of Family Studies.

Zeanah, C. H., Gunnar, M. R., McCall, R. B., Kreppner, J. M., & Fox, N. A. (2011). Sensitive periods. *Monographs of the Society for Research in Child Development, 76*(4), 147–162.

6

Post-adoption Contact and Relationships with Birth Family Members

Introduction

There is now considerable evidence that adopted children benefit from some knowledge and understanding of their birth family and antecedents, and that past practices, in which adoption was shrouded in secrecy, were detrimental to the wellbeing of adoptees as well as their birth parents (Brodzinsky, 2006; de Rosnay et al., 2015; Triseliotis, 1973). Nevertheless, open adoption remains a contentious issue in many countries and there is considerable debate as to what level and type of engagement with birth families is optimal (e.g. Boyle, 2017; Brodzinsky, 2006; Chateauneuf et al., 2017; Grotevant et al., 2011; Neil, 2009). New South Wales and the Australian Capital Territory appear to be unique in both legislating for and implementing regular face-to-face post-adoption contact with birth families as a prerequisite of the adoption order. This is reflected in the Barnardos programme, which has incorporated the core principles of transparency, communicative openness and post-adoption contact with birth family members throughout its history (see Chap. 1). An exploration of the nature and impact of these arrangements has implications for the development of adoption policy and practice not only in Australia, but also in a wider, international context.

© The Author(s) 2022
H. Ward et al., *Outcomes of Open Adoption from Care*,
https://doi.org/10.1007/978-3-030-76429-6_6

We have seen from the previous chapter that adoption enabled most of the children to achieve legal, residential and psychological permanence. This growing sense of permanence was part of the process through which the adoptees were able to become integrated into their adoptive families and develop close attachments which might form the foundations for healthier developmental trajectories. This chapter explores how far ongoing face-to-face contact helped or hindered this process. It presents data showing the prevalence of face-to-face contact and how long it lasted and then explores what the contact was like, what the advantages and disadvantages were for the adoptive parents, and how far it was thought to have benefitted the children concerned. Subsequent chapters also consider the impact of contact on outcomes.

Interpreting the Data

Data used in this chapter come from the responses to the survey (concerning 93 adoptees) and the interviews held with adoptive parents and adoptees who had completed it (20 interviews with adoptees and 21 with adoptive parents, concerning 24 adoptions). Two points should be noted. First, the majority of the follow-up sample spent a lengthy period living with their adoptive parents before the adoption order was made: about three-quarters (71/93: 76%) of them were there for two years or more, and about a quarter (24/93: 26%) for five years or more. During this period, most children had contact with birth family members, with extensive support from Barnardos. After the adoption order was made, face-to-face contact persisted, specified in the adoption order and left to the families to organise. The adoption plan may in some cases have required a change in frequency of contact, or a different venue, but there do not appear to have been radical alterations. Most interviewees did not clearly distinguish between the two periods, and it is likely that respondents to the questionnaire would not have done so either. So the data refer to experiences of contact from the time the child entered the adoptive home, rather than from the time the order was made. Second, many birth parents dropped in and out of contact arrangements, seeing the child for a few years, disappearing, and then perhaps reappearing when they were older. Some adoptees also refused to see birth relatives for a while and then later changed their minds. Both the survey and the interviews provide data concerning contact at a particular point in time; had they taken place a few months or years earlier or later, the picture might well have been different.

Post-adoption Contact

Birth Parents

Policy and practice concerning contact for children who have been separated from birth families tends to focus on the primary relationship between the child and the birth mother (Boddy et al., 2014). Less attention appears to be given to contact with birth fathers or to wider family networks in both practice and policy (Boddy et al., 2014) and research (Iyer et al., 2020). Set against this context, considerable effort appears to have been given to ensuring extensive contact between the Barnardos adoptees and their birth families. Table 6.1 shows the number of adoptees who had contact with birth parents after they moved to their adoptive homes. Altogether, 76 (87%) adoptees had contact with at least one birth parent. This group includes 35 children who saw both birth parents, 35 who saw their mothers only and 6 who had direct contact only with their fathers. Only 11 adoptees (13%) had no face-to-face contact with either birth parent. One of these children had indirect contact with

Table 6.1 Face-to-face contact with birth parents post-adoption (core follow-up sample *N* = 93)

	Frequency	Per cent
With both birth parents	35	40
With birth mother	35	40
With birth father	6	7
None	11	13
Total	87	100
Missing	6	

their birth mother; the birth parents of three others had both died before the adoption. Only eight adoptees whose birth parents were alive[1] had no contact at all.

Siblings

Child welfare legislation and policy in England and Wales (Children and Families Act 2014), the USA (Fostering Connections to Success and Increasing Adoptions Act 2008) and Australia (Department of Families, Housing, Community Services and Indigenous Affairs et al., 2011) promote the placement of siblings together wherever it is in their best interests to do so. These policies are supported by research which indicates that joint placements can provide greater stability and a greater sense of psychological permanence, and that separating siblings can leave an enduring sense of loss (see Selwyn, 2018, for summary). There are, however, some indications that siblings who have been abused within their birth families may not always benefit from being placed together (Farmer & Pollock, 1998; Selwyn, 2018) and that consideration needs to be given to the needs of each individual child within the sibling group. One of the objectives of the Find-a-Family programme was to find permanent placements with adoptive parents for children in large sibling groups, who often come under the category of 'hard to place'; throughout the period of the study, it was Barnardos' policy to place siblings together wherever possible.

Responses to the survey indicated the extent to which sibling relationships were preserved when children were placed in adoptive homes (Table 6.2). Thirteen of the follow-up sample were single children at the time they were placed and 80 had birth siblings; 46 (58%) of those who had brothers and sisters had been placed in a home with at least one sibling and so had daily contact. However, a further 29 children (88% of those who had been placed apart) had post-adoption face-to-face contact with siblings from whom they had been separated at some stage. Only four (5%) adoptees had no subsequent contact with any birth siblings after moving to their adoptive families.

---

[1] Strictly speaking these are children whose birth parents are not known to have died.

Table 6.2 Face-to-face contact with birth siblings after entering permanent placement (core follow-up sample N = 93)

	Frequency	Per cent	Cumulative per cent
Face-to-face contact with at least one sibling (adoptees placed together)	46	58	58
Face-to-face contact with at least one sibling (adoptees placed apart)	29	37	95
Placed apart and no face-to-face sibling contact	4	5	100
Total	**79**	**100**	
No siblings	13		
Missing	1		

Other Relatives

Children who are abused or neglected by birth parents often form close, compensatory relationships with grandparents or other members of their extended families (Hunt, 2018; Selwyn et al., 2014). Many of the adoptees had had close relationships with grandparents before being placed in out-of-home care. There is evidence from the interviews that several of them had been looked after by grandparents who had eventually decided they could not offer them a permanent home:

> [He was] left with [maternal grandmother and partner] until [maternal grandmother] finally said, "He's about to start school. You have to take responsibility". He had been with them for probably two to three years, maybe. (Adoptive parent of young man, aged 8 when permanently placed)

There is substantial evidence from both the survey and the interviews that efforts were made to preserve these relationships. As Table 6.3 shows, more than three-quarters of the children (59/76: 78%) who had a grandparent or other family members who could be traced continued to have contact with them after they moved to their adoptive homes.

Table 6.3 Face-to-face contact with grandparents and other extended family members after entering permanent placement (core follow-up sample *N* = 93)

	Frequency	Per cent
Face-to-face contact	59	78
No face-to-face contact	17	22
Total	76	100
Not known/not applicable	17	

Taken together, the data show a high level of continuing face-to-face contact with birth family members, indicating the strength of Barnardos' commitment to open adoption in practice. Eighty-eight (93%) of the adoptees had direct post-adoption contact with at least one member of their birth family; one of the five adoptees who had no face-to-face contact had indirect contact; only four children had no contact at all. There are also indications that efforts were made to reunite children who had previously been separated from siblings and to re-establish contact that had previously been lost. Nearly two-thirds (13/21: 62%) of the children whose case files indicated that they had no direct contact with a birth parent at the time they moved to their adoptive home had subsequent face-to-face contact.

Contact during childhood did not always translate into an enduring relationship through adulthood. Nevertheless, by the time of the survey, on average 18 years after placement,[2] at least 28 (40%) of the adoptees who had had contact with their birth mothers, and 14 (34%) of those who had had contact with birth fathers during the placement were still seeing them, and more than half of the adoptees (52/93: 56%) were still seeing at least one member of their birth family. The average age of those who were known to be still seeing at least one birth parent at the time of the survey was 16,[3] compared with 26[4] for those who had no contact with a living birth parent, indicating that post-adoption contact tended to reduce as the adoptees grew older. Although, as Chap. 5 has shown, about one in four adoptees had run away or temporarily left their adoptive home at some

---

[2] sd = 8.5; range 5–37 years.
[3] sd = 10.296; range = 6–40.
[4] sd = 9.523; range = 11–44.

stage, often with the intention of returning to birth parents, only two were known to be living with birth family members at the time of the survey.

What Was Contact Like?

It is clear from the quantitative data that contact happened, and that it persisted for a relatively high proportion of children: qualitative data from responses to open-ended questions in the survey and from the interviews with adoptive parents and children give a fuller picture of what contact was like and how it affected their wellbeing and that of their adoptive families. There are also some indications of how contact affected birth parents and other relatives, but we were unable to interview them (see Chap. 1), and so all these data come from third parties (adoptees and adoptive parents).

Before making an adoption order, the court had to be satisfied that there was no realistic chance of a child being successfully placed with a member of their extended family or of being safely reunited with birth parents. Chapter 3 has shown that almost all adoptees (91%) had been abused by birth parents, or were the siblings of children who had been seriously abused; more than two-thirds (69%) of them had had four or more adverse childhood experiences (ACEs) before being placed in out-of-home care, and a third of them (32%) had experienced at least one failed restoration before entering their adoptive homes. Nevertheless, face-to-face contact was part of the plan for almost every child. Children whose parents had seriously abused or neglected them still continued to have contact, including one child whose mother had thrown her across the room as a baby, causing brain damage; another whose parents had been convicted of murdering one of her siblings; and two others whose parents had 'rented them out' to paedophiles in return for cash. Contact in cases such as these inevitably raised complex and difficult issues.

The stipulation was not simply that adoptive parents would comply with the contact plan, they were also expected to facilitate it and, in most cases, to accompany the child to contact visits, so this entailed making a relationship with birth parents and other relatives. Most adoptive parents received some support from Barnardos until the adoption order was made, but not afterwards.

A relatively high proportion of the children (28/93: 30%) had initially been placed with long-term foster carers who later applied to adopt them. In these families, the post-adoption contact plan was to some extent a continuation of existing arrangements and birth parents and other relatives were already known to the adoptive parents. For other children, who were placed with prospective adopters with a view to adoption, new arrangements had to be made, with birth parents knowing from the outset that the child was likely to be adopted.

Once adoption became the permanence plan for the child, Barnardos did not envisage contact as a means of building close relationships with birth parents so much as a way of helping a child to understand their antecedents and develop a strong sense of identity. This was reflected in Barnardos' policy to recommend relatively infrequent contact meetings at between two- and six-monthly intervals. Most children who had contact saw their birth parents and birth siblings about four times in the first year of the placement. Meetings usually took place at a Barnardos office or in a neutral, public setting such as a park or a café, and an adoptive parent was expected to be present.

Uncomplicated Contact

In 34 (40%)[5] cases contact visits had not been problematic; many[6] of these adoptive parents indicated that they provided valuable opportunities to get to know the birth family and to reassure them about their children's wellbeing:

Important that birth parents see that their child is being cared for as they had hoped and that there is good long-term relationship made as possible as practical. (Adoptive parent of young man, aged 14 when permanently placed)

In our case it allowed us to form a friendship and that helped the child to feel comfortable. (Adoptive parent of young woman, aged 10 when permanently placed)

---

[5] All adoptive parents were asked: Did you ever find contact problematic? There were 84 responses: 50/84: 60% positive; 34/84: 40% negative.

[6] Adoptive parents of 11/84 (13%) children.

[Our child] enjoyed the contact and so did we. (Adoptive parent of young man, aged 3 when permanently placed)

I found it nice to be able to talk to [child's] birth family... and to just be supportive and involved in [child's] life. (Adoptive parent of young woman aged 1 when permanently placed)

Problems Concerning Contact with Birth Parents

However, the adoptive parents of more than half of the children (60%) indicated that, at least at times, there had been problems. A few cited practical difficulties as the primary issue: problems in arranging meetings through third parties because birth family members did not have phones; the stress of trying to pin down birth parents, who were leading chaotic lives, to a specific date or time; or the sheer hassle of getting to contact meetings when they entailed taking time off work to take small children on lengthy car journeys. As outlined in Chap. 2, many children came from fractured or multiply reconstituted families and this could result in complex contact plans which were difficult to fulfil:

There are too many contacts. We have four with the birth father, four with the birth mother and grandmother and six with siblings (these are six separate sibling contacts). (Adoptive parent of young man, aged 3 months when permanently placed)

Because some birth parents were considered to be a threat to the children's safety, there were also numerous issues concerning security and secrecy. Several children had their names changed before the adoption order, and their addresses concealed, so that birth parents could not find them; one reason why contact was so often arranged in neutral venues was to prevent birth parents from finding out where the children lived:

We maintained communication via mail through a solicitor which worked best for us to avoid birth families knowing where we lived, despite one of them objecting to that arrangement but we felt it kept our family more secure. (Adoptive parent of young woman, aged 2 when permanently placed)

So we didn't want them to know where we live. We didn't want them to see our car number plate, and no telephone contact. So we were a little bit careful or cautious to not meet these people.... Well, they may turn up on our front lawn and possibly camp there or something like this. We didn't want that to happen, because they had no home... (Adoptive parent of young man, aged 2 when permanently placed)

One child's birth relatives had previously abducted another child and this added to the concerns around contact:

He was under our guard at all times. We never left him alone anywhere. So we just thought maybe there is some criminal connection maybe to other people. So we just were very careful. I mean, we turned up to the initial meetings... in a taxi,... and... we couldn't be tracked home. (Adoptive parent of young man, aged 2 when permanently placed)

However, practical difficulties were a relatively minor issue. The most common reason[7] why adoptive parents found contact difficult related to the parents' continuing problems.

Parents' Problems and Their Impact on Contact

We have already seen (Chap. 2) that most birth parents struggled with complex and entrenched problems which had prevented them from safeguarding and nurturing their children. A wide body of research evidence indicates that changing such adverse behaviour patterns is a complex process that takes time to achieve (see Ward et al., 2014, for summary). Data from the interviews indicated that, by the time their children reached adulthood, only a very small minority of birth parents had succeeded in overcoming the difficulties that had led to the adoption order; many others continued to abuse drugs or alcohol, to maltreat other children in their care or to maintain relationships with abusive partners who had been the cause of the children's removal.

---

[7] Cited in 21/50: 42% responses.

Birth parents sometimes attended contact meetings under the influence of drugs or alcohol. Some abused, or threatened to abuse, the children during contact visits. The interview data concerning 24 adoptees included three cases in which birth parents came to contact visits accompanied by an unrelated adult who had previously sexually abused the child. There were also cases where parents became physically violent: for example, during one contact visit the birth father 'just went ballistic and was breaking everything and the police had to be called'; during another, the child was physically abused.

While the instances of physical assault or the threats of sexual abuse during contact are the most vivid, a more frequent issue was parents' emotional abuse or insensitivity. Some parents only wanted contact with one of their children or brought presents for one sibling but not the other; others constantly belittled the child. A common theme in the interviews was the adoptees' perceptions of rejection, and these were reinforced when birth parents broke promises to be more involved in their lives and/or to attend contact meetings. Survey responses from 8/50 (16%) adoptive parents cite birth parents' failure to turn up to contact meetings or last-minute cancellations as a significant issue. One of the unintended consequences of open adoption policy is that it makes such rejections more transparent: the adoptees knew that their parents could have contact, and questioned why they did not choose to do so:

> [Birth mother] is saying to him "I'll do this for you, and I'll see you and I'll write to you, and I'll send you this", and all of that sort of stuff, and I'm thinking 'Yes, but if you don't keep that promise, what does that do to a child?' and it was a little bit like when she brought him to Barnardos for the handover, saying "Yes, I'll write you letters and I'll send you this", and it was exactly the same spiel. And I'm thinking "But you didn't. You wrote him one letter...."
>
> ...And of course, nothing happened. She didn't write to him. She didn't contact him. She didn't send him anything, and that was it. I mean, in a very short space of time, [adoptee] isn't silly. He would say "Yeah, but she said that, and she wouldn't do it". (Adoptive parent of young man, aged 8 when permanently placed)

Some birth parents and other relatives refused to accept that the adoption order was permanent and tried to undermine the placement. These parents told the child they would soon be reunited; talked about the room they had prepared for the child's return; or tried to persuade the child to run away. They also tried to undermine the adoptive parent's relationship with the child, by denigrating them or by resuming a parental role:

> *She wanted to take control and she wanted to be the mother, and I'm thinking: "Hang on, but you've decided to relinquish your child, and he's now in our family".* (Adoptive parent of young man, aged 8 when permanently placed)

Almost all (94%)[8] adoptive parents who responded to the survey thought that they should be present during contact visits. The most common reason (given in respect of 76% adoptees)[9] was to protect or support the child, and particularly to monitor what happened:

> *We are now their legal guardians and we need to protect the child from possible abuse and misinformation being fed to the child by birth family contacts.* (Adoptive parent of young woman, aged 10 when permanently placed)

As the above quotation indicates, the legal status conferred by the adoption order was sometimes perceived as giving adoptive parents additional responsibilities to protect the child against potentially harmful interactions with birth family members:

> *I don't think young children should be left alone with criminals.* (Adoptive parent of young man, aged 5 when permanently placed)

> *By the time she [birth mother] attended visits she was like a stranger, which we would never leave our kids with unattended.* (Adoptive parent of young man, aged 9 when permanently placed)

---

[8] 81/86 responses: 94%, missing data on seven adoptees.
[9] 64/84 responses: 76%, missing data on nine adoptees.

Vulnerable children trying to make a new life shouldn't be exposed to criminal and drug using parents without supervision. (Adoptive parent of young man, aged 9 when permanently placed)

On the other hand, adoptive parents could feel that the change of status gave them less power to manage the child's interactions with birth family members. For instance, adoptive parents sometimes felt that, without the support of a child protection order, they could not prevent a young person from returning to their birth family:

Adoptive mother: *…and [the adoption] actually facilitated a situation where she was able to go back home because she was no longer a government child. So she didn't come under any jurisdiction….*
Adoptive father: *So we couldn't stop her from going home.* (Adoptive parents of young woman, aged 10 when permanently placed)

As the adoptees grew older, and they got to know birth parents better, adoptive parents sometimes became less worried about the potential dangers and allowed teenagers to go to contact visits unsupervised. Some of these meetings were successful—one young man, for instance, used to visit his birth mother regularly after school. However, some teenagers were exposed to potentially harmful situations:

There was one time I went and stayed with [birth father] for a week… and that was just – that should never have happened… Again, just the circles that he was involved in and he was still involved in drugs and didn't work and was in a housing commission place and it was just – what I was exposed to, and seeing that, and seeing people using drugs and it was… It should never have happened. (Young man, aged 2 when permanently placed, aged 41 when interviewed)

When he was 15 we'd agreed that he could go and spend a week with her, and live with her for a week. And we were all fine and happy about that, and then on the third night he rings up and says, "Mum, you've got to get me out of here. She keeps giving me marijuana". (Adoptive parent of young man, aged 2 when permanently placed)

Lack of Engagement

Contact could still be difficult where there was no threat to the child's safety. Birth parents and children who had never had a close relationship did not always find it easy to spend time in each other's company—parents could be 'difficult to relate to', 'hard to communicate with' or ignored the adoptee during contact:

> *I felt so let down by my birth mum, by my grandparents. It wasn't – I'd come home and we'd be driving back for two hours and I'd be sitting in the car crying until I fell asleep because we spent three months pretty much apart and I would see her and she wouldn't spend time with me. She'd be on her phone or she'd be off doing something else. Or when I'd spend time with her, she wouldn't want to talk to me. So it was hard for me to want to go back but she was my birth mum, so there was always a part of me that was very excited and I'd see her and it would be a huge let down.* (Young woman, aged 3 when permanently placed, aged 23 when interviewed)

Some children were also described as disengaged or bored during the visit:

> *So I felt so sorry for her. She'd come along to see this kid and to say, "Hi, I'm your mother", and [child] had nothing – really had no interest in engaging with her.* (Adoptive parent of young woman, aged 17 months when permanently placed)

> *It felt like a bit of an inconvenience in my life, even at a younger age, because there I was trying – not being forced but sort of being forced to do something which really had no meaning in my life or no – it wasn't going to be productive. I wasn't going to achieve anything out of it. I was just going to go and visit this lady and my sister. I could've done other stuff in that day's time. It wasn't for my benefit. It definitely wasn't benefiting me in any way.* (Young man, aged 2 when permanently placed, aged 19 when interviewed)

Those birth parents who had overcome past difficulties had sometimes 'moved on'; they could be insensitive when they talked about their new families, in which the adoptee continued to have no place:

My birth mum, she likes to brag about what her life is like now and it's hard to hear. She'll say she's married, and that the husband has a child and that that child will do Mother's Day with her and those sorts of things that of course are hard to hear because she's never taken any pride in my life or has done anything like that with me. (Young woman, aged 3 when permanently placed, aged 23 when interviewed)

Children's Difficulties Around Contact

Given their previous experiences of abuse and neglect and their birth parents' continuing adversities, it is perhaps unsurprising that most children became stressed before and after contact, an issue that was cited as significant by 30% (15/50) of survey respondents. Some children were frightened of birth family members who had previously abused them. Others found the whole experience confusing and destabilising: 'it just brings back emotions and feelings that don't really need to be there'. Some clearly did not want to attend:

It was stressful and sometimes inappropriate. My daughter did not want contact with her mother especially. (Adoptive parent of young woman, aged 3 when permanently placed)

Then it got to a stage where he really did not want to go. (Adoptive parent of young man, aged 12 when permanently placed)

She never wanted to go. (Adoptive parent of young woman, aged 4 when permanently placed)

It was also difficult for children and young people who had been leading relatively sheltered lives since they moved to their adoptive families to be confronted with parents who were under the influence of alcohol or drugs:

She was slurring her words and as a – however old I was, 12 or 13, I probably shouldn't have seen that. I didn't need to see it. I don't think she wanted it any more than I did. (Young man, aged 2 when permanently placed, aged 41 when interviewed)

Inevitably the tensions raised by contact were reflected in children's behaviour. Some children regressed or were described as angry, out of control or withdrawn. Those who had experienced significant abuse displayed bizarre or challenging behaviour both before and after the contact visits:

I understood it, but I didn't like it because it was so unsettling for him. Every three months he'd get better and better and then he'd go mental again, every time he saw her. He'd come home, he'd have those crazy eyes on and he just – it was horrible. (Adoptive parent of young man, aged 2 when permanently placed)

When her birth mother told her she was going to go back to court to get her home, [adoptee] let rip and broke the light bulbs in her bedroom and danced on them... she was like the girl from exorcist. Her eyes would go grey and she'd throw knives at you. (Adoptive parent of young woman, aged 10 when permanently placed)

[She] usually went backwards a little bit. Maybe started wetting herself and things like that. And she was very insecure again. She used to, like, hide in her room. But it took her a while to come out of it. She wasn't good after an access visit. It always upset her. Then she'd be fine. (Adoptive parent of young woman, aged 4 when permanently placed)

The interviews reveal only a handful of cases where contact was reduced or curtailed in the face of children's obvious distress. The adoption plans stated that 'from age 12 the child's wishes regarding contact will be a consideration but not the final determiner as to whether contact takes place'. This was the preferred wording of the Court. Before then, unless the birth parents dropped out, contact usually persisted regardless of the children's wishes.

Why Contact Ceased

Table 6.4 outlines the reasons why contact with birth mothers had ceased for the 42 (42/70: 60%) adoptees who had stopped seeing them by the time of the survey. The most common reason, cited in 15/42 (36%) cases, was that the adoptee had decided to curtail it, often when they reached their 12th birthday and their wishes could be taken into account. In almost as many cases (14/42: 33%), however, the birth mother had ended the contact, either by refusing to attend or by placing herself out of reach. By the time of the survey, contact with birth fathers had also come to an end for 21 (51%) children, with siblings for 14 (25%) children, and with other family members for 14 (24%) children. In the majority of these cases relatives had died, or contact had withered away as adoptees and relatives lost touch with one another. However, some adoptees had also made proactive decisions to end contact with birth fathers (3: 7%), siblings (2: 4%) or other family members (6: 10%). It is noteworthy that a higher proportion of adoptees took proactive steps to end contact with birth mothers than with other relatives.

Table 6.4 Reasons why contact with birth mothers ceased (N = 42)

Reason	Frequency	Per cent
I do not want to see my birth mother	15	36
I do not know where my birth mother is	8	19
My birth mother finds contact difficult and will not attend	6	14
My birth mother died after I went to live with my adoptive family	6	14
My birth mother is in prison and I cannot visit her	2	5
Other	5	12
Total	42	100

John

Before Entering His Adoptive Home

John's mother used drugs during her pregnancy and John believed that he experienced difficulties because of this. He remained at home with his birth parents for two years, during which time he could remember witnessing certain frightening events and being maltreated. By the time he was placed with his adoptive family, together with his younger sibling, he was almost three years old. He had a physical disability which had not been addressed, resulting in poor speech and language and communication difficulties. He presented as a nervous, anxious and insecure child, who was worried about being removed and who did not feel safe in his adoptive parents' home unless all the windows and doors were locked. Throughout his childhood, he was very loyal to his birth family and reluctant to talk about his abuse.

Contact After Placement

After being placed with his adoptive parents, John had regular contact with his birth parents, siblings and extended family. Initially John experienced contact as 'trying to have fun', but it became more difficult as his birth parents attended contact with people who had abused John, other family members were violent and John's birth mother was often drug-affected. John reacted to these events by becoming more stressed and anxious, both before and after contact, and by deliberately breaking toys his birth mother had given him. He saw contact as an ordeal which brought back bad memories and flashbacks from his early life experiences. Despite this, he remained respectful to his mother:

I know she's my birth mum. I know she gave birth to me. I give her respect. I'm not rude to her.

This attitude was encouraged by his adoptive parents:

If the boys see me be respectful and caring… they will follow suit and be like that themselves, so you have to lead them the right way. There's a lot of respect there because she got herself out of a dark place, and got herself together for seven years. She's not so good now, but within that seven years, she was trying her hardest, and it really showed, and the boys could see that.

John's adoptive parents encouraged him to attend contact, but also gave him the choice as to whether this continued into adolescence. John decided to cease contact when he was 13 years old but considered the emotional and physical health of his mother in his timing of this. His decision was

(continued)

(continued)
based on his growing awareness that his birth mother did not protect him from harm and that parents should not be given endless chances:

> *Just the fact that every time we went, something bad like – it went from being all right to something bad happening most times. And then it just got out of control. And then just we got over it, I got over it. And I said, "No, this is it. Can't do it anymore. Don't want to do it anymore".*

Impact of Contact on Birth Parents and Adoptive Parents

Contact was not only difficult for many of the adoptees. It could also raise painful issues for both birth parents and adoptive parents. Each contact visit could be a reminder to birth parents that the child was no longer theirs. Hearing birth children calling their adoptive parents Mum and Dad (and refusing to do the same for them) could be particularly painful. One adoptive mother who empathised with her child's birth parents explained:

> *There is that deep hurt and deep sadness if life doesn't turn out the way we want it to, and we've got no control over it to make it how we want it to.* (Adoptive parent of young woman, aged 6 months when permanently placed)

Birth parents' attempts to undermine the adoptive placement, as described earlier, could be seen as a way of dealing with their 'deep hurt and sadness'. There were also indications that some birth parents failed to turn up for contact meetings or stopped coming altogether because they found them too painful:

> *And I think it just brings back emotions and feelings that don't really need to be there. I don't know. I think it just really stuffs up your mind and your heart, and everything like that... And I think that's why it ended, because it got too much for [birth mother]. So I think that's why she stopped coming, which,*

again, I don't know, breaks your heart. (Young man, aged 9 when permanently placed, aged 36 when interviewed)

Contact could also be painful for adoptive parents. It shattered the illusion that theirs was a tightly knit biological family and reminded them that they were not the birth parents:

[Contact] probably just reminds you of reality, that you really don't want to think about too much, prefer to just have the illusion that she's your child, then you've got to face this reality, and she's not. (Adoptive parent of young woman, aged 10 when permanently placed)

Contact is a constant reminder to the adoptive parent that they are not the natural mother of the child. It is hard watching and encouraging a bond between a birth mother and child when you wish in your heart that YOU were the birth mother.... On an emotional level and everything else, I'd wish [contact] never happened, because it wasn't just upsetting for him, it was upsetting for me too. It was like a constant reminder, you're not his mum, you're not his mum. (Adoptive parent of young man, aged 2 when permanently placed)

There were some indications that contact was a particularly difficult issue for women for whom infertility had been their primary reason for adopting, as was the case for both the adoptive parents quoted above.

Why Did Contact Persist?

For many children, adoptive parents and possibly birth parents too, contact was extremely difficult. It was described as something to be endured, rather than enjoyed:

For me it was like wow we've got through another one and that's good. (Adoptive parent of young woman, aged 10 when permanently placed)

For me, personally, nothing, to be honest. I haven't got anything out of it. I don't think the girls have, only I know it's got to be ongoing and know it's the right thing. (Adoptive parent of young woman, aged 4 when permanently placed)

I used to tell him that morning because he used to get really anxious over it. His brother used to go, "It's only two hours, and we go to McDonald's afterwards". So, his brother was more at ease than [adoptee]. [Adoptee] used to get anxious, but then he started getting flashbacks of his past, and that made him more anxious. (Adoptive parent of young man, aged 2 when permanently placed)

Nevertheless, in spite of all the difficulties, data from the survey show that the adoptive parents thought that the majority (54/78: 69%) of their children had benefitted from face-to-face contact with birth parents. The same proportion of adult adoptees (22/32: 69%) also thought they had benefitted, though the interviews indicate that they were generally less positive about contact than their adoptive parents. Only one adoptive parent, whose child had eventually returned to his birth parents, indicated that issues around contact may have been a factor in destabilising the placement.

Contact with Grandparents, Siblings and Other Relatives

Grandparents

Most grandparents had been asked at some stage whether they could offer a home to the adoptee, but for various reasons this had not proved possible:

From what I've been told, my mum was a drug addict, and she already had two other children. She couldn't look after a third one. She couldn't look after the oldest one, and my biological father was an alcoholic, so, he couldn't look after another child either, and my biological grandparents on his side said, "No way, we're not looking after a child", and my biological mum's parents were already looking after one and said, "We can't look after another one". (Young woman, aged 6 months when permanently placed, aged 24 when interviewed)

Nevertheless, contact with grandparents was extremely important to many of these adoptees. The young woman quoted above, whose grandparents might appear to have rejected her initially, nevertheless developed a strong, positive relationship with them, despite being adopted:

> *I used to see them every day, and then when I started Year 7, I'd walk to my grandma's house, and I'd have afternoon tea with both of them every day. So, from Year 7 to Year 12, I would still see them every day, and then when my maternal grandma went into the nursing home, I'd visit her every Saturday and every Sunday, and then when my other grandma went into the nursing home, I would, yeah, still see her every Saturday and Sunday.* (Young woman, aged 6 months when permanently placed, aged 24 when interviewed)

Relationships with grandparents can be particularly important to children whose birth parents have not been able to provide safe and nurturing homes (Farmer et al., 2013; Grandparents Plus, 2017). Just over one in three (7/24) of the adoptees in the interview sample had a good relationship with grandparents, and contact visits with them appeared to be extremely positive:

> *So, with my birth grandparents, my birth father's parents, that was very positive. So, they were a regular part of our lives and I have very fond memories of their house at Christmas time, every year… It was a Brady Bunch, grandparent/grandchild relationship.* (Young man, aged 2 when permanently placed, aged 41 when interviewed)

> *She [grandmother]'s always been a constant, positive thing in my life.* (Young woman, aged 1 when permanently placed, aged 21 when interviewed)

> [Re contact visits] *I was like, really excited – exciting feeling, because, you know, it's grandparents, and they also love you.* (Young woman, aged 4 when permanently placed, aged 21 when interviewed)

[She] had a lovely grandmother. Her mother's mother was a big influence on her early life. She was a very caring lady. We had access visits with her in the earlier times, and I think she did a lot of caring for the children. She said, "I feel terrible they've gone into care, but I just feel I couldn't manage them". (Adoptive parent of young woman, aged 10 when permanently placed)

Maintaining the relationship was important for these grandparents as well as for the adoptees:

I think for [maternal grandmother], it was meaning that she wasn't losing her grandson, because there were no other grandchildren... I think, for her, it was important that she still was able to have that contact. (Adoptive parent of young man, aged 8 when permanently placed)

However, contact with extended family members was not always positive. Some grandparents and other family members were abusive themselves, or complicit in the parents' abusive behaviour. One young man 'would experience bad nightmares after the visit with grandmother'; the adoptive parents of another very vulnerable young woman had grounds for thinking that she was being groomed by her paternal uncle, with whom she claimed to have a very close relationship. The evidence suggests that contacts with both birth parents, grandparents and other family members should be promoted according to the needs of each individual child and carefully managed where there have been concerns about abuse.

Siblings: Placed Together

About half (46/93: 50%) of the adoptees in the core follow-up sample had been placed in a home with at least one birth sibling. The data from the interviews show that adoptees tended to regard all children living in the adoptive family as siblings—birth siblings, birth parents' biological children and other non-related foster and adopted children. Most continued to have close relationships with them into adulthood. Nevertheless, birth siblings were special. They had often been the only reliable source of support within the birth family, and relationships could be very close. Not all were beneficial: some adoptees felt they had no relationship with a birth sibling with whom they had not lived before entering the adoptive home; some birth siblings were intensely jealous of one another and risked jeopardising the placement. Moreover, some birth siblings were abusive; for instance, one young woman was placed with a brother who had been sexually abused in early childhood and became a perpetrator himself:

> *He was just weird and strange, and I never liked it. And he used to pull himself out – like pull his pants down and show his you-know-what and ask me to have sex with him while we were on holiday. I used to get sick a lot of a night-time, just freaking out. I used to have to go to sleep with the music on, because I'd hear [brother] walking around and stuff like that. I used to wake up and throw my guts up in the middle of the night. Just have a lot of nightmares.* (Young woman, aged 10 when permanently placed, aged 32 when interviewed)

This young woman was one of the few adoptees who questioned the decision to place siblings together. For others, even when the relationship was not particularly positive, it was symbolically important, representing a link with the past:

> *…[siblings placed together] can have someone to talk to if they don't want to turn to their parents. If they want someone there – like if they don't be separated, then they don't have that empty feeling.* (Young woman, aged 4 when permanently placed, aged 21 when interviewed)

Siblings: Placed Apart

Considerable efforts were made to facilitate contact between adoptees and siblings who had remained with birth parents or been adopted by other families. However, the interviews indicated that, by the time of the study, adoptees tended to be closer to the siblings and other young people who had lived in their adoptive home than to birth siblings from whom they had been separated many years previously, or who had been born after they had left. Several struggled to remember the names of these birth siblings or described them as follows:

I don't feel like they're my siblings – I don't know them. (Young man, aged 2 when permanently placed, aged 41 when interviewed)

[I think of them as] friends rather than relatives. (Young woman, aged 4 when permanently placed, aged 21 when interviewed)

They feel like a very extended family that you meet at the occasional family barbecue, and you'll talk to them, and then go for four years without seeing them, and not think twice about it. (Young woman, aged 6 months when permanently placed, aged 24 when interviewed)

One of the main reasons why close relationships were less likely between adoptees and birth siblings who remained with birth parents was that they often followed very different trajectories. As Chap. 7 will show, the majority of adoptees moved into a very different culture when they entered their adoptive homes: they were placed in families that were better off, better educated and more stable than their birth families, and efforts were made to help them overcome educational, social and emotional disadvantages. Siblings who remained at home had none of these experiences and many of them followed similar trajectories to their parents. Birth siblings could be jealous of an adoptee's good fortune, and adoptees could feel uncomfortable that their siblings had not had the same opportunities, but they often felt they had little in common. There may have been closer relationships between adoptees and siblings who had been placed in different adoptive homes:

I guess I do feel like I have more of a connection to them, and I don't know why, maybe because of the same thing, from the same mother removed, fostered, adopted. (Young man, aged 2 when permanently placed, aged 41 when interviewed)

However, maintaining these relationships requires commitment from both sets of adoptive parents, and this study shows little evidence that they endured (see also Ward et al., 2006).

Those adoptees who did have a relatively close relationship with birth siblings who remained with birth parents sometimes felt responsible for

them and tried to help them or to act as role models. After his elder
brother went to prison, one young man said:

> *The only ones I have in contact are the youngers now. And so I'm kind of that
> role model. I've got to be that role model and step up to the position that [elder
> brother] should have been in. And so I see it as my responsibility to show them
> what's right and what's wrong, rather than complaining to them about what's
> going on sort of thing. And so I've got to be that older brother that [elder
> brother] wasn't, sort of thing.* (Young man, aged 2 when permanently placed,
> aged 19 when interviewed)

Adoptees who continued to accept responsibility for siblings who
remained at home could, however, risk jeopardising their own life
chances. One young woman insisted on leaving her adoptive home at 15
and returned to her birth family to try to protect her siblings:

> *I just didn't feel that they were safe. I didn't think anyone was ever paying
> attention to them to actually help them. And from what my brother was saying,
> he was going on trips with this guy that was in my past, that did things to me,
> and stuff like that. And I feel that, you know, who was there to protect him?*
> (Young woman, aged 10 when permanently placed, aged 32 when
> interviewed)

However, she then became pregnant at 16, moved out to live with her
boyfriend and had two children who were placed in out-of-home care
following allegations made by her birth mother.

The interviews indicated that close relationships between separated
siblings might be established when adoptive parents included them as
additional 'honorary' members of their extended families. One birth sibling had been fostered by the adoptive parents before returning to birth
parents but continued to be seen as part of their family; other adoptive
parents actively promoted the relationship by including birth siblings in
family gatherings or becoming their advocates in negotiations with statutory services. The creation of an extended family through open adoption
is discussed later in this chapter.

Long-Term Consequences of Contact

The statutory grounds for maintaining contact with birth parents post-adoption are underpinned by the UN Convention on the Rights of the Child, which stipulates that states should respect 'the right of the child who is separated from one or both parents to maintain personal relations and direct contact with both parents on a regular basis, except if it is contrary to the child's best interests' (Article 9.3). While in the short term, contact with birth parents was often painful and frequently negative, in the longer term it might achieve two objectives: it could support children's need to develop a strong sense of identity by incorporating knowledge of their antecedents, and it could promote children's resilience by mitigating the difficulties with attachment, separation and loss experienced by those who had been transplanted from one family to another (Boyle, 2017). The data from the interviews show the part that face-to-face contact with birth parents and other family members played as adoptees sought to resolve these issues and achieve some form of closure.

Developing a Sense of Identity

Several studies have shown that a sense of belonging and connectedness are key factors in enabling young people to make the transition from adolescence to adulthood (Chandler et al., 2003; Ward, 2011). This is supported by a body of empirical research on young people's perceptions of self which has found that a key element of the identity formation process is:

> acquiring a working sense of one's own personal persistence in time (…an understanding that, despite all the changes that life and time has in store, you can claim confident ownership of your own past and feel a strong commitment to your own future). (Lalonde, 2006, p. 56)

The secrecy surrounding traditional, closed adoption is now known to be damaging to adoptees' sense of self (Brodzinsky, 2006; Kenny et al., 2012). Data from the interviews show how transparency about their origins and continuing contact with birth family members enabled adoptees to develop a strong sense of identity as they made the transition from one family to another. At a concrete level, photographs and life story books were valued as providing a sense of continuity with the past. Some face-to-face encounters were important for the same reasons:

> *The fact that I've met them as well. And I know what they look like. I know where I've come from, all that. I think if I didn't know any of that, I don't know. I think it would be a lot harder.* (Young woman, aged 6 months when permanently placed, aged 24 when interviewed)

Those who had not had such basic connections could feel cut off:

> *Yeah, because I don't know, aunties, uncles, cousins. I could walk past them in the street and wouldn't even know. I don't know anything about my family history. I don't even know what her frigging last name is because I can't remember it. I don't know what I should look out for.* (Young woman, aged 4 when permanently placed, aged 33 when interviewed)

Not only did these adoptees feel they had 'missed out on finding out who I am', they also found they had insufficient information about their family medical history and their genetic inheritance.

The interviews indicate that contact had often enabled young people to develop a sense of continuity and a sense of belonging to their past as well as their present. Grandparents and siblings could play a valuable role in this process:

> *Yeah. I think if I didn't have that contact when I was younger and now, I would have a lot more questions and I probably wouldn't be as comfortable talking about it…, I'm glad that we've stayed in contact because if I hadn't, I'm sure there'd be lots of questions I had unanswered, and both of them, my nan and [sister] have got photos from when I was younger and stories from when I was younger, and it's just nice to have the full picture. So I think if I didn't I might feel a bit empty.* (Young woman, aged 1 when permanently placed, aged 21 when interviewed)

Even those adoptees who were closely integrated into their adoptive families could value opportunities to retain this connection with their past:

Even though I'm adopted, there's a small emotional attachment towards a previous family. (Young man, aged 2 when permanently placed, aged 19 when interviewed)

Frank

Before Entering His Adoptive Home

Both of Frank's parents had drug and alcohol issues. Following multiple reports of domestic abuse and neglect, Frank was removed at the age of four and a half years. He then experienced several temporary placements, including kin care, and was abused in foster care. Following his placement with the foster carers who later adopted him, Frank experienced a protracted restoration attempt, which was distressing and unsettling for him, and it was eventually determined that he should return to his foster carers with a view to adoption. His birth mother did not agree with the plan of adoption, so Frank decided to delay it because he did not want to hurt or upset her.

Contact During Childhood

Throughout his childhood, Frank had regular contact with his mother and extended family on both sides, with contact with his mother varying from monthly to twice per year.

While contact with Frank's paternal family was always positive, his maternal family had drug issues and frequently dealt and used drugs from their home when Frank was there for contact. At times Frank felt very unsafe, scared and upset, being reminded of the chaos of his early life. When he was young, he did not quite understand his feelings and, as he grew older, he found the visits more difficult until he arrived at the stage where he could control his attendance, with the support of his adoptive parents:

When I was really young, I just had no idea how bad it really was. But as I grew older, I was just upset. Contact visits were just so awful for me... There's nothing else easier about it, really. Oh, as I get older, I know how to – I just leave as soon as it – now I just have this threshold. I just leave as soon as it turns bad. I just don't put up with it anymore at all.

(continued)

(continued)
Contact in Adulthood
   Frank's adoptive family helped him distance himself from his birth mother, as well as encouraging and showing respect for her, which helped facilitate an ongoing relationship. For Frank, much of his contact with his mother was extremely stressful; he became increasingly aware of her inability to be a parent, becoming angry, distressed and confused as he tried to "converge two separate identities". However, despite the difficulties, Frank was very clear about the importance of maintaining a relationship with his mother:

> So most of the time, she's stressed and anxious when I see her. Therefore, the contact just isn't enjoyable for me. But I still want to see my mum. She's still my mum. So even though it is not enjoyable, I wouldn't not want to see her....

Not all adoptees wished to retain this continuing connection. Once it had been acknowledged and understood, some felt ready to leave it behind:

Thanks for putting me up for adoption and giving me a fantastic life. Thank you that I could be part of your life for a little while, and now I'm saying goodbye, and closing that chapter. (Young woman, aged 6 months when permanently placed, aged 24 when interviewed)

Coming to Terms with Separation and Loss

Adoptive parents were very clear that contact was also necessary to help prevent children from fantasising about their birth families and to understand why they had been placed away from home. These were the major reasons why contact visits continued despite some children's obvious distress. For instance, one young man who was very frightened of his birth parents and convinced that they would try to kidnap him, nevertheless continued to have contact visits until after his 13th birthday. While he 'kind of just did as much as I can to keep my mind off it', his adoptive mother thought:

It's better for them to see the parents, because it makes it easier when they're older, because if they don't see them, they put them up on a pedestal, and they're more likely to stray back to them. But knowing them, and seeing them during the years, they know what they're like, so they don't have any questions. And I think that makes it easier for carers. (Adoptive parent of young man, aged 2 when permanently placed)

Contact was also seen as a means of reinforcing the message that birth parents were not good role models:

My emotions told me... I don't want all that. Let's just keep them isolated from it. But then my head tells me that's not the way to go because I didn't want her growing up and getting to 16 or 17 and have visions of this mother in a rosy light that she'll run off and look for her or want to go and live with her. Because I thought doing it gradually, she saw her for the warts and all. She saw the good part of her but she saw the warts. So she always left thinking, "Don't want to live there". (Adoptive parent of young woman, aged 4 when permanently placed)

I want her to know where she comes from and what the problems in the past were. That maybe she doesn't repeat them because up to now her family background has seemed to be in this cycle of abuse. It's gone on from the grandmother to the mother and passed down to [adoptee]. I don't want it to go on. (Adoptive parent of young woman, aged 4 when permanently placed)

In fact, in some ways, I think [contact] was positive for him, because she was such a terrible person, that he realised that the future was with us, and not with her. (Adoptive parent of young man, aged 9 when permanently placed)

Contact also meant that the adoptees became very conscious of the disparities between their current lifestyles in their adoptive homes, and those of their birth families. Some became concerned that they might revert to their birth parents' lifestyle in adulthood; one young woman who had decided to cut off all contact with her birth family when she was 12, arranged to see them again when she was older in order to reassure herself that she would not turn out like them:

I wanted to see them again when I was 15, just to – I don't really remember my reasons, but I think just to make sure that I wasn't actually like them, because I had put this – not so much phobia, but insecurity in me that I'm this bad person and I'm going to turn out like my biological parents. (Young woman, aged 6 months when permanently placed, aged 24 when interviewed)

However, most adoptees were more ambivalent and contact simply served to remind them of the distance they had travelled from families with whom they had increasingly little in common:

[birth mother] was a drug addict and I guess when I was younger [birth father] was a drug addict and had been in jail and how do you explain that to people? Again, being in an environment where you don't – I don't know anyone still. I don't know anyone now that's been in jail. (Young man, aged 2 when permanently placed, aged 41 when interviewed)

Regular contact with birth parents also helped adoptees understand the reasons why they could not safely live with them, and why they had been placed in adoptive homes. Ongoing contact with birth parents who had significant mental health problems could help adoptees maintain a positive relationship despite their parent's inability to look after them. When birth parents arrived at contact visits under the influence of drink or drugs, adoptees were reminded of the realities of previous adverse experiences. When birth parents brought an abusive partner with them, buried memories of maltreatment could be reawakened:

And then, as I was getting older, my understanding was getting stronger. And so I went from being a kid trying to have fun to, like, realising what these people, like, actually done. (Young man, aged 2 when permanently placed, aged 19 when interviewed)

Although knowing that they had been abused helped young people understand why they had been adopted, it could be painful to learn what had happened. It was difficult for birth parents to acknowledge and accept responsibility for the past and this became a sticking point for some adoptees, who resented what they perceived as a refusal to admit past mistakes or apologise for them.

Open adoption also meant that adoptees could access their case files and find out more about the reasons why they had been separated from birth parents; those who decided to do so could find this a harrowing experience:

> *After he read his files, he was pretty wild. I mean, we were having a fairly tricky time anyway. But he was really angry. And he was quite devastated, as you can imagine.... he had some more counselling, I think, around that time, to try and process that.* (Adoptive parent of young man, aged 6 when permanently placed)

Only two of the interviewees claimed that their adoptive parents had discouraged contact; neither of them had accepted the reasons for their separation, and both continued to fantasise about returning home to their birth families. On the other hand, there is ample evidence from the interviews that transparency and openness enabled other adoptees to come to terms with the separation and to understand why it had happened. Nevertheless, accepting that separation had been necessary could be a painful business, and the adoptees' experiences raise questions concerning whether it could have been achieved in a less stressful way.

Closure

The interviews provided data concerning the extent to which the experience of abuse and neglect, followed by separation and then adoption, continued to dominate the lives of the adoptees. Data were searched for evidence of whether the adoptee had come to terms with their birth parents' limitations; whether they understood and accepted the reasons for the adoption; and whether they perceived themselves as defined by their past experience. Of the 24 adoptees for whom these data are available, 9 appeared to have achieved closure in these areas; 9 appeared to be moving forward towards closure and 6 still seemed to be far from closure.

Coming to Terms with Birth Parents' Limitations

Achieving Closure Group (9/24 Adoptees)

Adoptees in the closure group had come to accept that their birth parents would never be able to provide them with a nurturing home. All of them had had face-to-face contact with birth parents since being placed in their adoptive homes, and six of them still continued to see them at the time of the interview (a few months after the survey). Those who continued to have contact were in control of the situation. They arranged the meetings, and guarded themselves against over-intrusive phone calls and texts by blocking them:

She calls me daily, but I don't answer every call. I talk to her – it depends. If I'm really stressed at uni, it can go for like two or three weeks. But I try to talk to her once every two or three weeks. (Young woman, aged 10 when permanently placed, aged 21 when interviewed)

These adoptees no longer expected that their birth parents would be able to support them; in fact, they tended to speak of a role reversal in which they were parenting the parent:

Why is she just such a dysfunctional parent? She's never going to be able to – we're never going to have a normal parent-child relationship. I'm basically the adult in our relationship. Every time I see her, I feel like I'm counselling her. I just listen to all her problems, and I'm the adult in our relationship. (Young woman, aged 10 when permanently placed, aged 32 when interviewed)

They also spoke about their parents objectively, as people with whom they might keep in contact, but would not expect to engage in a real relationship:

I'm happy to see them, I'm happy to interact with them, but I don't chase a relationship with them, because I don't feel there is one. (Young man, aged 2 when permanently placed, aged 41 when interviewed)

Those adoptees in this group who had decided to curtail contact had also benefitted by being in control of the situation:

No. I just think he's a grounded boy, because we gave him the choice in the beginning, "You tell us when you're finished with contact". We had to give him that, because we had to give the power back to him, and I think that's why he's so well grounded now, because we gave him that power back. (Adoptive parent of young man, aged 2 when permanently placed)

Adoptees in the closure group were often judgemental about their birth parents:

If a parent would rather take drugs than take care of its child, then it doesn't belong with them. And some people say, "Oh, send them to rehab. Give them another chance". I say do they really deserve that next chance if, like, they had one shot? It's not a video game. You don't just get chance after chance. You sort of mess up, that's it. (Young man, aged 2 when permanently placed, aged 19 when interviewed)

Nevertheless, one of the features of this group of adoptees was their ability to show kindness or empathy towards their birth parents, or at least to accept that they were people who had made bad decisions. Two of these adoptees delayed their adoptions so as not to upset their birth mothers. One young man who had dreaded contact visits because his mother would sometimes arrive under the influence of drugs or accompanied by someone who had abused him, nevertheless delayed curtailing them for several months because she was going through a difficult pregnancy when he reached the age at which he could make the choice, and he did not want to upset her at this time; another young man felt guilty that he had nothing in common with his birth parents; and a third was critical of the authorities because they had not removed his mother from an abusive household and given her the same chances that he had had.

Far from Closure Group (6/24 Adoptees)

The six adoptees in the far from closure group present a rather different picture. This group includes the only two interviewees who claimed that their adoptive parents had discouraged or prevented post-adoption contact with birth family members; both these adoptees had subsequently sought out their birth families. In fact, four of the adoptees in this group had returned to birth families at some stage after entering their adoptive home. However, none of the adoptees in this group were having face-to-face contact with a birth parent at the time of the interview, and relationships between them were sometimes acrimonious. Two adoptees who had returned to their birth parents' homes as adults had then been told to leave. One young woman hated her mother and refused to see her. Another young man had cut off all relationships with his birth family:

> There really isn't a relationship. Yeah, I don't have a relationship with them. Very, very miniscule on what is there. (Young man, aged 10 when permanently placed, aged 40 when interviewed)

While adoptees in the closure group had come to terms with their birth parents' limitations, those in the far from closure group were often still yearning for them to be able to nurture them:

> I just wanted my mum, my real mum. I just wanted my real mum. I just wanted my real mum… I never got the mother out of her that I wanted to see. And then she died. (Young woman, aged 4 when permanently placed, aged 33 when interviewed)

> I didn't really grow up with a mum, so I'd think about it, and I thought about it more as an adult than I did as a child. Not having a mum hurts… mums are supposed to love unconditionally. You should be able to go and talk to them about anything, and they'll back you up. I've never had that. (Young man, aged 10 when permanently placed, aged 40 when interviewed)

Accepting the Reasons for the Adoption

All nine of the adoptees in the closure group had positive relationships with their adoptive parents. Two of the adoptees in this group had been through an unstable time during which the relationship had reached breaking point: one had been 'kicked out of the house a number of times' and moved into lodgings at 18 because at that stage she and her adoptive mother 'could not live under the same roof successfully'. The other had walked out of his adoptive home in his 20s, had had no contact for three years and had since returned and been reconciled. Both these adoptees and their adoptive parents had been able to show sufficient flexibility to repair the relationship. Adoptees in this group had accepted that the adoption was permanent (and justified) and clearly regarded themselves as full members of their adoptive families, while at the same time often continuing a relationship with birth relatives.

Adoptees in the far from closure group had not accepted that the adoption was necessary:

Help should have got brought for the family, to deal with the situations, to deal with who I was, because I was obviously the black sheep and an emotional kid, rather than just remove a child, that's pretty bloody disgusting. I classify myself as part of the stolen generation, because I was just taken. The family unit wasn't helped, as far as I could see. (Young man, aged 10 when permanently placed, aged 40 when interviewed)

Three of the adoptees in the far from closure group had broken off the relationship with their adoptive parents, and the others had relationships that were troubled or uncertain. All the adoptees in this group had also broken off relationships with at least one birth parent or other family members, leaving themselves increasingly isolated.

I don't talk to [three of my brothers]. The only ones I do talk to is [my sister and another brother]... I prefer not to because they're on drugs, and I have no time for that. My sister, I know she's on drugs. I don't like it, but at least she talks to me.

Well, we had a disagreement with – [adoptive mother], and I left. And that was it. I came away to Sydney and started trying to look for my brother – my brothers and all my sisters. (Young man, aged 9 when permanently placed, aged 35 when interviewed)

Instead of successfully combining relationships with adoptive parents and birth family members, adoptees in this group were often left in limbo, feeling that they belonged neither to one family nor to the other.

Moving On

Almost all the adoptees who were interviewed had been displaying significant emotional and/or behavioural problems when they first entered their adoptive homes. They were commonly described as 'angry', 'out of control' or 'fearful' and were clearly demonstrating the consequences of past maltreatment, sometimes compounded by adverse experiences in out-of-home care (see Chap. 3). The factor which perhaps most clearly distinguished between the two groups of adoptees in adulthood is the extent to which, at least ten years after placement, the events of their early childhood continued to dominate their lives. Adoptees in the far from closure group were still suffering the consequences of the abuse they had experienced; for instance, the sister of one of the young men who had been sexually abused as a child explained that, by now, he had virtually cut himself off from both his birth family and his adoptive family:

But now that he's gone out and moved out and is on his own, I think that's what worries me the most because he's out there and – I don't know. He probably never leaves the house because he's a hermit sort of type thing. It still bothers me but I think, oh, geez, you know, are we one day going to get a phone call saying he's done something that we don't want to know about? Like that he's hurt someone or done something to a young person that he shouldn't have done. And I think even Dad, in a sense, sort of expects that too. I think he's waiting for the day that we get a phone call.... (Young woman, aged 10 when permanently placed, aged 32 when interviewed)

Many of the adoptees in this group were still angry at the way that they had been treated, and at times this dominated their conversations:

> *I like to talk about the issues of what went on with [adoptive parents who were perceived as abusive], and I think they just want to bury it. [My sister] just wants to bury it away and I get a lot out of talking stuff out, even now in relationships, I like to talk it out. I find that they don't like to talk it out. Families don't do that. They just forgive and forget, whereas that didn't really happen with me, so I haven't had that skill. I don't forget, and I sure as hell won't forgive unless you're apologising for it. So, I bring it up. I'm the bringer-up in front of everyone. I'll confront it head on, and they won't.* (Young man, aged 10 when permanently placed, aged 40 when interviewed)

Adult outcomes for this group of six adoptees were generally poor, with these young people engaged in violent behaviour and substance misuse, and becoming victims, or suspected perpetrators, of sexual abuse. Only two had educational qualifications; four members of this group had had no regular employment since leaving school and the others had a history of short-term, casual jobs. One of them told the researcher: 'I look at it as in I'm glad I never went to jail, then at least I was able to achieve that'.

The nine adoptees in the closure group had better qualifications and educational outcomes. They had not entirely overcome the consequences of abuse—even those who appeared outwardly successful indicated that there was an underlying fragility, an issue that will be discussed further in Chap. 8. Nevertheless, they had more insight into the way in which abuse had affected their development, and were able to take positive action to reduce its impact: for instance, one young man, who appeared to have achieved a very high degree of closure, was now trying to overcome a recurrent problem in his relationships:

> *I think it is tied to the unconscious memories of adoption. And I think I always was very – in my past relationships – always had a real inherent fear of being abandoned, a fear of people just – of them just leaving or me not being good enough. And that manifested itself in a lot of insecurities around relationships and would then manifest in behaviours that could be seen as controlling.* (Young man, aged 1 when permanently placed, aged 25 when interviewed)

The Impact of Contact on the Adoptive Parents' Roles

The policy of open adoption also had an impact on the adoptive parents' roles. Openness meant that they were aware of the abuse and neglect adoptees had experienced, and were involved in helping them come to terms with the past:

> *And I've always said to [adoptee], "Look, you treat your childhood in two ways. You can say, 'I had a terrible, traumatic, horrible childhood compared to a whole lot of other people around me, and I'm going to let that be the excuse for totally ruining my life, and getting into drugs, and doing this and that, or the other', or you can say, 'I had a really terrible, awful, horrible childhood. I'm not going to let it spoil my life.'"... You just make sure that [your birth father] and [birth mother] were not able to spoil your life by rejecting you when you were young, by actually making a success of your life and doing well.* (Adoptive parent of young woman, aged 8 when permanently placed)

Open adoption also meant that adoptive parents regularly arranged contact visits and accompanied adoptees to them; they also facilitated adoptees' attendance at birth family events such as weddings and funerals and sometimes went to them themselves. In the process they were obliged to develop some sort of relationship with birth parents and other family members. Just as with the adoptees, contact prevented adoptive parents from fantasising about the birth families in a manner that exaggerated their shortcomings, and helped them develop greater understanding. It was not always possible for adoptive parents to develop a relationship with birth parents and other family members, and, when these relationships did exist, they were not close, but they were rarely acrimonious. Over time, some adoptive parents saw themselves as having 'an extra strand of family' with 'all these extra layers of people in our world' and included birth family members in invitations to family events and on Christmas card lists. Some of them took on a parental role towards birth parents and siblings and gave professional advice to other birth relatives. Not all adoptees wanted this level of intermingling: one young woman cut up and threw away the Christmas cards her adoptive father had written for her birth relatives. However, others were thought to have found that such efforts helped bridge the gap between the two families:

It gives her that sense of belonging and feeling of being in their family, being in both families, alongside each other. (Adoptive parent of young woman, aged 3 when permanently placed)

These open, inclusive relationships were very different from the popular image of adoption as a closed and secretive institution which severed all family ties. One adoptive mother responded to a solicitor who accused her in court of trying to end all further contact between the child and her birth family through an adoption order:

Oh, funny you should say that. But last weekend, we had them over for a barbecue, and we're altogether for a barbecue. And in the summer, we had a holiday house in the Central Coast and we invited them over then. Oh, and by the way, I have just posted two parcels for the little ones' birthdays. So, no, I don't think so. (Adoptive parent of young woman, aged 4 when permanently placed)

All the nine adoptees in the closure group had adoptive parents who actively facilitated the relationship with birth parents; and all adoptive parents who regarded birth family members as an extra strand of family had adoptees in this group (although one also had an adoptive daughter in the far from closure group). Some, though not all, adoptive parents of young people in the far from closure group had had little contact with birth parents and had not had opportunities to get to know or understand them. These adoptive parents showed little empathy towards birth parents and were openly critical of them.

Conclusion

It seems clear that transparency and openness were necessary to enable adoptees to understand and accept the reasons why they had been removed from their birth parents, and to achieve some form of closure.

However, while contact ensured transparency, this could be painful to all parties involved. It forced adoptive parents to acknowledge that they were not birth parents; it clarified birth parents' problems and poor relationships with adoptees; and for some children, it brought back painful memories of the past.

Continuing contact with birth parents helped adoptees develop a strong sense of identity and understand where they had come from. This strengthened their sense of psychological permanence, enabling them to feel that they belonged to their past and their past relationships as well as to their present ones. It also prevented them from idealising their birth parents, helped them come to terms with their shortcomings, and decide whether they wished to continue with the relationship. There is only minimal evidence from this study to indicate that continuing post-adoption contact risks jeopardising adoptees' relationships with their adoptive parents or destabilising the placement (see also Neil et al., 2015).

However, many children had face-to-face contact with parents who had seriously abused them: they found it frightening and stressful. It needed to be carefully managed; it was important for adoptive parents to be there and for birth parents to be aware of appropriate boundaries. Where children were reluctant to attend, more consideration might have been given to supporting indirect contact arrangements. The adoptees benefitted from being able to control contact as they grew older, and from being able to decide whether they wanted it to continue.

A recent evidence review of contact following placement away from birth parents concluded that the key issue was not how much contact was most beneficial, but 'how best to facilitate positive experiences and the meaningful involvement of people who matter to the child' (Iyer et al., 2020, p. i). Other studies have found that contact needs to be tailored to the needs of each child (Neil et al., 2015; Quinton et al., 1997). The experiences of the Barnardos adoptees confirm the importance of these messages.

Key Points

- New South Wales and the Australian Capital Territory appear to be unique in both legislating for and implementing face-to-face post-adoption contact with birth families as a prerequisite of the adoption order.

- Altogether, 76 (87%) adoptees had face-to-face post-adoption contact with at least one birth parent. Only 11 adoptees (13%) had no face-to-face contact with either birth parent.
- Forty-six (58%) of those adoptees who had brothers and sisters had been placed in a home with at least one sibling and so had daily contact. Only 5% of adoptees had no post-adoption contact with their birth siblings.
- More than three-quarters of the children (78%) had post-adoption contact with grandparents or other extended family members.
- Ninety-three per cent of the adoptees had direct post-adoption contact with at least one member of their birth family; only four children had no contact at all.
- Most children had face-to-face contact with birth parents and siblings about four times in the first year of the placement; adoptive parents accompanied them to contact visits.
- By the time of the survey, on average 18 years after placement, more than half of the adoptees (56%) were still seeing at least one member of their birth family. However, younger adoptees appeared to have more contact than those who were older, indicating that contact tended to diminish over time.
- Contact visits had not been problematic for 40% of adoptees; it had given adoptive parents valuable opportunities to get to know the birth family and to reassure them about their children's wellbeing.
- Contact had been problematic for 60% of adoptees. Issues included complex practical arrangements, and safety and security. Birth parents' adverse behaviour during contact was the most significant problem.
- Contact also introduced painful transparency: it reminded adoptive parents that they were not birth parents; clarified birth parents' problems and poor relationships with adoptees; and prevented children from fantasising about their birth family and helped them understand why they had been adopted.
- Almost all adoptive parents thought that they should be present during contact visits, to protect or support the child, and to monitor what happened. However, some adoptive parents felt that the change of sta-

tus gave them less authority to manage the child's interactions with birth family members.

- A third of the adoptees became stressed before and after contact. They found contact frightening, confusing or destabilising and their behaviour deteriorated.

- Unless the birth parents dropped out, contact persisted regardless of children's wishes until they were 12, when the courts allowed their wishes to be taken into account.

- The most common reason given for the cessation of contact was that the adoptee had decided to curtail it.

- While, in the short term, contact with birth parents was often painful, in the longer term it could support children's need to develop a strong sense of identity by incorporating knowledge of their antecedents, and it could mitigate the difficulties with attachment, separation and loss experienced by children who are transplanted from one family to another. Over two-thirds of both adoptive parents and adoptees (69%) thought that contact had ultimately been beneficial.

- The evidence suggests that contacts with both birth parents, grandparents and other family members need to be promoted according to the needs of each individual child, and carefully managed where there have been concerns about abuse.

- Adoptees tended to regard all children living in the placement as siblings. Relationships with same-placed birth siblings could be very close—but not all siblings benefited from being placed together.

- Adoptees' relationships with birth siblings who remained with birth parents were often distant, particularly when they followed different life trajectories.

- Adoptees who had come to terms with their birth parents' limitations understood and accepted the reasons for the adoption. They no longer perceived themselves as defined by their past experience. They appeared to have achieved closure and moved on with their lives.

- All the adoptees who had achieved closure had adoptive parents who actively facilitated the relationship with birth parents: many had incorporated birth family members as 'honorary' family members. Adoptive parents of some adoptees who were far from closure showed little empathy with birth parents, were openly critical of them and had had little contact with them.

- Adoptees who had achieved closure had more positive adult outcomes than those who had not.

References

Boddy, J., Statham, J., Danielsen, I., Geurts, E., Join-Lambert, H., & Euillet, S. (2014). Beyond contact? Policy approaches to work with families of looked after children in four European countries. *Children and Society, 28*(2), 152–161.

Boyle, C. (2017). What is the impact of birth family contact on children in adoption and long-term foster care: A systematic review. *Child and Family Social Work, 22*(S1), 22–33.

Brodzinsky, D. (2006). Family structural openness and communication openness as predictors in the adjustment of adopted children. *Adoption Quarterly, 9*(4), 1–18.

Chandler, M., Lalonde, C., Sokol, B. & Hallett, D. (2003). Personal persistence, identity development and suicide: A study of native and non-native North American adolescents. *Monographs of the Society for Research in Child Development, 68*(2), Serial No. 273.

Chateauneuf, D., Page, D., & Decaluwe, B. (2017). Issues surrounding post-adoption contact in foster adoption: The perspective of foster-to-adopt families and child welfare workers. *Journal of Public Child Welfare, 12*(4), 436–460.

de Rosnay, M., Luu, B., & Conley Wright, A. (2015). *I guess I was an accident at first, but then I was chosen: Young children's identity formation in the context of open adoption in New South Wales. An examination of optimal conditions for child wellbeing.* University of Sydney Institute of Open Adoption Studies.

Department of Families, Housing, Community Services and Indigenous Affairs together with the National Framework Implementation Working Group Families (2011). *An outline of National Standards for out-of-home care. A Priority Project under the National Framework for Protecting Australia's Children 2009–2020.* Commonwealth of Australia. http://www.dss.gov.au/sites/default/files/documents/pac_national_standard.pdf. Accessed 14 Nov 2020.

Farmer, E., & Pollock, S. (1998). *Sexually abused and abusing children in substitute care.* John Wiley.

Farmer, E., Selwyn, J., & Meakings, S. (2013). 'Other children say you are not normal because you don't live with your parents': Children's views of living with informal kinship carers: Social networks, stigma and attachment to carers. *Child and Family Social Work, 18*, 25–34.

Grandparents Plus. (2017). *State of the nation 2017 survey report.* https://www. grandparentsplus.org.uk/wp-content/uploads/2020/02/Grandparents_Plus_ State_of_the_Nation_Survey_2017.pdf. Accessed 17 Nov 2020.

Grotevant, H. D., Rueter, M., Von Korff, L., & Gonzalez, C. (2011). Post-adoption contact, adoptive communicative openness, and satisfaction with contact as predictors of externalizing behaviour in adolescence and emerging adulthood. *Journal of Child Psychology and Psychiatry, 52*, 529–536.

Hunt, J. (2018). Grandparents as substitute parents in the UK. *Contemporary Social Science, 13*(2), 175–186.

Iyer, P., Boddy, J., Hammelsbeck, R., & Lynch-Huggins, S. (2020). *Contact following placement in care, adoption, or special guardianship: Implications for children and young people's well-being. Evidence review.* Nuffield Family Justice Observatory.

Kenny, P., Higgins, D., Soloff, C., & Sweid, R. (2012). *Past adoption experiences: National research study on the service response to past adoption practices* (Research report No. 21). Australian Institute of Family Studies.

Lalonde, C. (2006). Identity formation and cultural resilience in aboriginal communities. In R. J. Flynn, P. Dudding, & J. G. Barber (Eds.), *Promoting resilience in child welfare* (pp. 52–71). University of Ottawa Press.

Neil, E. (2009). Post-adoption contact and openness in adoptive parents' minds: Consequences for children's development. *British Journal of Social Work, 39*, 5–23.

Neil, E., Beek, M., & Ward, E. (2015). *Contact after adoption: A longitudinal study of post adoption contact arrangements.* Coram BAAF.

Quinton, D., Rushton, A., Dance, C., & Mayes, D. (1997). Contact between children placed away from home and their birth parents: Research issues and evidence. *Clinical Child Psychology and Psychiatry, 2*(3), 393–413.

Selwyn, J. (2018). Sibling relationships in adoptive families that disrupted or were in crisis. *Research on Social Work Practice, 29*(3), 165–175.

Selwyn, J., Wijedasa, D., & Meakings, S. (2014). *Beyond the adoption order: Challenges, interventions and adoption disruptions, RR 336.* Department for Education. https://assets.publishing.service.gov.uk/government/uploads/system/uploads/attachment_data/file/301889/Final_Report_-_3rd_April_2014v2.pdf. Accessed 30 Dec 2020.

Triseliotis, J. (1973). *In search of origins: The experiences of adopted people.* Routledge and Kegan Paul.

Ward, H. (2011). Continuities and discontinuities: Issues concerning the establishment of a persistent sense of self amongst care leavers. *Children and Youth Services Review, 33*(12), 2512–2518.

Ward, H., Brown, R., & Hyde-Dryden, G. (2014). *Assessing parental capacity to change when children are on the edge of care: An overview of current research evidence. RR369.* Department for Education. http://www.gov.uk/government/publications. Accessed 17 Nov 2020.

Ward, H., Munro, E. R., & Dearden, C. (2006). *Babies and young children in care: Life pathways, decision-making and practice.* Jessica Kingsley Publishers.

7

Progress After Placement

Introduction

Studies of children who have experienced acute adversity in infancy have shown strong evidence of recovery-to-normal developmental trajectories following placement with sensitive and supportive substitute parents (Masten, 2001, 2014; Rutter et al., 2007; Sonuga-Barke et al., 2017; Zeanah et al., 2011). The majority of the Barnardos adoptees found stability and security in their adoptive homes and became fully integrated into their adoptive families; most of them also felt that they had always or often experienced 'sensitive parenting' from their adoptive parents (Chap. 5). Factors such as these are known to strengthen resilience and facilitate a sense of psychological permanence (Masten, 2006). The policy of open adoption also enabled most adoptees to have continuing contact with their birth families; although contact was not always beneficial and raised numerous complex issues (Chap. 6), nevertheless it enabled the adoptees to retain a sense of continuity with their past and an understanding of their origins. The data on stability and contact explored in the two previous chapters suggest that, after they reached their adoptive homes, most of the Barnardos children found themselves in a supportive environment. However, the fundamental question is whether the

© The Author(s) 2022
H. Ward et al., *Outcomes of Open Adoption from Care*,
https://doi.org/10.1007/978-3-030-76429-6_7

experience of adoption promoted developmental recovery and increased the children's long-term chances of achieving 'satisfactory wellbeing in adulthood' (Parker et al., 1991).

This chapter explores the progress made by the 93 adoptees in the core follow-up sample in terms of their physical and mental health and their education. Chapter 8 then focuses on the 60 adoptees who were 18 or older at the time of the survey and asks how they had progressed on a range of adult outcomes including education, mental health, ability to make friends and relationships and wellbeing. Both chapters draw on quantitative data collected through the survey and qualitative data collected through interviews with 20 adoptees and 21 adoptive parents, focusing on 24 adoptees. In order to understand the outcomes achieved by the adoptees, it is useful to look at their position first, at the time they joined their adoptive families, and then when they completed the survey, on average 18 years later.

It should be noted that in the New South Wales child welfare system, the adoption order was granted, on average, four years after the adoptive placement began. The data included in this chapter relate to the children's status at entry to the adoption placement, rather than at the time the adoption order was made. In addition, many of the placements commenced as long-term foster care placements and it was only after several years that the plan was changed to that of adoption. To avoid confusion, we refer to all these placements as 'adoptive placements', regardless of the original plan for the child.

Developmental Status of the Adoptees When They Joined Their Adoptive Families

Chapter 3 explored the information held on social work files and presented to the courts showing the many factors that are likely to have had an impact on the development of the adoptees before they entered the Find-a-Family Programme. We know that 69% of the full cohort had had four or more adverse childhood experiences (ACEs) while living with their birth parents, and about half had encountered further negative experiences in out-of-home care before entering their adoptive homes. As a result, 57% were classified as highly vulnerable to poor outcomes. We also know (Chap. 1) that there were no significant differences in previous experience between the full cohort and the 93 adoptees who responded to the survey; 70% of the core follow-up group had had four or more ACEs and 54% were classified as being highly vulnerable to poor outcomes. It is not surprising, therefore, that at entry to their adoptive homes, the impact of past adversities was evident in the developmental trajectories of some (though not all) of the adoptees.

Physical Health

When they entered their adoptive homes, just under half (44%) of the adoptees in the core follow-up sample had a diagnosed health condition, and just over one in four (27%) had two or more conditions. Table 7.1 shows how the adoptive parents rated their children's physical health at this stage. In their view, about two-thirds (55/86: 65%) of the adoptees were in 'good' or 'excellent' health, and just over one in ten (11/86: 13%) were regarded as being in poor or very poor health. There is evidence that some adoptees had significant health conditions and disabilities that were the direct result of previous experiences of abuse and neglect. For instance, two children had experienced brain damage that was thought to be the consequence of physical abuse.

Table 7.1 General physical health of adoptees when they joined the adoptive family: adoptive parents' ratings (core follow-up sample N = 93)

General physical health	Frequency	Per cent*
Excellent	9	11
Very Good	24	28
Good	22	26
Fair	20	23
Poor	8	9
Very Poor	3	4
Total	86	100
Missing	7	

*Percentages have been rounded

Developmental Delay

At entry to their adoptive home, 37 (40%) adoptees in the core follow-up sample had been identified as having some form of developmental disorder or delay. The prevalence is similar to that found in the full cohort (37%) and likely to be more than 2.5 times that found in the general population (see Chap. 3). Most of these children had more than one type of developmental delay. Table 7.2 shows the prevalence of the different types of developmental disorders and delays that were identified. Twenty (22%) adoptees had a cognitive or language delay; ten (11%) had delayed physical or motor skills, and seven (8%) had developmental disorders including autism and ADHD. Before they were adopted, the carers of 14 (38%) of these children had received extra funding in response to their high levels of need.

Although some children suffered from congenital impairments, the high prevalence of developmental delay in the Barnardos sample is also likely to reflect early experiences of abuse and neglect (see Chap. 3). Physical abuse had affected the development of some children; others had been affected by poor nutrition and inadequate stimulation, others by substance misuse when they were in the womb, and others by inattention to health conditions or congenital abnormalities that required early intervention. For instance, one three-year-old had a minor physical condition (tongue-tie) that had not been corrected by the time he entered his adoptive home, and that had adversely affected the development of his language and communication skills.

Table 7.2 Developmental delays and disorders in core follow-up sample (*N* = 93)

Developmental disorders and delays	Frequency*	Per cent*
Developmental disorder/behavioural and emotional disorders including autism/Aspergers/ADHD	7	8
Cognitive/language delay	20	22
Physical/motor skills	10	11
Unspecified developmental delay	18	19
AT LEAST ONE of the above	37	40
NONE of the above	56	60

*Responses allowed for more than one type of delay or disorder

Mental Health and Manifestations of Distress

As Table 7.3 shows, adoptive parents rated the mental health of well over half (53/86: 62%) of the children as between 'fair' and 'excellent' when they joined the family. However, the mental health of 33 adoptees (38%) was considered to be 'poor' or 'very poor'.

Eleven (12%) adoptees were perhaps showing signs of incipient psychiatric illnesses in that they went on to develop conditions such as schizophrenia, bipolar disorder, depression and anxiety disorder as they grew older. However, many adoptees whose adoptive parents regarded them as having 'poor' or 'very poor' mental health were also showing signs of acute distress, and this is likely to have been related to their earlier experiences. These adoptees were also, on average, 33 months[1] older than those with better mental health ratings when they entered their adoptive homes, indicating a relationship between poor mental health and length of exposure to adverse experiences.

Table 7.3 General mental health of adoptee when they joined the adoptive family: adoptive parents' ratings (core follow-up sample N = 93)

General mental health	Frequency	Per cent*
Excellent	6	7
Very Good	8	9
Good	17	20
Fair	22	26
Poor	19	22
Very Poor	14	16
Total	**86**	**100**
Missing	7	

*Percentages have been rounded

---

[1] Mean age at entry to adoptive homes 6 years and 9 months (sd = 42.43) vs 4 years (sd = 44.82); $t = -3.328$; $df = 84$; $p = 0.001$.

The 24 adoptees who were the subjects of interviews[2] were all aged 18 or over at the time of the study. All except five had shown evidence of emotional or behavioural difficulties at the time they joined their adoptive families. The interview data give vivid descriptions of their behaviour at the beginning of their placements. Some adoptees showed internalising problems; they described themselves (or were described as) unhappy, depressed, fearful, anxious and insecure.

When she came to live with us, she was just so withdrawn, lacking in self-esteem. She was just like a mouse and was always cowering.... When she came to live with us, it wasn't easy to see a lot of positives with [daughter] in the beginning. She was a lot harder to be a parent to because of this negative attention-seeking behaviour, withdrawal, sulking.... (Adoptive parent of young woman, aged 6 when permanently placed)

Other adoptees found it hard to cope with physical contact or had difficulty forming attachments. These children could be 'hard to get through to', wary of trusting adults and/or difficult to comfort:

No, she wasn't easy. She developed quite quickly after she came. She learnt to speak pretty well straightaway. But I found her not easy to comfort, and she was just difficult. She wasn't naughty. I just found her not easy to comfort, I suppose. She was different... (Adoptive parent of young woman, aged 3 when permanently placed)

Some children had learnt to develop manipulative relationships as a survival skill:

He was fun, he was wonderful, but his behaviours... this is right from when he was two, and trying to play that person off against that person, trying to play on his cuteness. He knew how to do all that, at the age of two. He knew: "If I can't get what I want from that person, I'll suck up to that person, in a specific way, and they'll help me out". He had these little survival skills at the age of two. (Adoptive parent of young man, aged 2 when permanently placed)

---

[2] There were 20 interviews with adoptees, and 21 with adoptive parents, focusing on 24 adoptions.

Many adoptees had had numerous moves when living with their birth families and/or in out-of-home care before entering their adoptive homes. Adoptive parents reported them as being fearful of further instability:

Every time someone came to the door, he was anxious. He would scurry under the bed, because he thought he'd be removed. (Adoptive parent of young man, aged 2 when permanently placed)

or wary of making new relationships:

He'd got to that stage where he'd decided that he would no longer make friends, because he was not going to be in one place long enough to make friends. (Adoptive parent of young man, aged 8 when permanently placed)

I think, in terms of him as a little boy who was taking it and not putting very much into it because – I mean, we were the seventh house he'd lived in, and so he just was going through the motions... (Adoptive parent of young man, aged 6 when permanently placed)

Externalising Problems

However, many of the adoptees externalised their distress. Some were described as 'difficult', 'oppositional', 'argumentative' or 'disobedient'. 'Anger' was the word that both they and their adoptive parents most frequently used to describe their emotional state when they joined their new families: 'I was an angry child', 'I was very, very angry and I'd often have flip outs and temper tantrums':

She was very difficult in the first few years, I think, very defiant and angry. She actually made it very difficult with [adoptive father].... She used to bite him and hit him and kick him, and just a lot of anger and violence...

I remember once, feeling really quite disturbed because she'd got these Barbies,... and she'd painted their faces purple, cut all their hair off, and then torn them limb from limb. And I remember thinking: "Oh, my God, what's this?" I was just – and luckily, she went for a visit to the psychologist after that, and the psychologist said: "Look, she's just got a lot of anger, and she's taking it out, and I don't think you need to worry. She's going to be all right". (Adoptive parent of young woman, aged 8 when permanently placed)

As one adoptee explained, reflecting on his younger self in adulthood:

I was such an angry person before, both with my mum and my relationships and that was a direct reflection of how much anger I had for myself. (Young man, aged 2 when permanently placed, aged 25 when interviewed)

In addition, many of the adoptees were described as 'out of control' or 'needing structure', 'boundaries' or 'routine' when they first joined their adoptive families:

He was like a wild child when he first came. You had to be with him most of the time, keep an eye on him, because he really didn't have any self-discipline at all. (Adoptive parent of young man, aged 9 when permanently placed)

In care, yeah, he lived in a dirty place with a lot of older children. He had no rules or boundaries. The carer mother was very nice and very supportive, but it was just chaos and there were no boundaries or anything. (Adoptive parent of young man, aged 2 when permanently placed)

Children whose needs had previously been ignored sometimes expressed their distress by over-eating or hoarding food:

She had all the characteristics of a child who hadn't had much to eat. She used to hide food.... Because she was this obsessive about food – she would be this – she was really focused on McDonald's, so, sometimes she'd have sport, or something like that, we'd take her out to McDonald's, about three or four in the afternoon.... And once she'd go there and have this big Happy Meal and whatever – and I just assumed she wouldn't want dinner, and at six o'clock she'd go: "Where's my dinner? Where's my dinner?" and I was like: "But you just ate an hour ago". "I want my dinner". And I can relate that as actually a security thing. She needed to know that her dinner would appear, even if she didn't eat it. (Adoptive parent of young woman, aged 8 when permanently placed)

Others stole from their adoptive parents and their friends:

Some of the worst things were when he started stealing from our friends; not just us. You know, going to a family friends' – really good friends' places, and then finding out later he'd stolen their son's watch, and the repercussions.... And that was just like really feeling pretty bad about that.... We know you steal from us. We know that. But to do that – and it wasn't just the once. There were a couple of people that he stole from, that we know of. (Adoptive parent of young man, aged 6 when permanently placed)

Five (5%) of the adoptees for whom there were survey responses had been involved in criminal behaviour before they entered their adoptive homes, although most had been below the age of criminal responsibility at the time.

Even when adoptees had no obvious behavioural difficulties, they could still require high levels of support from adoptive parents. One boy, for instance, insisted on being carried everywhere by them:

I carried [adoptee] for a year, close to a year, which completely, like, threw me. I was just never expecting that I was going to be cooking dinner carrying a seven-year-old with me.... But that was sort of nice, too. He wasn't hard – defiant – it was just hard because I wasn't expecting it. It was practically hard when I'm trying to cook dinner, and the neediness that it showed was sort of like oh, my god, this poor little kid. (Adoptive parent of young man, aged 6 when permanently placed)

Another needed intensive developmental support:

So we had to go through all that process of going to all different organisations to teach him how to understand language, and how to play with other children, and how to play, just in general, and how to eat properly and stuff like that.... Taught him to be a little kid. He didn't know – you'd sit him in front of blocks and he didn't know what to do. He didn't know how to ask for a drink. He always sat back until someone went to him. So, yeah being a little kid. (Adoptive parent of young man, aged 3 when permanently placed)

The boy whose adoptive parent is quoted above had been in out-of-home care for a year before he was placed with his adoptive family. The 93 adoptees in the core follow-up sample had been in out-of-home care for an average of just over two years before they entered their adoptive placements; more than half of them had been separated from abusive parents for over a year.[3] The prevalence of developmental delays, behavioural problems and manifestations of distress, reported by adoptive parents indicates that greater attention might have been paid to helping these children address some of their difficulties during the lengthy period between separation and permanent placement.

School Performance

Inevitably, the adoptees' poor developmental progress and their emotional and behavioural problems had an adverse impact on their school performance. Some had also been frequently absent from school or had experienced numerous changes before entering their adoptive homes and were consequently significantly behind their peers. According to their adoptive parents, three-quarters of the adult adoptees (42/55: 76%)[4] had had problems at school. About a third of this group had experienced difficulties related to delayed or impaired cognitive development, developmental disorders or missed schooling. However, it was the adoptees' emotional and behavioural problems that posed particular challenges in the school environment and often compounded, or were compounded by, their developmental delays and disorders. Examples include one boy whose adoptive parents described him as having an 'intellectual disability and emotional instability leading to poor peer relationships' and who had kicked the teacher in the shins on his first day at school; another who became 'defiant, uncooperative and disruptive' when his teacher left half way through the school year; and a girl who had 'poor maths and English skills, poor social skills' and who 'got into the wrong crowd' and began 'leaving school at lunchtime with boys' and 'stealing from a local chemist'. As Table 7.4 shows, by the time they reached adulthood, the parents of 33 (60%)[5] of the adoptees had had to attend their children's school because of their poor behaviour, 12 of them on numerous occasions.

---

[3] Months between separation and permanence: Mean = 25 months; sd = 26 months; median = 16 months; range = 123 months.

[4] Adoptive parents of adult adoptees were asked: Did your child have any academic or other problems at school? Missing data for five adoptees.

[5] Adoptive parents of adult adoptees were asked: Did you ever have to attend your child's school because of their poor behaviour? Missing data for five adoptees on this variable.

Table 7.4 Adoptive parents: Did you ever have to attend your child's school because of their poor behaviour? (core follow-up sample: adult adoptees N = 60)

Response	Frequency	Per cent
No	22	40
Yes occasionally	21	38.2
Yes often	12	21.8
Total	55	100
Missing	5	

Stigma

Some of the adoptees also found school difficult because they were stigmatised by other students and, occasionally, by staff. When asked what the worst thing was about being adopted, interviewees frequently identified the way in which their situation was viewed by others. Being adopted meant that they were different from other children, and could be singled out for unwanted attention; as a result, many adoptees did not want others to know about their history:

He only ever did it once at prep school, and he told his very best friend at the time, who then told the other boys, so, [adoptee's] reaction to that was: "Well, I told him, and he wasn't meant to tell anybody, and I basically called him a liar", and the other boys then turned against the boy he'd told, and it was never mentioned after that. He would not tell anybody, and we never mentioned it to any of the parents. (Adoptive parent of young man, aged 8 when permanently placed)

I feel if I tell anyone where I actually came from, they're going to judge me... they're going to be like: "Ew". So, I don't tend to talk about it. (Young woman, aged 6 months when permanently placed, aged 24 when interviewed)

The worst thing about being adopted I would say is going through school and telling people you're adopted and I found that people used that against me when they wanted to, and that, to me, would be the worst thing, telling people about it and not knowing what response you might get, what their opinions are of adoption, when they might use it against you... (Young woman, aged 6 when permanently placed, aged 29 when interviewed)

Others experienced overt stigmatisation, with other children bullying them because they did not look like their adoptive parents, because their adoptive parents were not their 'real' parents, or because of their birth parents' problems:

> So, basically, the comment which came from both [bullies] but not exactly the same words were: "If your own dad can't love you, then why would anyone else?" So, the other, in primary school, it was just slightly different words. I think it was 'parents', but it was still a comment that I definitely haven't let go of. (Young woman, aged 6 when permanently placed, aged 29 when interviewed)

Any indication of their status, such as a contact visit during school time, could emphasise their difference:

> I didn't care about him missing school per se. But it was another thing that made him different to other kids, and the reasons… was more ammunition for kids to give him a hard time. (Adoptive parent of young man, aged 6 when permanently placed)

While most of the bullying came from peers, one young woman described in some detail how staff at her school had been prejudiced against her because of her antecedents:

> There was a lot of judgement and prejudice and I felt like I was always on trial and everyone: "Be careful of her. She's come from this bad family." And these tutors would tell other girls not to be friends with me, because I was a bad influence… I was the devil child. I was made out of sin. I remember leaving and the principal was like: "By the time you're 25, you will", what did she say? "You will have had a baby and you will be in jail." I'm 24. I've never had a criminal record. Don't have a baby…. And she was like: "You know, I just know it. People like you never turn out well". (Young woman, aged 6 months when permanently placed, aged 24 when interviewed)

Issues Facing Adoptive Parents

Not all the adoptees had to deal with the difficulties described above, and some of them only encountered problems when they reached adolescence. However, 57 (61%) were described by their adoptive parents as showing signs of poor mental or physical health or developmental delay when they entered their adoptive homes, and 14 more encountered problems at school, with the result that at least three out of four (71/93: 76%) faced specific challenges which required specialist help from adoptive parents and other professionals if they were to be adequately supported.

Given the range of difficulties faced by the adoptees, it is not surprising that the adoptive parents of almost half the children found the first year of the placement to be 'stressful' or 'very stressful'. Less than a third of the children had adoptive parents who rated the first year as 'always good' or 'OK' (see Table 7.5). Parents who had adopted more than one child gave different responses for 17 of them.

Parents' perceptions of stress in the first year of the placement were not significantly associated with their motivation for adopting, the total number of children in the household or the number of children they had adopted. However, adoptees who had been 'only' children were significantly[6] more likely to perceive themselves as always having received 'sensitive parenting' than those who had grown up with other children in the household.

It is important to note that many of the adoptees' difficulties were closely related to their experiences before joining their new families. Adoptees whom we had classified as being highly or extremely vulnerable to poor outcomes on entering their adoptive homes were significantly

Table 7.5 Adoptive parents: How did you find the first year of your child's placement? (Core follow-up sample N = 93)

Response	Frequency	Per cent	Cumulative per cent
Always good	16	18.6	18.6
OK	10	11.6	30.2
Mainly OK	18	20.9	51.2
Stressful	30	34.9	86
Very stressful	12	14	100
Total	86	100	
Missing	7		

[6] X^2 = 6.217; df = 1; p = 0.013.

more likely than others to be considered by their adoptive parents as having poor or very poor mental health at this time.[7] Moreover, adoptive parents who had made this assessment were significantly more likely to have rated the first year as 'stressful' or 'very stressful'.[8] They were also significantly more likely to rate the first year as stressful if the child had had face-to-face contact with their birth father[9] (but not their birth mother) during the placement. It is not clear why this should have been the case; contact with birth fathers was not, for instance, related to perceptions of the child's mental health.

Some (23/53: 43%) families received respite care and/or continuing post-adoption support from the agency after the adoption order had been made. Almost all of them would also have been eligible for a post-adoption allowance (see Chap. 1). Nevertheless, some adoptive parents faced additional stress because of the financial impact of the adoption. The 93 adoptees in the core follow-up group were placed with 60 adoptive families. At least 24 (40%) of the primary carers had given up work to look after their adoptees. Only 4 had returned to work after a year, and 13 within five years. Six of the others had never returned to work, or never returned fully, sometimes explicitly because the children appeared to need them at home. This had caused financial difficulties for almost half of these families (11/24: 46%), and two families claimed that these had been significant. Most of those (8/11) for whom the placement had caused some financial strain had also found the first year stressful.

Adoptive parents experienced financial stress not only because the adoptees' needs made it difficult for primary carers to return to work, but also because accessing appropriate services for them could be expensive. During the time that the child was fostered, Barnardos covered these costs. However, as part of the normalisation process, this ceased when the child was adopted:

I think before adopting, people need to realise that some of these children have ongoing problems which need ongoing therapies etc. which after adoption can put a huge financial strain on the family budget. I know I get a post-adoption

---

[7] $X^2 = 7.97$; $df = 1$; $p = 0.005$.
[8] $X^2 = 6.813$; $df = 1$; $p = 0.009$.
[9] $X^2 = 5.565$; $df = 1$; $p = 0.018$.

allowance but with three kids all with additional needs the financial impact is huge, especially with all the therapies, doctors' visits, psychology visits… and when fostered Barnardos covered those costs so impact wasn't felt as much. Plus a lot of the psychological issues not having occurred till the kids got older. I wouldn't swap any of this but I think people do need to realise this. (Adoptive parent of young woman, aged 18 months when permanently placed).

These findings have profound implications both for the recruitment and training of prospective adoptive parents and for policies concerning the provision of post-adoption support; we discuss them in the final chapter of this book.

Progress

There is considerable evidence to show that children who have suffered extreme deprivation and adversity in infancy can show dramatic improvement in developmental progress when placed in well-functioning families. For instance, Rutter and colleagues' study of infants who suffered gross deprivation in Romanian orphanages found that, following removal and placement with adoptive families in the UK, their developmental catch-up was 'spectacular' (Rutter et al., 2007; Sonuga-Barke et al., 2017). The Barnardos adoptees had not suffered the extreme institutional neglect that had been the experience of the Romanian adoptees, but they had experienced significant adversity before entering their adoptive homes (see Chap. 3) and, as we have seen, they showed considerable evidence of poor physical and mental health, developmental delay and poor academic achievement. The responses to the survey showed how far their developmental trajectories changed after they entered their adoptive homes. Although there would inevitably have been changes as the adoptees grew older, as we shall see, there were also other factors at play.

Changes in Physical Health

According to their adoptive parents (Table 7.6), three-quarters (63/85: 74%) of the adoptees saw an improvement in their physical health after they entered their new families. These included 10 of the 11 adoptees

Table 7.6 Adoptive parents: Did your child's general physical health change after they came to live with you? (core follow-up sample *N* = 93)

Response	Frequency	Per cent
Yes, improved	63	74.1
Stayed the same	20	23.5
No, deteriorated	2	2.4
Total	**85**	**100**
Missing	8	

whose health had been rated as poor or very poor on entry; data are not available for the other adoptee. Those whose health showed little change had all been previously assessed as having good, very good or excellent health. The health of only two adoptees, both of whom had significant developmental problems, appeared to have deteriorated.

Some adoptees experienced significant changes to both their physical health and their developmental progress. Corinne's case study may be an extreme example, but other adoptees had similar, though less dramatic, experiences.

Corinne

Before Entering Her Adoptive Home

Corinne's mother would strap her in her cot and leave her on her own all day while she went out to beg. Corinne was not changed and was often apparently left covered in faeces. She was given no opportunity to move around or play like other children and had no one to communicate with. She was 19 months old when the police found her and removed her. At that time her development had been grossly delayed, and she was assessed as having the mental and physical abilities of a two-month-old baby. She 'did not react if you put a hand in front of her face'. She was thought to be probably brain damaged. She also had hip flexion contractures, possibly caused by staying in the same position for long periods of time. She was placed with her adoptive parents just before she was two, and they rated both her physical and mental health as 'very poor'. According to the case papers, she had 'developmental delay, speech delay, and gross and fine motor skills impairments'.

Progress During Childhood and Adolescence

(continued)

(continued)

Corinne's speech had been significantly delayed because she had not had anyone to communicate with for the first 19 months of her life. She was five when people could eventually understand what she was trying to say. As a child she also had very bad physical coordination, because her motor skills had not adequately developed:

I was always the last kid picked on a sports team, that kind of stuff, which was very – it was at the time, the type of thing that really sucks when you're a kid, because those sorts of things mean a lot to you, because I'd want to be as good as the other kids at sport. And I just couldn't catch the ball.

She finally began to catch up at puberty. When interviewed at the age of 25, she said:

And now I don't feel it affects me at all, physically. I feel – I train a lot, I'm physically strong, I eat well and I don't feel any need – I feel I've well and truly caught up. Who knows? Perhaps I'd be even better if I didn't have that, but I don't feel like I'm in anyways below par in my physical abilities now.

Changes in Mental Health

In addition to completing the survey, parents of adoptees aged under 18 were asked to complete the Child Behaviour Checklist (CBCL) (Achenbach & Rescorla, 2000; Achenbach & Rescorla, 2001), a standardised measure designed to assess socio-emotional development in pre-school and school-aged children and young people. Twenty (20/33: 60%) responded. The results show that while the socio-emotional development of 13 of the adoptees who were still of school age fell within the normative range, 4 were borderline and 3 were in the clinical range. At the time of the survey, one of the adoptees in the clinical group had returned to live with their birth parents, and another was living with another member of the adoptive family, but not their adoptive parents. Some CBCL scores did not match adoptive parents' assessments of adoptees' mental health status: the mental health of one adoptee whose score was in the clinical range was assessed by his adoptive parents as 'very good' and that of another in the borderline range was assessed by adoptive parents as 'fair'.

Table 7.7 Adoptive parents: Did your child's general mental health/psychological state change after they came to live with you? (core follow-up sample *N* = 93)

Response	Frequency	Per cent
Yes, improved	57	66.3
Stayed the same	23	26.7
No, deteriorated	6	7
Total	86	100
Missing	7	

Four of the adoptees whose CBCL scores were in the clinical or the borderline range had been assessed as in 'poor' or 'very poor' mental health when they entered their adoptive homes, although three of them were thought to have improved by the time of the survey. The reports from adoptive parents (Table 7.7) indicated that the mental health of two-thirds (57/86: 66%) of the adoptees improved after placement. These included 26 of the 33 (79%) adoptees whose mental health had been rated as 'poor' or 'very poor', and 15 (75%) of those who were aged nine or over at entry. Almost all (35/39: 90%) of those whose mental health had been rated as between fair and excellent at entry were considered to have improved or stayed the same. The six adoptees whose mental health had deteriorated had originally been rated as 'good' (2), 'fair' (2) or 'poor' (2).

Altogether there were 11 adoptees whose mental health either had deteriorated (6) or had not changed following an initial rating of 'poor' or 'very poor' (5). At entry to their adoptive homes, these adoptees were, on average, 17 months older than those whose mental health improved, and five of them were over 9 years old. Seven of these adoptees had disabilities resulting in significant impairment or had developed mental illnesses such as schizophrenia or bipolar disorder. One had died; others were likely to be dependent on services for most of their lives:

[Adoptee] has a global developmental delay, so hard to know how she feels sometimes. Our worry is now [she] is approaching 18 getting the right services for her so she can live independently. (Adoptive parent of young woman, aged 2 when permanently placed).

Other adoptees whose mental health was thought to have deteriorated had seen an increase in the distress they had shown on entry to their adoptive homes. These included one young woman who had become heavily involved in drugs and prostitution; a young man whose anger and aggression had increased to the point at which he was subject to a restraining order; and another who had become addicted to drugs. These three young people all had unresolved issues concerning their relationship with their birth families.

Those adoptees whose mental health had improved had not necessarily overcome all their difficulties or even overcome them sufficiently to achieve fulfilment in adulthood. For instance, one young man whose mental health was thought to have improved was living alone as an adult at the time of the survey and struggling with 'a gambling addiction; depression, anxiety and a borderline personality disorder'. The following chapter explores in greater detail the mental health of those adoptees who were aged 18 or over at the time of the survey and considers the implications for those who continued to experience difficulties into adulthood.

Academic Progress After Joining the Adoptive Family

As the adoptees became more settled and their mental health improved, so did their school performance. As Table 7.8 shows, survey responses from their parents indicated that the academic progress of two-thirds (57/84: 68%) of the adoptees improved after they joined their new

Table 7.8 Adoptive parents: Did your child's performance at school change significantly after they came to live with you? (core follow-up sample *N* = 93)

Response	Frequency	Per cent
Improved	57	67.9
No change	24	28.6
Deteriorated	3	3.6
Subtotal	84	100
Missing	9	

families; better school performance was significantly associated with better mental health.[10]

The trend for performance to improve is supported by the evidence that only six adoptees (10%) were reported as having repeated a grade during their school career. All but one of these adoptees repeated a school year because of learning disabilities or developmental delay. Altogether 20 (20/55: 36%) of the adult adoptees had been diagnosed with learning disabilities by the time they left school. Almost all of these (17/20: 85%) had experienced a significant improvement in their academic performance, and this may have been due to the additional support that such a diagnosis brought them (see Chap. 8). It is noteworthy that only 14 of the 22 adult adoptees who had been identified as experiencing developmental delay when they entered their adoptive homes had subsequently been diagnosed as having learning disabilities, suggesting that improvements in both physical and mental health may have helped other adoptees, such as Corinne above, to catch up lost ground.

Contact with Birth Parents and Progress

Finally, quantitative data collected through combined responses to the survey questions from adoptive parents and adoptees shed a little light on the question of whether face-to-face post-adoption contact with birth parents had an impact on the adoptees' developmental progress. There was no statistically significant association between improvements in the adoptees' mental health and face-to-face post-adoption contact with either birth mothers or birth fathers, although higher percentages of those children who had no contact saw positive changes.[11] However, the 28 adoptees who still had face-to-face contact with either birth mothers or birth fathers at the time of the survey were significantly less likely to

---

[10] $X^2 = 5.285$; $df = 1$; $p = 0.02$.

[11] Data on 80 adoptees: 42/66 (64%) of those who had face-to-face contact with birth mothers, and 11/14 (79%) of those who did not were rated as having improved mental health: $X^2 = 1.152$; $df = 1$; $p = 0.283$. Data on 55 adoptees: 22/38 (58%) of those who had face-to-face contact with birth fathers, and 11/17(65%) of those who did not were rated as having improved mental health: $X^2 = 0.227$; $df = 1$; $p = 0.634$.

have experienced improvements in their school performance.[12] Given that the qualitative data presented in Chap. 6 also showed that many adoptees found face-to-face contact extremely stressful, these findings could, perhaps, be interpreted as further indications that the nature and the timing of contact needs to be carefully managed and tailored to the needs of each individual child.

Conclusion

The data explored in this chapter raise a number of important issues. First, it is evident that a high proportion of the adoptees were displaying significant developmental deficits and problematic behaviour when they entered their adoptive homes; these added to the challenges facing the adoptive parents, half of whom found the first year to be stressful or very stressful. Face-to-face contact with birth parents, particularly birth fathers, may have added to the stress. There are implications here for the recruitment and preparation of adoptive parents and also for the provision of post-adoption support. These will be discussed further in the final chapter of this book.

Second, a high proportion of the adoptees made progress in terms of their physical and mental health and their academic performance after they had entered their adoptive homes. Greater stability (Chap. 5) is likely to have been a contributing factor. The contribution made by better access to professional services, the personal efforts of adoptive parents and both adults' and children's understanding of the change of status brought by adoption will be discussed in the following chapter.

---

[12] Data on 52 adoptees: 14/28 (50%) of those who still had face-to-face contact with a birth parent and 19/24 (79%) of those who did not were rated as having improved school performance: $X^2 = 4.741$; $df = 1$; $p = 0.029$.

Key Points

- At entry to their adoptive placements, 37 (40%) adoptees showed signs of developmental delay; most of them displayed more than one type of delay. Twenty (22%) of these children had a cognitive or language delay, ten (11%) had delayed physical or motor skills, and seven (8%) had developmental disorders including autism and ADHD.
- Eleven (13%) adoptees were rated by their adoptive parents as being in poor, or very poor, physical health when they entered the placement.
- The mental health of 33 adoptees (38%) was considered to be 'poor' or 'very poor' when they joined the adoptive families: 11 (12%) were perhaps showing signs of incipient psychiatric illnesses in that they went on to develop conditions such as schizophrenia and bipolar disorder.
- Many adoptees whose mental health was considered 'poor' at the time of placement were showing signs of acute distress, and this is likely to have been related to their earlier experiences.
- Although adoptees showed both internalising and externalising emotional and behavioural problems, 'anger' was the word that both they and their adoptive parents most frequently used to describe their emotional state.
- Three-quarters (42/55: 76%) of the adult adoptees had had problems at school; the parents of 33 (60%) adult adoptees had had to attend school because of their child's poor behaviour.
- At least three out of four adoptees faced specific challenges which required specialist help from adoptive parents and professionals to support their progress.
- The adoptive parents of almost half the children found the first year of the placement to be 'stressful' or 'very stressful'; parents of less than one-third found it 'always good' or 'OK'.
- At least 24 (40%) of the primary carers had given up work to look after their adoptees. Only just over half (13: 54%) had returned to work within five years. This had caused financial difficulties for almost half of these families (11/24: 46%).
- After entering their adoptive placements, about three-quarters (74%) of the adoptees saw improvements in their physical health and two-thirds (66%) in their mental health. About two-thirds (68%) also saw

improvements in their school performance. Better school performance was significantly associated with better mental health.

- Improvements in both physical and mental health may have helped about a third of the adoptees who had been experiencing developmental delay to catch up lost ground.
- The challenges faced by adoptive parents provide a powerful case for careful preparation and extensive, long-term post-adoption support.

References

Achenbach, T. M., & Rescorla, L. A. (2000). *Manual for the ASEBA preschool forms and profiles*. University of Vermont Research Centre for Children.

Achenbach, T. M., & Rescorla, L. A. (2001). *Manual for ASEBA school-aged forms and profiles*. University of Vermont Research Centre for Children.

Masten, A. S. (2001). Ordinary magic; resilience processes in development. *American Psychologist, 56*(3), 227–238.

Masten, A. S. (2006). Promoting resilience in development: A general framework for systems of care. In R. J. Flynn, P. M. Dudding, & J. G. Barber (Eds.), *Promoting resilience in child welfare* (pp. 3–17). University of Ottawa Press.

Masten, A. S. (2014). *Ordinary magic: Resilience in development*. Guildford Press.

Parker, R., Ward, H., Jackson, S., Aldgate, J., & Wedge, P. (1991). *Looking after children: Assessing outcomes in child care*. HMSO.

Rutter, M., Beckett, C., Castle, J., Colvert, E., Kreppner, J., Mehta, M., Stevens, S., & Sonuga-Barke, E. (2007). Effects of profound early institutional deprivation: An overview of findings from a UK longitudinal study of Romanian adoptees. *European Journal of Developmental Psychology, 4*(3), 332–350.

Sonuga-Barke, E., Kennedy, M., Kumsta, R., Knights, N., Golm, D., Rutter, M., Maughan, B., Schlotz, W., & Kreppner, J. (2017). Child-to-adult neurodevelopmental and mental health trajectories after early life deprivation: The young adult follow-up of the longitudinal English and Romanian adoptees study. *Lancet, 389*, 1539–1548.

Zeanah, C. H., Shauffer, C., & Dozier, M. (2011). Foster care for young children: Why it must be developmentally formed. *Journal of the American Academy of Child and Adolescent Psychiatry, 50*, 1199–1201.

8

Adult Outcomes

Introduction

Studies of childhood development have identified a range of dimensions along which children need to progress if they are to achieve 'long-term wellbeing in adulthood' (see Parker et al., 1991). This overall concept of adult functionality is dependent on a constellation of positive, interlocking outcomes across the spectrum of dimensions. Positive outcomes include having achieved educational qualifications and employment; being able to make positive relationships; having reasonable mental and physical health and wellbeing; and an absence of criminal or addictive behaviour patterns. Finding safe, stable and suitable accommodation is also often included because it is interrelated with positive developmental outcomes (Parker et al., 1991; Stein, 2012; McGloin & Spatz Widom, 2001; Cashmore & Paxman, 2007).

As we have seen, some adoptees made significant progress on a range of developmental dimensions after they entered their adoptive homes. Although a small group failed to reduce developmental deficits, or developed new problems, the majority managed to overcome many of the consequences of their early adversities. However, although we have been

© The Author(s) 2022
H. Ward et al., *Outcomes of Open Adoption from Care*,
https://doi.org/10.1007/978-3-030-76429-6_8

able to explore their progress, it was only after they were 18 or older that we could assess adult functioning. This chapter explores the quantitative data concerning the 60 adoptees who were aged 18 and over at the time they and/or their adoptive parents responded to the survey, supplemented with the qualitative data from the interviews with 21 adoptive parents and 20 adoptees, concerning a total of 24 adoptees. It presents the outcomes they achieved on each of these key domains and explores how they compared both with those of the normative Australian population as well as with those of the care leavers studied by Cashmore and Paxman (2007). The adult adoptees covered a wide age range, so many of them were at different stages in their developmental trajectories; this needs to be borne in mind when considering the outcomes they achieved.

Education and Training

Qualifications[1]

We have already seen (Chap. 7) that about two-thirds of the adoptees made significant academic progress after they reached their adoptive homes. Table 8.1 shows the highest educational qualifications those who were aged 18 or over had obtained at the time of the survey. At that time, at least 35 (63%) of the adult adoptees had completed Year 12[2] or obtained a further education qualification and 19 (34%) had no qualifications. Two adoptees had 'other' qualifications, the level of which is unclear. One 18-year-old was still at school. The percentage of adult adoptees who had completed Year 12 is very similar to that of the Australian population, 66% of whom had reached this level of education

---

[1] Cashmore and Paxman's (1996, 2007) Wards Leaving Care studies excluded young people with an intellectual disability on the grounds that their leaving care experiences would be very different, but included 'several young people with only mild intellectual disabilities' (Cashmore & Paxman, 1996, p. 7 footnote). In the Barnardos study, adoptive parents provided information concerning diagnoses of intellectual disabilities. Some of these responses are inconsistent with internal data from interviews. We therefore decided not to exclude Barnardos adoptees with learning disabilities from calculations concerning education and employment.

[2] Australian equivalent of high school graduation.

Table 8.1 Educational qualifications (core follow-up sample: adult adoptees N = 60)

Qualification level achieved	Frequency	Percent
No Qualification	19	34
Year 12 Certificate	13	23
TAFE or Apprenticeship complete	11	20
Higher Education: Degree	11	20
Other	2	3
Total	56	100
Still studying	1	
Missing	3	

in 2016, the year of the survey (Australian Bureau of Statistics, 2017).[3] It should, however, be noted that, unless otherwise indicated, the population data referred to in this chapter covers a wider age range (15–64 years) than that of the adult adoptees (18–44 years).

Higher Education

About one in four (13: 23%) of the adult adoptees had their Year 12 Certificate only, one in five (11: 20%) had a trades or vocational certificate, and approximately one in five (11: 20%) had an undergraduate or postgraduate degree. The prevalence of higher education qualifications was likely to increase, as about a quarter of the group were still studying (15: 27%), including three who were apprenticed to a trade and six who were at university, four of whom were undergraduates. If they all completed their courses, 15 (27%) of the sample would have a degree. This is only marginally lower than the normative Australian population, 30% of whom had a bachelor's degree or postgraduate qualification at the time of the survey (Australian Bureau of Statistics, 2017).

---

[3] See: https://www.abs.gov.au/AUSSTATS/abs@.nsf/DetailsPage/6227.0May%202016?Open Document: Table 30 1.13. Educational attainment: Year 12 (or equivalent) or non-school qualification at Certificate III level or above, persons aged 15–64 years—2004 to 2017.

Employment[4]

Nearly two-thirds of the adoptees (33/53: 62%) were in full-time work, full-time study or both part-time work and study at the time of the survey. This is similar to Australian population data which indicate that, at the time of the survey, 65% of Australians were fully engaged in employment or study (Australian Bureau of Statistics, 2017, Table 33.1.13), although the age range (15–64) is larger than that of the adult adoptees (18–44).

NEET Status

Most OECD countries have introduced policy initiatives to reduce the number of young people who are not engaged in any education, employment or training (NEET). Table 8.2 shows that almost three-quarters (37/53: 70%) of the adoptees were engaged in some form of education or employment at the time of the survey. There were 16 (30%) adoptees who were NEET: five indicated they were not in work or looking for employment due to a disability; two were parenting full-time and one was a full-time carer. There are no explanatory data concerning the nine others.

It is difficult to compare these findings with Australian population data. An analysis of OECD data on Australian young people (Australian Institute of Health and Welfare, 2017) indicates that in 2016, 5% of

Table 8.2 Number of adult adoptees in education, employment or training, or not, at the time of the survey (core follow-up sample: adult adoptees N = 60)

Adult adoptees	Frequency	Percent
In education, employment or training	37	70
Not in any education, employment or training	16	30
Total	53	100
Missing	7	

---

[4] Data were available on 53 adult adoptees; data missing for 7 adoptees.

15–19-year-olds and 12% of 20–24-year-olds were NEET.[5] The findings presented above relate to the adult adoptees in the Barnardos sample across the full age range (18–44 years). The number of Barnardos adoptees who fell within the population age ranges (15–19 and 20–24) are too few for meaningful analysis, and there are no data on those aged 15–17 years. The closest approximation shows that of the 15 Barnardos adoptees aged 18–24 for whom such data are available, 20% (3) were NEET in comparison with 17% of the general population.

The numbers of young adults who are not in education, employment or training are a cause for concern for any society because NEET status is known to have a negative impact on physical and mental health and to increase the likelihood of risk-taking behaviours such as substance misuse and crime (e.g. Henderson et al., 2017; Allen, 2014). By the time they are 21, young people who have been NEET for six months or more are more likely than their peers to be unemployed, to be poorly paid, to have no training, to have a criminal record and to suffer from poor health and depression (Allen, 2014). Of the 16 Barnardos adoptees who were NEET, 6 were involved in crime, 4 were involved in substance misuse and 9 had poor mental health. Six of them displayed more than one of these outcomes. Although these data indicate an association between NEET status and negative outcomes, there are too many missing data items, and the numbers are too small for meaningful analysis.

Criminal Behaviour

Although a relatively high proportion of the adult adoptees who were NEET (6/16: 38%) had committed offences, in the sample as a whole the prevalence of crime appears to have been relatively low. Only one of the five adoptees who had committed a criminal offence by the time they joined their adoptive families continued to offend after placement. Most of the adult adoptees had no record of offending behaviour after

---

[5] https://www.aihw.gov.au/getmedia/9e8a7231-f19e-474b-9ebb-ce41e8df39c6/aihw-australias-welfare-2017-chapter3-1.pdf.aspxp.4

adoption (50/60: 83%).[6] Ten adoptees, however, had some involvement with the criminal justice system after joining their adoptive families: four had committed offences for which they received custodial sentences; two had been fined; and four had been cautioned. Four other adoptees had apparently committed criminal offences, but the police had taken no further action. A caution does not constitute a conviction, and therefore these are not included in conviction rates. Altogether six adult adoptees (6/60:10%) had a criminal conviction by the time of the survey. It is difficult to ascertain how this figure compares with that for the general population. Australian data on the percentage of the population with a criminal record are not available.[7] In England and Wales, over 11 million adults have a conviction (31% of the adult population), significantly more than the Barnardos adoptees.[8] It should be noted, however, that the average age of the adult adoptees was 29 (sd = 7.4; range 18–44), and the British data on criminal convictions cover a lifespan, so exact comparisons are impossible.

Alcohol Consumption and Substance Misuse[9]

In view of their birth parents' experiences, many of the adoptees were concerned that they would become addicted to alcohol or illicit drugs:

He went through a stage where he was going, "Mum, am I going to be a drug addict? If I take a tablet or something am I going to end up on drugs?" (Adoptive parent of young man, aged 2 when permanently placed)

---

[6] Adoptees were categorised as having been involved in criminal activities if they had any involvement with the police resulting in an official caution or conviction. If the adoptee had been involved with police but they took no further action, then this was not categorised as criminal behaviour.

[7] See Australian Institute of Criminology 2015, Response to FOI request: https://www.right-toknow.org.au/request/percentage_of_australians_with_c

[8] Home Office, 2017, response to Freedom of Information request ref.: 44921, http://www.unlock.org.uk/policy-issues/key-facts/

[9] Adoptees were categorised as misusing substances if they said they used non-prescription drugs and it was a problem, or if they were currently accessing rehab or detox services. If no adoptee survey data were available, then the response of the adoptive parent was used and misuse established if they indicated alcohol or drugs use was a behaviour of their adoptee that was of current concern to them. Data were available for 43 adult adoptees.

My mum would be like, "Now, you know what your mum is, you know what your dad is, so, don't you ever try drugs". And I went, "Okay". Not that I ever intend to, and I'm allergic to alcohol, so we're safe on that one. (Young woman, aged 6 months when permanently placed, aged 23 when interviewed)

Self-reported findings on alcohol consumption and substance misuse are notoriously unreliable. Nevertheless, the following responses to the survey tend to complement rather than contradict what we know of the adoptees from other sources.

Most adult adoptees indicated that they did not drink alcohol (25/37[10]: 68%) or only at low levels (7:19%, 1–2 units per week). However, 16 (16/43[11]: 37%) adoptees were using non-prescription drugs at the time of the survey. This is about three times higher than the prevalence found within the normative population (12.6%) (Australian Institute of Health and Welfare, 2017).

Although a high proportion of the adoptees used non-prescription drugs, this was not always regarded as an issue of concern. There were concerns about substance misuse for seven (7/43:16%) adoptees. Only one (2%) adoptee reported ever accessing a detox programme or rehabilitation services for drug or alcohol use.

Mental Health

A well-established body of research has identified associations between risk-taking behaviours such as misuse of illicit drugs and/or alcohol and crime and/or depression and other mental health issues (e.g. Conway et al., 2006; Torrens et al., 2011; Beautrais, 2000); the high prevalence of substance misuse amongst the Barnardos adoptees may therefore be related to their continuing struggles with mental health issues. Although, for most adoptees, these were less intense than they had been at the start of the placement (see Chap. 7), they had rarely been fully overcome.

---

[10] Missing data on 23 adult adoptees.
[11] Missing data on 17 adult adoptees.

The responses to the survey indicated that in adulthood, 11 adult adoptees (11/59[12]: 19%) had a diagnosed classifiable mental disorder according to the ICD10[13] criteria. These included schizophrenia (two adoptees), bipolar disorder (two), chronic depression (four), anxiety/stress-related disorders (six) and personality disorder (two). Four adoptees had been diagnosed with more than one mental health condition.

An analysis of data collected for the Australian National Survey of Mental Health and Wellbeing focuses on experiences of affective disorders; anxiety disorders and substance misuse disorder. This found that 20% of Australians had experienced at least one of the above disorders in the previous year, and 45% over a lifetime (Slade et al., 2009, para 2.1). The Barnardos cohort showed a similar recent prevalence (10/59[11]:17%). However, the data were collected differently[14] and may not be strictly comparable.

We also explored mental health issues more broadly. In this analysis we interrogated the survey responses to find out whether adoptees who did not necessarily have a diagnosed psychiatric disorder indicated that they had continuing issues concerning depression, anxiety and substance misuse.[15] Responses from the adoptive parents that showed whether they had current concerns around adoptees' self-harming behaviours, eating disorders or obsessive-compulsive behaviours were also included as indicators of ongoing mental health issues. The data indicated that 35 (35/60: 58%) adult adoptees met these criteria. This is a high prevalence; it is markedly greater than that found in Cashmore and Paxman's (2007) sample of care leavers (46%), where similar data are presented, and is an issue to which we will return.

---

[12] Missing data on one adoptee.

[13] ICD10 chapter V used, various subsections.

[14] Responses to the question: Do you/does your child have a diagnosed health condition? What is your/your child's diagnosed health condition?

[15] Those who indicated they at least 'very often' experienced low mood, anxiety or depression or reported problematic use of non-prescription drugs, were considered to have mental health issues. Where there were no data from adoptees, responses from adoptive parents indicating they had current concerns about these issues were also included.

The Barnardos study only has data from personal reports rather than standardised instruments, and our criteria may have been broader than those used in other research; as a result, our findings may not be fully comparable. Nevertheless, we can say with some certainty that a relatively high proportion of the Barnardos adoptees continued to have ongoing mental health issues in adulthood. This is consonant with research on the developmental trajectories of the Romanian children adopted from institutional care which found that severe adversity in early childhood 'can have a profound and lasting psychological impact despite subsequent enrichment in well-resourced and supportive families' (Sonuga-Barke et al., 2017 p. 1545).

However, despite a high prevalence of mental health issues, many of the adult adoptees had good educational qualifications and secure and fulfilling employment. On most criteria they appeared to be functioning exceptionally well. It is also evident from their interviews that several adoptees had developed considerable insight into the consequences of their past and had resolved many of the emotional and behavioural problems that had been so evident at placement.

As the years progressed, gradually I was healing, because I was getting exactly what I needed, emotionally, physically and psychologically. I was just gradually healing. And over time, I am where I am now.... So it took years and years and years of counselling and just routine at the home, and someone [adoptive mother] that was emotionally giving me what I needed, actually spoke to me about what was going on.

I feel like what I've been through has turned me into an extremely resilient adult and also teenager. My resilience is just — when I compare myself to people my age, I just seem to bounce back from shitty things so quickly. And I just kind of like shrug it off. I think it's because anything that has happened from after my childhood is just nowhere near worse than what it was before. So that's why I have resilience when things happen now. Because I'm like: "This will pass". (Young woman, aged 10 when permanently placed; aged 21 when interviewed)

Some of the adoptees, such as the young woman quoted above, appeared to have overcome their antecedents by the time of the interview. The interviews show numerous indicators of personal strength and resilience. Nevertheless, almost all the interviews also reveal an underlying vulnerability. For instance, one adoptive mother described her adult son, now in his 20s and with a good job and a stable relationship:

He seems happy. He seems mostly at peace with himself. His demons have sort of gone. I think they're at the surface sometimes. I think they're not far. They're waiting to come out if there's adversity. So I think they're still – as we all have, things to deal with in our lives. I probably over-worry for him because I don't want this world that he's created to crash around him... (Adoptive parent of young man, aged 6 when permanently placed)

Even those adoptees who appeared to be functioning exceptionally well as adults nevertheless often showed an underlying enduring vulnerability. For instance, one young man, who was 'happier than he'd ever been' with a wife and child and a reasonable job, was still aware of his unresolved, underlying anger:

I'd say I'm a strong-headed person that knows where he's going in life now. I have a loving family. Weaknesses: I'm highly emotional. I'm angry... Nothing's really changed. I guess maybe not – like I think I have dealt with those sort of things. But I guess I can get to points, emotionally and all that sort of stuff, that just makes me go over the top and overboard. I don't know. I'm a very defensive person. So maybe that's why. I just put up a massive shield or wall, and that's how I deal with things. (Young man, aged 9 when permanently placed, aged 35 when interviewed)

The case study of Geoffrey is an example of the positive trajectories and also the underlying vulnerability displayed by some of the most successful adult adoptees.

Geoffrey

Before Entering His Adoptive Home

Geoffrey was six when he and his sister were placed with their adoptive parents. While living with their birth parents, they had witnessed domestic violence and been exposed to neglect, physical abuse and sexual abuse. Geoffrey had been placed in out-of-home care at the age of ten months but had then had four placements, some of which had been abusive, before entering his permanent home. When Geoffrey was first placed with his adoptive parents, he was very withdrawn, anxious, lacking in self-esteem and prone to negative attention-seeking behaviour.

Progress During Childhood and Adolescence

Because of his previous experiences, Geoffrey found it very difficult to trust people.

Trust for me is really difficult and I would always build up a wall... If I felt [someone] coming too close to me, I would do anything in my power to test them and to push them away.

Both he and his adoptive parents recognised that this had been a dynamic in his early relationship with them, resulting in lengthy periods when he would withdraw, testing out how they would respond to the 'black hole of emotional need' he displayed.

As Geoffrey settled into his adoptive home, he gradually became more relaxed.

And so we'd say 90% of the time Geoffrey was miserable. But then it was 80% of the time he was miserable. And then there was a time when he was happier more than he was unhappy. And when he was happy, he was delightful.

As a teenager and young adult, Geoffrey had to come to terms with unwanted information about the details of his childhood experiences of abuse as well as a definitive rejection by his birth mother. He went through a difficult period when he became very depressed and decided to end the relationship with his birth family. He also continued to suffer from anxiety and low self-esteem. His lack of trust and fear of abandonment impacted on his relationships with partners, who he continued to push away.

Both Geoffrey and his adoptive parents were interviewed when he was 29, By that time, Geoffrey had overcome many of his difficulties.

And to see him develop as a teenager and as a young man..., to see that transition happen with Geoffrey was fantastic...

He had very good educational qualifications, a steady job and had been living as an independent adult for several years. It was also clear from interviews with both him and his adoptive parents that he was aware of his tendency to low self-esteem and his issues with trust and that he had developed a number of coping strategies. He was now in a stable relationship with a supportive partner whom he had 'not been able to push away'.

Relationships

Partners

As Table 8.3 shows, nearly two-thirds of adult adoptees (26/42: 62%) were in a long-term relationship at the time of the survey. Only five of them had never had a partner. As one would expect, the older adoptees were more likely[16] to have a long-term partner than those who were still under 30: 78% (18/23) of those aged 30 or over were in a long-term

Table 8.3 Do you currently have a partner? (Core follow-up sample: adult adoptees N = 60)

Relationship Status	Frequency	Percent	Cumulative percent
Yes, I am in a long-term relationship	26	61.9	61.9
Yes, I have a partner but would describe as short-term	2	4.8	66.7
No, I have had a partner in the past but do not have one now	9	21.4	88.1
No, I have never had a partner	5	11.9	100
Total	**42**	**100**	
Missing	18		

---

[16] X^2 = 5.768; df = 1; p = 0.016.

relationship, and only one adoptee in this age group had never had a partner.

Nevertheless, the adoptees' underlying vulnerability sometimes appears to have had an impact on their relationships with partners. We have already seen how some adoptees tended to push people away for fear that they might be abandoned again if they got too close. One young man's solution had been to avoid relationships altogether:

Look, I've been hurt a few times in my life and it taught me a lot about my... how to deal with my emotions, my feelings and what I don't want to get myself into, and that is to the point where I'm in a depression and I want to kill myself, because someone has hurt me terribly. I've never been in a relationship, have gone out, yes, and they've broken me. (Young man, aged 9 when permanently placed, aged 39 when interviewed)

Others reacted by being over-controlling:

My relationships were always very connected and close but also there was always a very consistent theme, and a very consistent negative theme... and it took me until the most recent break up..., before I finally got it. And I think that this actually is quite relevant to your research, because I think it is tied to the unconscious memories of adoption. And I think I... always had a real inherent fear of being abandoned, a fear of people just – of them just leaving or me not being good enough. And that manifested itself in a lot of insecurities around relationships and would then manifest in behaviours that could be seen as controlling. (Young man, aged 23 months when permanently placed, aged 25 when interviewed)

And one 18-year-old who was living with his adoptive parents still found it hard to cope with physical affection, 15 years after he came to live with them:

It's hard for him to just walk up and give you a hug, and if you go to hug him, he goes: "What are you doing?" (Adoptive parent of young man, aged 2 when permanently placed)

Domestic Abuse

Nine adoptees (26%[17]) had been in relationships in which their partner's anger or aggression had been a problem—five in past relationships and four at the time of the survey. The overall rate of domestic abuse does not appear very different from that in the Australian population, where 23% of women and 7.8% of men aged 18 or over have experienced violence by an intimate partner since they were 15 years old. However, it should be noted that the prevalence of male victims (5/14: 36%) is much higher in the Barnardos sample. Although the numbers are too small for statistical comparison, it is noteworthy that the two adoptees who had Apprehended Violence Orders (AVOs)[18] made against them to protect others from their aggressive behaviour were also women.

Friends

The adoptees' underlying vulnerability appears also to have had an impact on their ability to make friends. Six (16%) of the adult adoptees who responded to the survey claimed that they had no friends,[19] and only just over half this group (20/37: 54%) said they had four or more. The interviews revealed how some adoptees struggled to make and retain friendships:

> I mean, he did make friends, but he hasn't got long-term friends, even today... He's quite happy being by himself. He gets on well with people, and he can sit down and have a conversation with anyone, but he hasn't got that closeness... I think the damage that was done back in those early years, affected him, to some degree, because he just – the making of friends was not easy, and he hasn't kept friends. (Adoptive parent of young man, aged 8 when permanently placed)

---

[17] Data from 35 adoptees, 14 men and 21 women; missing data on 25 adoptees.
[18] Used in cases of domestic violence as well as other forms of personal violence.
[19] Adult adoptees who responded to the survey were asked: How many close friends do you have? Missing data on 23.

My ability to keep – make, keep and hold closeness with people. I don't have that. It's very hard, because you want it, but you just don't know how to achieve it. (Young man, aged 10 when permanently placed, aged 39 when interviewed)

But he's still not terribly fabulous at engaging with people. So that's an ongoing thing – superficially, but, you know... He just doesn't put himself out very much for anyone. (Adoptive parent of young man, aged 6 when permanently placed)

Isolation

While many adoptees displayed some degree of vulnerability, and this had an impact on their relationships with peers and partners, a small number appeared to struggle with relationships more extensively. Six of the adoptees who had experienced (or were experiencing) domestic abuse had no friends or just one friend. Two of these adoptees were estranged from their adoptive families, and one was also estranged from his children. This group appeared to be very isolated and only three of them had achieved sufficiently positive outcomes on other dimensions to meet the criteria for 'successful adult functioning' (see below).

Outcomes for the Barnardos Adoptees, Australian Care Leavers and the Wider Australian Population

Comparison with the Australian Population

The first three columns of Table 8.4 (pp. 238–240) summarise the data discussed so far concerning the adult outcomes for the Barnardos adoptees and how they compare with those for the general population in Australia. It should be noted that these are not exact comparisons—the adoptees were aged 18–44 years, while the adult population data covers a much wider range—from 15 (or sometimes 20) to 64 years. There were

Table 8.4 Adult outcomes: Barnardos adoptees compared with normative Australian population and with care leavers

Outcome	Australian national statistics %	Barnardos adoptees (N=60) Ages 18-44, mean age 30 Frequency	%	Cashmore and Paxman (2007) Care leavers (N=41) Ages 20-23 Frequency	%
Education and employment					
Educational qualification (Year 12 or more)	66%[a] (Ages15-64)	35[b]	63%	17	42%
Expected or completed bachelor's degree or higher	Data not available	15	27%	4	10%
Completed bachelor's degree or higher	30%[c] (Ages 20-64)	11[d]	23%	N/A sample too young	N/A sample too young
In full-time education, employment or training or part-time study and work concurrently	65%[e] (Ages15-64)	33 (n=53)	62%	14	34%
Not in any education, employment or training	5% (Ages 15-19)[f] 12% (Ages 20-24)	16 (n=53) 3 (n=15)	30% (Ages 18-44) 20% (Ages 18-24)	18	44%
Mental health					
Substance misuse	12.7% 16-24 year olds[g]	7 problematic use (n=43)	16% problematic use	4 serious use	10% serious use
Substance use	12.6% - recent use, any use[h]	16 (n=43)	37%	7	17%
Mental health diagnosis (*Criteria matched to ICD 10. Includes substance misuse[i], depression[j], anxiety[k], schizophrenia[l] and personality disorder*)	Data not available[m]	11 (n=59)	19%	7	17%
Mental health diagnosis as reported in National Survey (Slade et al, 2007) (*Criteria matched to ICD 10. Includes substance misuse disorder, affective disorders, anxiety disorders*)	[n]One year prevalence (community): 20.0% Lifetime prevalence (community): 45.0%	10 (n=59)	17%	Not reported	
Mental health issues (*Criteria include substance misuse, mood disorders, and anxiety*)	No comparison	35 (n=60)	58%	19	46%

(continued)

Table 8.4   (continued)

Outcome	Australian national statistics	Barnardos adoptees (N=60) Ages 18-44, mean age 30		Cashmore and Paxman (2007) Care leavers (N=41) Ages 20-23	
	%	Frequency	%	Frequency	%
Criminal activity					
Criminal convictions since living with adoptive family	Comparable Australian data on criminal convictions unavailable. Over 11 million UK adults have a conviction (31% of the adult population). In 2017, 33% of males and 9% of females born in 1953 had a conviction[c]	6 (n=60)	10%	Not reported	
Domestic abuse	23% (2.2 million) Australian women and 7.8% (703,700) men aged 18 or over have experienced violence by an intimate partner since they were 15 years old[e].	9 (5 men; 4 women) (n=35:14 men, 21 women)	26% (36% men; 19% women)	12	29%
Adult functioning					
Successful functioning as an adult	No comparison	20 (n=38)	53%	17	41%
Help with mental health issues[g]	No comparison	28 (n=34)	82%	13/19	68%
Living independently of a parental figure	Women[f]: 18-21: 14% 22-25: 52% Men: 18-21: 19% 22-25: 40%	40 (Full sample, n=58) 5 (Ages 18-25, n=19)	70% 26%	37	90%

[a]Educational attainment Year 12 or equivalent: Table 30.1.13, persons aged 15–64 years old, http://www.abs.gov.au/AUSSTATS/abs@.nsf/DetailsPage/6227.0May%202017?OpenDocument

[b]One adoptee still studying and three adoptee educational outcomes not known.

[c]Completed bachelor's degree or higher: Table 27 1.13 persons aged 20–64 years old, http://www.abs.gov.au/AUSSTATS/abs@.nsf/DetailsPage/6227.0May%202017?OpenDocument

[d]This includes those adoptees who are under the age of 21 therefore cannot have completed an undergraduate degree

[e]Table 33.1.13, persons aged 15–64 years old, http://www.abs.gov.au/AUSSTATS/abs@.nsf/DetailsPage/6227.0May%202017?OpenDocument

[f]https://www.aihw.gov.au/getmedia/9e8a7231-f19e-474b-9ebb-ce41e8df39c6/aihw-australias-welfare-2017-chapter3-1.pdf.aspx, p.4

[g]Table 3, Publication Data Tables, National Survey of Mental Health and Wellbeing: Summary of Results, 2007, Australian Bureau of Statistics

(*continued*)

Table 8.4   (continued)

[h]Table 5.4, National Drug Strategy Household Survey, 2017, The Australian Institute of Health and Welfare

[i]ICD10 (V) F10–19 Mental and behavioural disorders due to psychoactive substance use

[j]ICD10 (V) F30–39 Mood [affective] disorders

[k]ICD10 (V) F40–48 Neurotic, stress-related and somatoform disorders

[l]ICD10 (V) F20–29 Schizophrenia, schizotypal and delusional disorders

[m]Australian National Survey of Mental Health and Wellbeing collected data on selected mental disorders which were: expected to affect more than 1% of the population; could be diagnosed through the World Health Organisation Composite International Diagnostic Interview (CIDI); and were likely to be identified through a household survey. This excluded schizophrenia and personality disorder

[n]Slade T, Johnston A, Teesson M, Whiteford H, Burgess P, Pirkis J, and Saw, S. (2009). The Mental Health of Australians 2: Report on the 2007 National Survey of Mental Health and Wellbeing. Canberra: Department of Health and Ageing

[o]Home Office, 2017, response to Freedom of Information request ref.: 44921, http://www.unlock.org.uk/policy-issues/key-facts/

[p]http://www.abs.gov.au/ausstats/abs@.nsf/mf/4906.0

[q]Only those identified as having or having had mental health issues

[r]Wilkins, R. (2017) The 12th annual statistical report of the HILDA Survey, Melbourne: Melbourne Institute: Applied Economic & Social Research The University of Melbourne

also only 60 adult adoptees, and the percentages shown for each outcome often relate to very small subsets, reducing the likelihood of accurate comparisons with the much larger population database. Notwithstanding these caveats, the data indicate that on the following variables the Barnardos' adoptees had similar positive outcomes to the rest of the Australian population[20]:

- education (year 12 or more): 63% vs 66%
- completed bachelor's degree (or expected completion): 27% vs 30%
- in full-time education, employment or training: 62% vs 65%.

The adoptees also had similar adverse outcomes to the wider population on the following variables:

---

[20] That is, percentages within five points of the Australian population.

- substance misuse: 13% vs 16%
- mental health diagnosis: 17% vs 20% one year prevalence
- domestic abuse (women): 19% vs 23%

However, on the following variables the Barnardos adoptees had markedly more negative outcomes than the Australian national population:

- NEET: 20–30% vs 5–12%
- substance use: 37% vs 13%
- victim of domestic abuse (men): 36% vs 8%.

Comparison with Care Leavers

Setting the Barnardos' data alongside the Australian national statistics provides a context for exploring how the adoptees fared when compared with the rest of the population. The fourth and fifth columns of the table show how the outcomes for the Barnardos adoptees compared with those of other young people who had had similar antecedents: the cohort of care leavers whose trajectories were followed for five years by Cashmore and Paxman (1996, 2007). Once again, the comparisons are not exact. Although very similar questions were asked, they were not always phrased identically. The care leavers cohort was smaller than the Barnardos adult adoptees sample and the age range was much shorter (20–23 years vs 18–44 years). Moreover, the care leavers were all interviewed four to five years after they aged out of the system, while the adult adoptees in the Barnardos sample were followed up between 10 and 37 years after they were placed with their adoptive parents. Not only was there a much wider timeframe for the Barnardos' follow-up, but the average time after leaving their adoptive home was much greater (10 years; sd = 7.42). This is important as there is some evidence to show that outcomes for care leavers, particularly concerning education, improve as they grow older, because a number return to further and higher education as mature students (Jackson et al., 2011); outcomes for the care leavers in the Cashmore and Paxman study might therefore have been more positive had they been followed up when they were older. On the other hand, the findings from the Cashmore and Paxman study might insufficiently reflect the difficulties that care leavers encounter, because those who participated had more stable care careers than those who could not be accessed (Cashmore & Paxman, 1996, p.22).

Keeping these caveats in mind, the data nevertheless indicate that the Barnardos adoptees had significantly more positive outcomes than the Cashmore and Paxman care leavers on the following variables:

- educational qualification (Year 12 or more): 63% vs 42%[21] (p = 0.04)
- expected or completed bachelor's degree or higher: 27% vs 10%[22] (p = 0.037)
- in full-time education, employment or training: 62% vs 34%[23] (p = 0.007)

The care leavers were too young to have completed their degrees when they were interviewed. However, only three were at university, and a fourth was about to go the following year, with her fees paid by her employer (Cashmore & Paxman, 2007, p. 33). Although some others might eventually enter university as mature students, at the time of the study it seemed likely that four (10%) care leavers would become graduates, substantially fewer than the adoptees. There were also significantly more adoptees in full-time work and/or education or training. However, although there were fewer adoptees who were NEET (30% vs 44%),[24] the difference was not sufficient to reach statistical significance.

The Barnardos adoptees did markedly better than the care leavers on positive outcomes such as employment and education, and on many of these variables they were similar to the general population. However, although the only one to reach statistical significance was the use of non–prescription drugs, their outcomes were markedly worse than those of the

---

[21] 35/56 adoptees and 17/41 care leavers had qualifications: X^2 = 4.212; df = 1; p = 0.04.

[22] 15/56 adoptees and 4/41 care leavers had degrees or were studying for them: X^2 = 4.358; df = 1; p = 0.37.

[23] 33/53 adoptees and 17/41 care leavers were in full-time education, employment or training or concurrent part-time education and employment: X^2 = 7.311; df = 1; p = 0.007.

[24] 16/53 adoptees and 18/41 care leavers were NEET: X^2 = 1.883; df = 1; p = 0.170.

care leavers on the following variables, all of which are indicative of negative outcomes:

- substance use: 37% vs 17%[25] (p = 0.039)
- substance misuse (i.e. problematic substance use): 16% vs 10%[26] (not significant, p = 0.376)
- mental health issues: 58% vs 46%[27] (not significant, p = 0.235)

The Barnardos adoptees had similar outcomes to the care leavers on the following variables:

- victim of domestic abuse: 26% adoptees vs 29% care leavers
- mental health diagnosis: 19% adoptees vs 17% care leavers

Overall, therefore, the adoptees appear to have done much better than the care leavers in terms of education and employment, but worse, or equally unsatisfactorily, in terms of mental health issues and related adverse outcomes such as substance misuse and domestic violence.

Successful Adult Functioning

So far, we have looked at each outcome area separately. It is, however, possible to produce a composite measure that combines positive and negative outcomes and balances them out to provide an overall indication of adult functioning, which 'operationalises the concept of resilience' (Cashmore & Paxman, 2006). Cashmore and Paxman (2007) developed an overall measure of success to show how well the young people in their sample had fared, four to five years after leaving care, basing this on previous work undertaken by McGloin and Spatz Widom (2001). They calculated how the care leavers had fared over seven outcomes domains: those who showed positive outcomes on at least five domains were regarded as

---

[25] 16/43 adoptees and 7/41 care leavers used non-prescription drugs: X^2 = 4280; df = 1; p = 0.39.
[26] X^2 = 0.785; df = 1; p = 376.
[27] X^2 = 1408; df = 1; p = 0.235.

Table 8.5 Adult functioning: Outcomes domains and criteria for success

Outcome Domain	
Employment, education or training	Employed or studying throughout
Living arrangements	No homelessness
Qualification	Completed year 12 or further education
Substance misuse	No self-reported problems
Mental health**	No reported depression or suicide ideation
Criminal behaviour	No admissions/self-reports, no cautions or convictions
Relationships	No domestic violence issues

*Adapted from Cashmore and Paxman, 2007, p.102
**Cashmore and Paxman criteria included depression and suicidal ideation (p102). Data on suicide ideation was not available for . the Barnardos adoptees. Adoptees were categorised as negative on this variable if there was evidence of a diagnosis of depression or other affective disorder and/ or if there were ongoing concerns about self-harming behaviours and/or if they had answered 'Always' or 'Very Often' to the WHOQUOL Question (26): How often do you have negative feelings such as blue mood, despair, anxiety, depression?

functioning successfully as adults. Table 8.5 shows the outcomes domains and the criteria for success.

The same methodology was used to assess how the Barnardos adoptees functioned as adults. Although just over a third (22/60: 37%) had to be excluded from the analysis because of missing data on too many domains, there were no significant differences between those who were included and those who were not. Those who could not be included were the same age (77 months) when they entered their adoptive homes and of similar age when they completed the survey (27.5 vs 30); there was also a similar gender split between the two groups (41% male vs 47% male); they also showed similar levels of vulnerability (64% of those who were excluded vs 66% of those included were classified as at high risk of adverse life trajectories). Although they did not have data on enough outcomes variables to be included, the data that *were* available indicated that the excluded group had a higher proportion of positive versus negative outcomes (70% vs 30%) than those who were included (62% vs 38%), suggesting that, had there been sufficient data, the overall results might have been more positive.

Key Factors Contributing to Success

According to our composite measure, over half (20/38: 53%) of the adult adoptees for whom there were sufficient data available met the criteria for functioning successfully in adulthood. Although higher percentages of young women and adoptees aged under 30 met these criteria, neither gender[28] nor age (under or over 30) was significantly associated with successful adult functioning.[29] In Chap. 3 we explored the extent to which the adoptees had encountered one or more of the following risk factors, all of which are known to be associated with adverse outcomes in adulthood and/or disrupted adoption placements (Farmer et al., 2011; Felitti et al., 1998; Finkelhor et al., 2011; Nalavany et al., 2008: Osborn & Delfabbro, 2006; Rousseau et al., 2015; Selwyn et al., 2014; White, 2016):

- four or more adverse childhood experiences
- sexual abuse
- polyvictimisation
- more than 15 months between notification of abuse and separation
- aged two or older when separated from birth parents following abuse
- two or more years between separation and permanence
- two or more failed reunifications
- three or more placements in care
- behavioural problems at entry to permanent placement
- aged four or older before entering permanent placement
- more than 12 months between permanent placement and adoption order

As Tables 8.6 and 8.7 show, the data indicate trends, but very few statistically significant relationships, between each of these factors and the adoptees' successful (or unsuccessful) adult functioning. In comparison with those who were successful, adoptees who had not achieved successful adult functioning tended to have waited on average 9.5 months more between notification and separation, and 2.4 months more between separation and permanence. Consequently, they were on average 12 months

---

[28] About 55% young women versus 50% young men achieved successful functioning in adulthood. $X^2 = 0.095$; $df = 1$; $p = 0.758$.

[29] About 59% adoptees aged under 30 vs 48% aged over 30 achieved successful functioning. $X^2 = 0.473$; $df = 1$; $p = 0.492$.

Table 8.6 Key vulnerability factors (1): differences between successful and unsuccessful adult functioning in adult adoptees (means, standard deviations and t-tests)

Variable	Success group	n	Mean	SD	t	df	p
Months between notification and separation	Successful	20	10.35	16.31	1.148	34	0.259
	Not successful	16*	19.94	32.68			
Months between separation and permanence	Successful	20	27.65	29.00	0.27	36	0.788
	Not successful	18	30.11	26.88			
Age (months) at separation	Successful	20	42.45	41.34	0.879	36	0.385
	Not successful	18	54.78	45.09			
Age (months) at permanence	Successful	20	70.15	46.23	0.977	36	0.335
	Not successful	18	84.94	46.98			
Months between placement and adoption order	Successful	20	59.65	69.31	0.542	36	0.591
	Not successful	18	49.78	35.71			
Total number of placements, incl. adoption	Successful	20	4.25	2.86	0.277	36	0.784
	Not successful	18	4.5	2.68			
Number of ACEs (out of 9)	Successful	20	4	1.95	1.774	36	0.085
	Not successful	18	5.1	1.91			

*Data missing for two adoptees (not successful group)

older at separation, and 15 months older when they entered their adoptive homes. In comparison with the group who achieved successful adult functioning, this group had, on average, spent ten months less in their adoptive homes before the adoption order was made, but a lengthy postplacement period is unlikely to be such a powerful risk factor in the Australian context, where children were often fostered for several years before there was an adoption plan, and some adoptions were delayed to take account of birth parents' situations (see Chap. 6). The group who did not achieve successful adult functioning had also experienced slightly

Table 8.7 Key vulnerability factors (2): differences between successful and unsuccessful functioning in adult adoptees (frequencies, percentages and X^2 tests)

Variable		Successful		Not Successful		X^2	df	p
		n	%	n	%			
Failed reunification	None	16	80	10	56	2.62	1	0.106
	Any	4	20	8	44			
Sexual abuse	None	15	75	10	56	1.591	1	0.207
	Any	5	25	8	44			
Behaviour difficulties at permanence*	None	12	63	10	58	0.071	1	0.790
	Any	7	37	7	41			
Types of abuse	0–3	20	100	12	67	7.917	1	0.005**
	4	0	0	6	33			
Vulnerability group	Medium	8	40	5	28	0.629	1	0.428
	High	12	60	13	72			
Sensitive** parenting	Always	15	75	4	31	6.310	1	0.012***
	Not always	5	25	9	69			

*Data missing for 2 adoptees (one in each success group)
**Significant at p<0.01
***Data missing for 5 adoptees (not successful group)
****Significant at p < 0.05

more placements in care, and more of them had had a failed attempt at reunification. They had also, on average, encountered one more adverse childhood experience (ACEs), more of them had been sexually abused and more of them had behavioural difficulties when they entered their adoptive homes.

The only one of these risk factors that was significantly related to adult functioning was polyvictimisation: adoptees who had experienced all four types of maltreatment (physical abuse, sexual abuse, neglect and emotional abuse), were significantly less likely to be functioning successfully in adulthood than those who had experienced three or less. While more of the adoptees who had been placed in our high vulnerability group[30] failed to achieve successful adult functioning, and more of those in our medium vulnerability group were successful, the differences are small and do not reach statistical significance. Adoptees in the subgroups at the extreme ends of the vulnerability spectrum did show significant differences: all five adoptees who had been classified as extremely vulnerable[31] to adverse outcomes were unsuccessful, and the one adoptee for whom there were sufficient data who was classified as at low risk met the criteria for success; however, the numbers are too small for further analysis. Nevertheless, it seems possible that the adoption acted as a powerful protective factor, albeit not sufficient to counteract the most damaging previous experiences. One other factor that we found to be significantly associated with adult functioning lends weight to this hypothesis: adoptees who thought their adoptive parents had always parented them sensitively were significantly more likely to have achieved successful adult functioning than those who thought this had never, or only sometimes been the case; however, there are considerable missing data on this variable.

Contact with Birth Parents and Adult Functioning

It is also noteworthy that we found very little statistical association between face-to-face contact with birth parents and either adoptees' ongoing mental health issues or their functioning in adulthood. The only finding that reached statistical significance was that those adoptees who appeared to have mental health issues at the time of the survey were more likely to have had face-to-face contact with their birth fathers post

---

[30] The high vulnerability group had reached the threshold for adverse outcomes on six or more risk factors; the medium group had reached the threshold on less than six risk factors.

[31] Extremely vulnerable children had reached at least twice the threshold on six or more risk factors; those whose vulnerability score was low had no extreme scores and had reached the threshold on one or two factors.

adoption.[32] So few adoptees had had no post-adoptive contact with birth mothers that the numbers are too small for comparative analysis. Although again the numbers are too small for statistical analysis, it is noteworthy that six of the nine adoptees whose interviews indicated that contact had enabled them to come to terms with their past had achieved successful functioning in adulthood, while four of the six whose interviews indicated that they still had unresolved issues with their birth family and they were 'far from closure' were not functioning successfully (and there were insufficient data on the other two).

As Chap. 6 has shown, the qualitative data indicate that post-adoption contact was generally thought to be beneficial and that it brought considerable advantages. However, poor management of contact and the issues some birth parents brought to contact sessions may have negated these benefits for some adoptees.

Differences Between Care Leavers and Adoptees' Experiences: Understanding Disparate Outcomes

Table 8.8 shows how the 38 Barnardos adoptees who had sufficient data to be included in the composite measure of adult functioning compared with the care leavers in Cashmore and Paxman's (2007) study. According to this measure, over half of the adult adoptees (53%) were able to function successfully as adults, in comparison with 41% of the care leavers. Of particular interest is the finding that half (50%) of the male adoptees were functioning successfully. This is a markedly higher proportion than that found in the care leavers study (31%) and, indeed, in numerous other studies which have tended to show that young men are significantly less resilient than young women (McGloin & Spatz Widom, 2001; Stein, 2004). However, neither of these disparities between the adoptees' and the care leavers' samples are statistically significant.

---

[32] 75% (15/21) of adult adoptees whose mental health was assessed as 'poor' had had face-to-face post-adoption contact with birth fathers vs 29% (6/16) who had had no contact: $X^2 = 5.143$; $df = 1$; $p = 0.023$.

Table 8.8 Successful adult functioning: Barnardos adult adoptees (*N* = 38) compared with care leavers (*N* = 41)

	Barnardos Sample successful		Cashmore & Paxman sample successful	
Gender	n	% of gender group	n	% of gender group
Female	11/20	55	13/28	46
Male	9/18	50	4/13	31*
		% of sample		% of sample
	20/38	53	17/41	41**

*Not significant X^2 = 1.146; df = 1; p = 0.284
**Not significant X^2 = 0.988; df = 1; p = 0.32

So far, we have seen that the adoptees tended to be more vulnerable than care leavers in terms of their mental health and substance use, but nevertheless they often did better in terms of education and employment. They also appeared to be more likely than care leavers to function successfully as adults.

It is important to be aware that the datasets are not strictly comparable and that there are substantial missing data. Both these factors could have distorted the analysis. However, as noted in Chap. 1, there are no indications of bias in the Barnardos dataset,[33] and there is also ample evidence from the interviews to support the quantitative data from the survey. A more likely explanation of the disparities in outcome between adoptees and care leavers is to do with the different experiences that adoption provides, particularly over the period when young people are making the transition from adolescence to adulthood. There is substantial evidence to show that the period of emerging adulthood can be a difficult time for vulnerable young people who still need parental support as they move towards independence (Mann-Feder & Goyette, 2019). We have already

---

[33] For instance, missing data led to the exclusion of a slightly higher number of young women (13) than young men (9) from the analysis of composite outcomes. Because most studies find that young men do worse than young women, we would expect the Barnardos findings to show greater evidence of poor outcomes if the dataset had been skewed.

seen (Chap. 5) that, as emerging adults, the adoptees were more likely to have experienced greater stability and to have received more long-term emotional and practical support from their adoptive parents than is generally available to care leavers from previous foster parents. They were also more likely to have received both personal and professional support to help them overcome the consequences of their early childhood experiences.

Living Arrangements

Table 8.9 shows the adult adoptees' living arrangements at the time of the survey. As we have already seen (Chap. 5), 18 (31%) were still living with their adoptive parents after their 18th birthdays. Two other adult adoptees were living with an older sibling (one a birth sibling and one an adopted sibling) who was providing quasi-parental support.

There is evidence from the interviews that several of the 19 adult adoptees who had run away or prematurely left their adoptive parents' home had briefly gone back to their birth families; these attempted returns had often ended acrimoniously. Only one adult adoptee was living with a birth family member at the time of the survey; this was a young man with

Table 8.9 Living arrangements (core follow-up sample: adult adoptees N = 60)

Who do you/does adoptee live with?	Frequency	Percent
With partner	23	40
With adoptive parents	18	31
With another member of adoptive family	1	2
With an adult birth sibling	1	2
With friends	6	10
Alone	4	7
In an institution (residential unit or prison)	2	3
Other	3	5
Total	**58**	**100**
Missing	2	

mild learning disabilities who had formed a relationship with an elder birth brother who was supporting him.

The majority of adoptees who were not living with members of their adoptive family or birth relatives (23/38: 61%) were living with long-term partners. Most of these (17/22: 77%)[34] were buying their own homes or living in long-term rented accommodation. Six adoptees were living with friends, and only four were living alone. However, five others had 'other' living arrangements, and we know that at least one of these was in prison and another in supported accommodation for adults with mental health problems. Both these young people were still receiving extensive support from their adoptive parents.

Four (4/21: 19%) adoptees[35] had couch surfed or slept rough for more than seven nights since leaving their adoptive homes. This was a similar level of homelessness to that experienced by the care leavers in Cashmore and Paxman's (2007) study (9/41: 22%). However, in other respects the adoptees' experiences of being able to make the transition to adulthood were significantly different from that of care leavers. Only 5 of the 19 adult adoptees (26%) who were aged between 18 and 25 had left their adoptive parents' home in comparison with 90% (37/41)[36] of care leavers who were no longer living with foster carers or members of their family by their early 20s (Cashmore & Paxman, 2007, p.17). Of the 11 adoptees in this age group for whom there were sufficient data available, 8 (73%) met the criteria for successful adult functioning, all but one of whom were living with their adoptive parents (or a member of their family) at the time of the survey. This is further evidence, to add to that discussed in Chap. 5, of the adoptive home providing the 'safe and secure home base' that a wealth of research has shown to be conducive to successful adult outcomes (e.g. Schofield, 2002; Stein, 2004).

---

[34] Missing data on accommodation for one adoptee.

[35] Data on this variable are available for 21/39 adoptees who had left home.

[36] 37/41 care leavers and 5/19 adoptees of a similar age were living independently in their early 20s (X^2 = 6.292; df = 1; p = 0.012).

Support with Education and Employment

Education

Adoptive parents did not only provide a secure home base from which adoptees could launch themselves into adult life, they also took steps to ensure that they acquired the skills and confidence they needed to support themselves. It is evident from the interviews that many adoptive parents had gone to considerable lengths to rectify the deficits in their adoptees' education.

> *We had special needs teaching at both primary and high school. Plus, remedial teaching after school, speech pathology, occupational pathology, remedial eyesight… every form of intervention imaginable.* (Adoptive parent of young man, aged 9 when permanently placed)

> *I hadn't been to school properly from zero to eight… School was hard in primary school, because I started late and I didn't have a lot of the basics, and Mum had to get a lot of tutoring for me. I had English tutoring, I had maths tutoring, I had French tutoring, I had everything.* (Young woman, aged 8 when permanently placed)

> *I think we really, really tried hard to tackle the learning difficulty issues. She got into uni, which I think is amazing. So I think we have given her opportunities.* (Adoptive parent of young woman, aged 6 months when permanently placed)

> *I used to read all her essays and correct them. I never wrote them for her. I used to read them, correct them, explain what she'd done wrong and make her rewrite. Sometimes, she would write two or three drafts.* (Adoptive parent of young woman, aged 8 when permanently placed)

This level of support could be intrusive, and it was not always appreciated. Nevertheless, it is likely to have been a major factor in the adoptees' educational success. It was also very different from the common experience of care leavers, which is often one of missed opportunities, ignorance of available compensatory support and the absence of an adult prepared to go out of their way to help them succeed (Jackson, 2001;

Cashmore & Paxman, 2007; Skuse & Ward, 2003). Those care leavers in the Cashmore and Paxman study who had achieved educational success tended to have been in long-term stable placements with supportive foster carers whose level of commitment to them was similar to that of adoptive parents (Cashmore & Paxman, 2007, pp. 39–40).

Another factor that contributed to the adoptees' educational success was that it provided them with tangible evidence of the distance they had travelled. Open adoption meant that adoptive parents could use this as a means of encouraging their children to succeed:

But, one thing he did, when he graduated from Year 12 he goes: "I wonder what [birth grandmother] and [birth mother] would think now?".... So, I took a picture, exact of him, just so I'll show her when we do see her, yeah, that he did graduate. So, that was a big thing. He had to prove a point that he was going to be better than them. (Adoptive parent of young man, aged 2 when permanently placed)

It could also help to reconcile birth parents to the adoption:

She actually walked up to me in the supermarket one day and she said: "I want to thank you". And I said: "Oh, what for?" She said, "It's really good to sit back and see my boys successful and well educated, and it's because of you. Thanks for doing that." She said, "Now I've got two kids I can be really proud of". (Adoptive parent of young man, aged 2 when permanently placed)

Employment

Most adoptive parents also continued to offer encouragement and support through the early years of employment. They went to considerable efforts to help their young people find employment, offering them work in their own businesses, or asking friends or colleagues to give them work experience, or helping them make enquiries about vacancies:

So we had to find work for [adoptee] and of course he had this real, real desire to be a deckhand. So I typed up a CV... and physically he and I walked... [to]

all of the marinas around here… there are dozens of marinas.' (Adoptive parent of young man, aged 9 when permanently placed)

They also supported them through crises until they were settled. It was not unusual for these young people to be sacked from their jobs, but they had parents who were willing to help them overcome the difficulties that had led to this setback and find further work.

We give him constant support around his financial situation, support, and or advice… [Adoptee] has this explosion every 18 months, two years where things build up and something goes horribly wrong and he quits his job and he's without a job for weeks or a month and he continues to pay rent and he might – because he's under pressure he goes gambling and he might drink and he does other things.

So, we're there. We try – we're very connected with him… So, I guess what I'm trying to say there is that we're happy to help, but on our terms, and we're not prepared to just give him money to bail him out. (Adoptive parent of young man, aged 5 when permanently placed)

Mental Health

The young person whose adoptive parent was quoted above was in his mid-20s at the time of the survey. Like many of the other adoptees he had received both continuing informal, personal support from his adoptive parents and professional support to help him with the periods of depression and anxiety that continued to affect him. Forty-two (42/59: 71%)[37] of the adult adoptees had had access to mental health support services at some point in their lives[38] and eight of them had been admitted to hospital. Twenty-eight (28/34: 82%)[39] of those adoptees who had continuing mental health issues had received professional help in dealing with them. At least nine adult adoptees were still receiving professional support at

---

[37] Missing data on one adoptee.

[38] Adoptees were asked if they had ever accessed mental health support services from a counsellor, psychologist or psychiatrist. Adoptive parents were also asked if their child had ever accessed similar mental health services.

[39] Missing data on one adoptee.

the time of the survey. Considerably more adoptees than care leavers who had mental health issues received professional mental health support (82% vs 68%) (Cashmore & Paxman, 2007, p. 93), although the disparity did not reach statistical significance.

Risk Factors and Protective Factors in the Relationship Between Adoptive Parents and Children

Adoption, therefore, provided some protection against the consequences of the adoptees' adverse antecedents. Most adoptive parents were able to provide a secure base, and both informal and professional support to help their children overcome their earlier problems and develop the skills and confidence to make a successful transition to adulthood. The body of international research on out-of-home care indicates that these are likely to be the most significant ways in which the adoptees' experiences differed from those of most care leavers (Cashmore & Paxman, 2007; Mann-Feder & Goyette, 2019).

There were also two other factors that appear to have contributed to adoptees' functioning in adulthood. First, those adoptees whose parents had rated the first year of the placement as 'stressful' or 'very stressful' were significantly less likely to achieve successful functioning in adulthood than those whose parents had not.[40] Second, those adult adoptees who regarded themselves as having 'always' experienced sensitive parenting from their adoptive parents were also significantly more likely to be functioning successfully.[41] The significance of these two factors—adoptees' perceptions of parental sensitivity and adoptive parents' perceptions of the first year of the placement—indicate the importance of the relationship in promoting adoptees' resilience. They also provide useful pointers to both training needs and support needs of adoptive parents, issues that are discussed in the final chapter.

---

[40] $X^2 = 9.795$; $df = 1$; $p = 0.02$.
[41] $X^2 = 6.310$, $df = 1$; $p = 0.012$.

Commitment

A final protective factor was the adoptive parents' commitment to the children. This is not possible to quantify, but it was clearly at the basis of the adoptees' strong sense of security that was likely to have contributed to positive outcomes.

The change in legal status underpinned the adoptive parents' and adoptees' commitment to the relationship; it was identified by one of the interviewees as 'the difference between marriage and cohabitation'. The security that the adoption order brought was of great, and sometimes unexpected, significance:

I was very surprised (nobody warned me about this) that there was this huge emotional release when the judge signed the adoption order. I didn't think that would happen. A huge sense of security for both of us. (Adoptive parent of young man, aged 2 when permanently placed)

After adoption my son said: we are a real family now, can we get the stick figures for the car? We thought at the time we were a real family, adoption gave him more security that he wasn't going to be moved anywhere. (Adoptive parent of young man, aged 3 when permanently placed)

The change in legal status was identified by numerous adoptees as the identifying factor that distinguished adoption from their previous experiences. Both the survey responses and the interviews include numerous statements in the same vein as the following:

There was no negative side to being adopted. I mean, one of the other good things about it, it did formalise my position. (Young man, aged 2 when permanently placed, aged 40 when interviewed)

I think having that sense of comfort, that, okay they're my family now, I don't have to worry about anything else, that I don't have to do this soul searching, or searching for biological relatives. I just go: "Oh, you're mine, actually". (Young man, aged 9 when permanently placed, aged 39 when interviewed)

Table 8.10 Adoptive parents' ratings of the adoption (core follow-up sample *N* = 93)

Rating	Frequency	Percent*	Cumulative percent
Very positive	34	40	40
High and lows, mainly highs	33	39	79
High and lows, mainly lows	2	2	81
It was/is difficult and challenging	16	19	100
Total	85	100	
Missing	8		

*Percentages have been rounded

Nevertheless, as Table 8.10 shows, many of the adoptive parents found that adoption had not been easy. While they described 40% (34/85) of the adoptions as very positive, more than 1 in 5 (21%: 18/85) had been mainly negative, including 16 (19%: 16/85) which had been 'difficult and challenging'.

Adoption had also taken a toll on some adult relationships: one in six (16%) adoptive parents thought that the adoption had had a negative impact on their relationship with their partner. It had also sometimes had a negative impact on adoptive parents' relationships with their birth children:

> *And I think [adoptee] came with a lot of baggage that we found really difficult, which has impacted on the whole family... and now they're getting penalised because this child I've taken in, who is my daughter but is really putting me through hell and back, and now the others are saying: "But we're not going to visit".* (Adoptive parent of young woman, aged 3 when permanently placed)

Some adoptive parents who had found the experience 'difficult and challenging' regretted their decision to adopt a child:

I feel angry and bitter. I feel abandoned by my child, and never a word of thanks from him. He exercised his options and preferred to return to his birth family... and I hope he has found happiness. I think he currently lives with one of his older female siblings. However, I don't know. He doesn't keep in touch. In fact, I don't know if he is alive or dead. When we put our toe in the 'adoption water' and spent the many, many months with Barnardos in their excellent training programme, I remember my goals... 'a completion of my family... enrichment of my family... and to give two abused kids a "better second chance in life". Significant elements have gone wrong... Promise I'll never do it again. And will never recommend it to anyone else. (Adoptive parent of young man, aged 10 when permanently placed)

However such comments were rare. Other parents who had found the adoption difficult and challenging nevertheless had few regrets:

Challenging but have no regrets. Am a much better person for having had the children. (Adoptive parent of young woman, aged 4 when permanently placed)

The early and later teenage years were very destructive to us as a family but you will never know how much of that you can put down to adoption. Thankfully now many years later our communication has improved and our relationship is much more positive and happy. (Adoptive parent of young man, aged 8 months when permanently placed)

We are glad we did it, but it was quite challenging. I think the child got something that they could not have gotten otherwise. (Adoptive parent of young woman, aged 11 when permanently placed)

Perhaps the most important finding to come from the study is that, however unsatisfactory the adult adoptees' lifestyles, and however difficult the relationship, adoptive parents very rarely rejected them. They had come to consider themselves as the adoptees' parents and consequently they were there for the duration. Adoptive parents continued to support adoptees who had become heavily involved in prostitution; who had become addicted to drugs; who had developed long-term mental health problems. Darren's case study provides a typical example.

Darren

Before Entering His Adoptive Home
Darren was diagnosed with autism and epilepsy at an early age. He also had learning disabilities. He experienced physical and sexual abuse before being placed in foster care. His foster parents decided to keep his siblings but asked for him to be removed. He was placed with his adoptive parents when he was eight years old and was described as aggressive but not assertive.

Progress
Darren was described as 'a difficult kid to manage, a difficult teenager, difficult young man'. He left his adoptive parents to return to his birth parents, but then returned to his adoptive parents when that broke down.

As an Adult
It became apparent that Darren would not be able to live independently. He could not manage his financial affairs; he could not keep his home clean or look after himself properly. When he was in his 20s, his adoptive parents moved him into supported accommodation. However, they continued to visit him and to support him in numerous ways. In their view:

What would it be like for Darren if he did not have anyone that he could rely on? He truly would be one of those homeless bag people because he does not have the inner resources.

Adoptive parents also welcomed back adoptees who had comprehensively rejected them. The following quotation comes from an adoptive mother whose son left them and had no contact for three years before he returned:

He said when he got in touch with us: "A lot of people, whether it was their natural parents or not... they would not have taken me back. They may not have wanted to talk to me", and he said, "And I know people, after having met people over that time... I know people whose parents have not wanted to know them, after what's happened". And he said: "But you..."

I can't understand why a parent would not want – even if it is years on, if a child finally realised that they needed to speak to the parent, wanted to come back to the family, no matter what happened... I find it hard to understand why a parent wouldn't want to, then, take that opportunity to reconnect and try and work something out. Home was always here, if he ever needed to come back. (Adoptive parent of young man, aged 8 when permanently placed)

We do not know enough about the process by which adoptive parents come to regard themselves as the parents of a child to whom they did not give birth. Greater understanding of this issue would better inform the recruitment and training of adoptive parents and indicate how placements might be better supported.

Conclusion

Adult outcomes for the Barnardos adoptees were relatively positive. They did well educationally, and most of them were in employment. Although many of them had continuing mental health issues, nevertheless they were more likely to function successfully as adults than young people who age out of out-of-home care. Our composite measure of outcomes showed that 55% of the adult adoptees appeared to be functioning successfully as adults. Ten were highly successful, showing positive outcomes on six or seven indicators. Only one adoptee showed negative outcomes on all seven indicators, and two more had negative outcomes on five. However, adoption was not an easy task; many of the adoptive parents had found it challenging and stressful, both for themselves and partners and sometimes for their birth children. Their long-term commitment despite the challenges, their sensitivity and their determination to help the adoptees succeed are likely to be key factors associated with successful outcomes.

Key Points

- Educational outcomes of adult adoptees tended to be similar to those of the general population and markedly better than those of a comparable sample of care leavers.
- Adoptees were also more likely to be in work and less likely to be NEET (not in education, employment or training) than care leavers.
- There were indications that continuing mental health issues and reports of substance misuse were more common amongst the adoptees than care leavers.

- Nevertheless, more adoptees than care leavers achieved 'successful functioning in adulthood'.
- Adult adoptees who had good qualifications, a steady, satisfying job and were in an established partnership still showed signs of underlying vulnerability.
- The presence of a committed and supportive adoptive parent helped adoptees both access the services they needed and function satisfactorily in adulthood despite ongoing consequences of earlier abuse. This was the major difference between the experiences of adoptees and care leavers.
- Adoption appears to have acted as a powerful protective factor. Only extreme indicators of vulnerability at entry to the adoptive home correlated with poor adult outcomes.
- Adoptees who felt that they had received sensitive parenting were significantly more likely to function satisfactorily in adulthood.
- Those whose adoptive parents had found the first year of the placement challenging were significantly less likely to achieve success.
- Almost all adoptive parents considered the adoptees to be their own children and continued to support them into adulthood, regardless of what were sometimes severe behavioural problems and challenging mental health issues. Better understanding of how this parental bond is formed would enhance recruitment, training and support programmes.

References

Allen, M. (2014). *Reducing the number of young people not in education, employment or training (NEET)* (Health equity evidence review No. 3). Public Health England and Institute of Health Equity.

Australian Bureau of Statistics. (2017). *Education and work Australia.* May 2016. https://www.abs.gov.au/AUSSTATS/abs@.nsf/DetailsPage/6227.0May%20 2016?OpenDocument. Accessed January 2021.

Australian Institute of Health and Welfare. (2017). *Australia's Welfare 2017.* Australian Government: AIHW.

Beautrais, A. (2000). *Risk factors for suicide and attempted suicide among young people.* Commonwealth Department of Health and Aged Care.

Cashmore, J., & Paxman, M. (1996). *Wards leaving care: A longitudinal study.* NSW Department of Community Services.

Cashmore, J., & Paxman, M. (2006). Predicting after-care outcomes: The importance of 'felt' security. *Child and Family Social Work, 11,* 232–241.

Cashmore, J., & Paxman, M. (2007). *Wards leaving care: Four to five years on.* University of New South Wales.

Conway, K. P., Compton, W., Stinson, F. S., & Grant, B. F. (2006). Lifetime comorbidity of DSM-IV mood and anxiety disorders and specific drug use disorders: Results from the National Epidemiologic Survey on Alcohol and Related Conditions. *Journal of Clinical Psychiatry, 67*(2), 247–257.

Farmer, E., Sturgess, W., O'Neill, T., & Wijedasa, D. (2011). *Achieving successful returns from care: What makes reunification work?* BAAF.

Felitti, V. J., Anda, R. F., Nordenberg, D., Williamson, D. F., Spitz, A. M., Edwards, V., Koss, M. P., & Marks, J. S. (1998). Relationship of childhood abuse and household dysfunction to many of the leading causes of death in adults. The adverse childhood experiences (ACE) study. *American Journal of Preventive Medicine, 14*(4), 245–258.

Finkelhor, D., Turner, H., Hamby, S., & Ormrod, R. (2011). Polyvictimization: Children's exposure to multiple types of violence, crime and abuse. *US Department of Justice Juvenile Justice Bulletin.* https://www.ncjrs.gov/pdf-files1/ojjdp/235504.pdf. Accessed 28 Nov 2020.

Henderson, J. L., Hawke, L. D., Chaim, G., & National Youth Screening Project Network. (2017). Not in employment, education or training: Mental health, substance use, and disengagement in a multi-sectoral sample of service-seeking Canadian youth. *Children and Youth Services Review, 75,* 138–145.

Jackson, S. (2001). *Nobody ever told us school mattered: Raising the educational attainments of children in public care.* BAAF.

Jackson, S., & Cameron, C. (2011). Young people from a public care background: Pathways to further and higher education in five European countries. Final report of the YIPPEE Project. University of London Thomas Coram Research Unit.

Mann-Feder, V. R., & Goyette, M. (2019). *Leaving care and the transition to adulthood. International contributions to theory, research and practice.* Oxford University Press.

McGloin, J. M., & Spatz Widom, C. (2001). Resilience among abused and neglected children grown up. *Development and Psychopathology, 13,* 1021–1038.

Nalavany, B. A., Ryan, S. D., Howard, J. A., & Smith, S. L. (2008). Pre-adoptive child sexual abuse as a predictor of moves in care, adoption disruptions, and inconsistent adoptive parent commitment. *Child Abuse and Neglect, 32*(12), 1084–1088.

Osborn, A., & Delfabbro, P. H. (2006). Research Article 4: An analysis of the social background and placement history of children with multiple and complex needs in Australian out-of-home care. *Communities, Children and Families Australia, 1*(1), 33–42.

Parker, R., Ward, H., Jackson, S., Aldgate, J., & Wedge, P. (1991). *Looking after children: Assessing outcomes in child care.* HMSO.

Rousseau, D., Roze, M., Duverger, P., Fanello, S., & Tanguy, M. (2015). *Etude sur le devenir à long terme des jeunes enfants placès à la Pouponnière Sociale Saint Exupéry entre 1994 et 2001.* Rapport Recherche St-Ex 2013–2014. Unité de Psychiatrie de l'Enfant et de l'Adolescent du CHU d'Angers.

Schofield, G. (2002). The significance of a secure base: A psychosocial model of long-term foster care. *Child and Family Social Work, 7*, 259–272.

Selwyn, S., Wijedasa, D., & Meakings. (2014). *Beyond the adoption order: Challenges, interventions and adoption disruptions, RR 336.* Department for Education. https://assets.publishing.service.gov.uk/government/uploads/system/uploads/attachment_data/file/301889/Final_Report_-_3rd_April_2014v2.pdf. Accessed 30 Dec 2020

Skuse, T., & Ward, H. (2003). *Children's views, the importance of listening. An interim report to the Department of Health.* Loughborough University Centre for Child and Family Research.

Slade, T., Johnston, A., Teesson, M., Whiteford, H., Burgess, P., Pirkis, J., & Saw, S. (2009). *The mental health of Australians 2: Report on the 2007 National Survey of Mental Health and Wellbeing.* Department of Health and Ageing.

Sonuga-Barke, E., Kennedy, M., Kumsta, R., Knights, N., Golm, D., Rutter, M., Maughan, B., Schlotz, W., & Kreppner, J. (2017). Child-to-adult neurodevelopmental and mental health trajectories after early life deprivation: The young adult follow-up of the longitudinal English and Romanian Adoptees study. *Lancet, 389*, 1539–1548.

Stein, M. (2004). *What works for young people leaving care?* Barnardos.

Stein, M. (2012). *Young people leaving care: Supporting pathways to adulthood.* Jessica Kingsley Publishers.

Torrens, M., Gilchrist, G., Domingo-Salvany, A., & Psycobarcelona Group. (2011). Psychiatric comorbidity in illicit drug users: Substance-induced versus independent disorders. *Drug Alcohol Depend, 113*(2–3), 147–156.

White, K. R. (2016). Placement discontinuity for older children and adolescents who exit foster care through adoption or guardianship: A systematic review. *Child and Adolescent Social Work Journal, 33,* 377–394.

Wilkins, R. (2017). *The 12th annual statistical report of the HILDA survey.* Melbourne Institute, Applied Economic & Social Research, The University of Melbourne.

9

Conclusion: Implications for Policy and Practice

Introduction

In Chap. 1, we explored the current discourse around adoption. Past adoption practices have been rightly criticised for a number of systemic and blatant injustices and also for a common lack of transparency. However, it is important to be transparent not only about children's origins but also about the reasons why some are permanently removed from birth families. Child maltreatment does occur and can have permanent, serious and sometimes fatal consequences. We argued that in spite of the injustices of the past and concerns about some current practices, if practised within a robust rights and ethics framework, adoption can be an appropriate intervention for the small group of abused and neglected children in out-of-home care who cannot safely return to their birth families (Palacios et al., 2019). For these children, the question professionals have to resolve is not whether or not they should return home, but whether it would be in their best interests to be adopted or remain in out-of-home care.

This book has traced the outcomes of a cohort of children who, following such a best interests decision, were adopted from care through

© The Author(s) 2022   **267**
H. Ward et al., *Outcomes of Open Adoption from Care*,
https://doi.org/10.1007/978-3-030-76429-6_9

Barnardos' Find-a-Family in New South Wales, Australia. Almost all of them had been significantly abused or neglected and none could safely return to their birth parents. We have examined the characteristics and experiences of these children, their adoptive parents and birth parents and attempted to identify factors which contributed to their resilience. A fundamental feature of the programme was the expectation of regular face-to-face contact with birth family members as part of the adoption plan, mandated and upheld by the courts; we explored the value of contact for the adoptees and their adoptive parents, and its impact on life trajectories. The findings have implications for adoption policy and practice throughout Australia; but they are also relevant in the many jurisdictions such as the USA, the UK and parts of Europe where the adoption of children from care, and particularly open adoption, are hotly debated issues.

The Study

All 210 adoptees were traced from notification of abuse or neglect to placement in permanent homes. Almost half of them (93: 44%) were traced from entry to their adoptive homes until the follow-up cut-off date, an average of 18 years after permanent placement.

The study supports the findings from international research on adoptions of children from out-of-home care (e.g. Grotevant et al., 2007; Selwyn et al., 2006; Selwyn et al., 2014; Thomas, 2013). These show that the profile of this population is very different from that of infants relinquished for adoption by lone parents in the twentieth century (see Parker, 1999). Almost all of the adoptees in the Barnardos cohort had been seriously abused or neglected while living with their birth families; most had been exposed to a range of other adverse childhood experiences that are known to be associated with poor physical and mental health outcomes in adulthood, including premature mortality (Felitti et al., 1998). Birth parents were struggling with complex combinations of substance misuse, mental health problems and domestic abuse; there is no evidence that they had sufficient capacity to change and provide safe homes for their children within an appropriate timeframe. Apart from a very few children who were voluntarily relinquished, also in response to maltreatment concerns, all the children in the study were the subject of child protection orders. Those who were not placed for adoption were expected to remain in long-term foster care until they aged out at 18.

Delays in professional decision-making, repeated experiences of separation and loss, and unstable placements in out-of-home care had compounded the vulnerability of the Barnardos adoptees: by the time they entered their adoptive homes, all had reached the threshold for significantly increased risk of poor adult outcomes on at least one of 11 criteria; almost half of them had reached it on six. The children's previous experiences were reflected in developmental delays, high levels of behavioural disturbance and emotional problems at entry to their adoptive homes.

Data from the core follow-up sample (N = 93) show that at entry to their homes, adoptive parents rated 13% of the adoptees as in poor physical health and 38% in poor or very poor mental health. Three-quarters of them had problems at school, and at least three-quarters faced specific challenges which required specialist support. Almost half the adoptive parents found the first year of the placement stressful. However, most adoptees saw improvements in their physical and mental health after being permanently placed, and about two-thirds saw improvements in their academic performance.

Data from this core follow-up sample show that most adoptees established permanent relationships with adoptive parents who came to regard them as their own children and supported them into adulthood. Most adoptees stayed in their adoptive homes until they were at least 21 and then left for normative reasons. Twelve left their adoptive homes before they were 18, indicating a disruption rate of 13%. About a quarter of the adoptions showed an underlying fragility in that the adoptee had run away or temporarily left home on at least one occasion. However, the distinguishing feature was that adoptees could return and that most adoptive parents continued to support them after they had left. There were no dissolutions and no evidence that any child returned to out-of-home care. The adoptees were less likely to maintain close relationships with their adoptive parents than the normative Australian population, but the relationship was twice as likely to persist as that between care leavers and former foster carers.

Data concerning the 60 young people who were 18 or over at the time of follow-up show that, in comparison with the normative Australian population, adult adoptees had similar, though slightly less positive, outcomes in terms of basic and higher education, and a similar proportion were in full-time education, employment or training. However, they showed markedly more negative outcomes in terms of being NEET (not in education employment or education), substance misuse and being the victim of domestic abuse (men).

In comparison with a sample of care leavers (Cashmore & Paxman, 2007), the adoptees showed significantly more positive outcomes in terms of basic and higher educational qualifications and employment. However, they showed significantly worse outcomes in terms of substance use and some indication of greater levels of substance misuse and mental health problems. A higher proportion of adult adoptees showed evidence of successful adult functioning than care leavers, but the difference was not statistically significant.

Adoptees who met the criteria for success on our composite measure of adult functioning (Cashmore & Paxman, 2007) tended to have had less exposure to recognised risk factors than those who did not succeed, but the differences were not statistically significant. The only factors that were found to have a significant relationship with adult functioning were exposure to polyvictimisation (all four types of abuse) before separation from birth families (associated with less successful functioning) and experiences of sensitive parenting in adoptive homes (associated with those who met the criteria for success). Our overall classification of vulnerability (Chap. 3) was not a reliable predictor of adult outcome, except for those adoptees at the extreme ends of the spectrum. Adoption by parents who could meet children's therapeutic needs appeared to act as a powerful protective factor in promoting resilience and facilitating developmental recovery, but it was not sufficient to counteract the most damaging early experiences (see also Rutter et al., 2007; Sonuga-Barke et al., 2017).

Most adoptees (87%) had face-to-face post-adoption contact with at least one birth parent. They also had face-to-face contact with grandparents and siblings. More than half were seeing at least one birth relative at the time of the follow-up. Adoptive parents accompanied their children to contact meetings. Contact was difficult for 60% of the sample, the most significant issue being birth parents' continuing problems. Although it was painful, most (69%) adoptees and adoptive parents thought that contact had been beneficial. There is no evidence that open adoption jeopardised the stability of adoptive homes; it was the placements where adoptive parents were less open to face-to-face contact and had less empathy with birth parents that were the most fragile (see also Grotevant et al., 2007; Neil, 2003).

Evidence concerning the impact of contact on adoptees' outcomes was mixed. There was little statistical association between face-to-face contact and adoptees' mental health or adult outcomes, except one finding that, for some adoptees, contact with birth fathers had a detrimental impact. However, there are indications that contact helped adoptees develop a strong sense of identity, come to terms with their parents' limitations, accept the reasons why adoption had been necessary and move on. Those who did so appeared to have better outcomes.

The ability of adoptive parents to accept adoptees as their own children was perhaps the most significant factor in facilitating successful outcomes. The presence of committed substitute parents, who regarded them as their own children and supported them through the transition from adolescence to adulthood regardless of enduring and challenging emotional and behavioural difficulties, was the feature that distinguished the experiences of adoptees from those of most care leavers; it is likely to have had a major impact on adult outcomes. The change of legal status conferred by adoption underpinned the development of a committed relationship between most adoptive parents and adoptees and helped mitigate the consequences of their past adversities. Ongoing contact with birth parents facilitated the development of this relationship.

Implications for Child Protection Policy and Practice

Evidence from this study supports the wide body of research that has found that abuse and neglect in early childhood have long-term consequences that are difficult to escape (see Brown & Ward, 2013, for summary). We know that, like other children adopted from care, the Barnardos adoptees had experienced high levels of abuse and neglect before being separated, that there was a continuing risk of maltreatment within their birth families and that they could not safely return home (see also Selwyn et al., 2006). It was also Barnardos' policy to focus on children who were 'hard to place', indicating that even within this very vulnerable population, the Barnardos adoptees had been exposed to exceptionally poor early childhood experiences. Abuse and neglect in early childhood, in many cases compounded by adverse experiences in out-of-home care, are likely to lie behind the high levels of emotional and behavioural difficulties evident at entry to their adoptive homes and the ongoing mental health issues present amongst adult adoptees. Although the adult adoptees did well in terms of education and employment, many were nevertheless reliant on continued support from adoptive parents and partners to help them function in an adult world; even those who were living very successful adult lives showed an underlying vulnerability.

Evidence of the continued impact of abuse and neglect indicates a need for a focus on policies aimed at addressing parents' difficulties when they start to emerge and then effectively preventing maltreatment from occurring. Addressing abuse and neglect as a public health issue, with a whole population focus on improving parenting, has been found to be effective in some countries (Davies & Ward, 2012). Where abuse and neglect have occurred, there is also a need for long-term support for those affected, whether they are adopted, placed in long-term foster homes, or remain living with birth parents (see Brown et al., 2016).

Children Who Cannot Remain with Birth Parents

Delays in Professional Decision-Making

The study has important implications for professional decision-making where children cannot safely remain at home. Polyvictimisation was significantly associated with poor outcomes in adulthood. Long-term exposure to abuse pending a decision to separate them from birth families, repeated failed attempts at restoration and instability in care pending a permanent placement are also likely contributors to the adoptees' vulnerability (Brown et al., 2016). There is no evidence that birth parents had been able to overcome their difficulties by the time the children were adopted; more timely decision-making and more robust assessments of parental capacity to change might have reduced the adoptees' exposure to abuse and neglect and their consequences (Ward et al., 2014, 2019).

Quality of Out-of-Home Care

The study raises questions about the quality of out-of-home care, although it should be noted that, because it spans a 30-year timeframe, some of the deficits underlying the adoptees' experiences may have since been addressed. Nevertheless, it is noteworthy that 100 (48%) adoptees had had three or more placements before entering their adoptive homes, and 10 had moved more than ten times. Placement moves happened both before and after entry to Barnardos. The impact of these experiences is evident from the interviews, where adoptive parents described children who hid from visitors for fear they had come to move them again and where remarks from adoptees such as the following were commonplace:

> But I feel like I – you know, moving around to different homes so often and changing primary schools was just really – there was no stability in that, and that's what a child needs: they need stability growing up. (Young woman, aged 10 when permanently placed, aged 21 when interviewed)

Placement instability is a recognised and continuing problem in the Australian child welfare system (Wulczyn & Chen, 2017). It is also an issue in the USA (Blakey et al., 2012), Sweden (Vinnerljung et al., 2014), England (Ward, 2009) and many other countries. In England, about 30% of moves in out-of-home care occur because of a breakdown in the relationship between carer and child. However, over half (54%) are administrative moves, engendered as part of the case management process (Ward, 2009); Delfabbro et al. (2005) found around 60–70% of placement moves occurred for the same reason in Southern Australia. Action should be taken to monitor moves within out-of-home care and their reasons and to reduce them wherever possible.

There is also evidence of poor quality day-to-day care in foster homes. Interviews provided some evidence of sexual and emotional abuse in foster care, but this appears to have been disclosed and addressed at the time. However, adoptive parents also described children being placed in their homes after many months (or years) in out-of-home care who were developmentally delayed because of lack of stimulation, or who had no experience of rules or boundaries. The following quotation is from a young woman who had spent seven years in foster care before entering her adoptive home:

> I think I probably many times would've thought, "Oh, she's the worst. She's giving me all these rules and not letting me do these things". But now when I look back on it, that was just a healthy adult providing boundaries for a child, which I never had in my life. (Young woman, aged 10 when permanently placed, aged 21 when interviewed)

Implications for Permanency Planning

We do not know how many foster homes were abusive or of sub-optimal quality. Some of the adoptees had experienced highly supportive, stable long-term foster placements, many of them with carers who went on to adopt them. Nevertheless, the findings do throw into sharp relief the differences between long-term foster care and adoption. Adoption provided the children with greater stability than most had previously experienced in foster care. At the time they were followed up, those who were still living with their adoptive parents had been there for an average of 13 years, and this includes adoptees who had had numerous previous foster or residential placements. We do not know how many adoptees would have gone on to achieve stability had they remained in foster care. The breakdown rate (13%) is lower than that of the placements of children in the Pathways of Care Longitudinal Study (POCLS) of out-of-home care in

New South Wales, which gives a 'conservative' estimate of 17% 'following the Wave 1 interview' (Wulczyn & Chen, 2017). It is also substantially lower than the 28–30% found for placements in long-term foster care in the UK (Biehal et al., 2010), or the 24% found for similar placements in Sweden (Vinnerljung et al., 2014). However, it is slightly higher than that found in a study of children in long-term foster care in Norway, in which 12.5% of placements with kinship and non-kinship carers who 'believed that the child should grow up in their family' disrupted after an average of 8.9 years (Holtan et al., 2013). The authors of this study point out that in Norway, as in other Nordic countries, long-term stable foster care is the preferred route to permanence, and adoption is seldom an option; their findings suggest that, given the appropriate support, long-term foster carers can provide similar levels of stability if the expectation is that they will provide a 'family for life'.

Comparison with Cashmore and Paxman's (2007) study of wards leaving care, who were of similar age to many of the Barnardos adoptees, showed that adoptees tended to do better in terms of education and employment than care leavers. In part this may be due to the determination with which adoptive parents sought out specialist help to enable their children to overcome past deficits in education as well as their psycho-social difficulties. However, the findings also showed that most adoptive parents provided much greater support for young people making the transition from adolescence to adulthood than foster carers were able to offer. Adoptees were approximately three years older than care leavers when they left home, they could and did return when plans went awry, and they continued to receive practical and emotional support from adoptive parents after they had achieved independence. This type of enduring parental support was rarely available to care leavers; it is likely to be a key reason why, despite stronger evidence of enduring mental health issues, adoptees were more likely to achieve satisfactory functioning in adulthood.

Finally, the change in legal status that adoption brought seems to have given the children the sense of belonging and security they needed to achieve a positive sense of identity. It provided the foundation for the formation of a new family, to which both adoptive parents and adoptees developed a life-long commitment. Triseliotis' (2002) review of research literature on outcomes of long-term foster care and adoption concluded that 'even when long-term fostering lasts, the children still feel less secure and have a weaker sense of belonging than those who are adopted' (p. 28). He identified the legal status the adoption order gave them as a key element in adoptees' greater sense of belonging.

As well as showing the benefits of adoption, the findings also indicate that, where this is not a suitable option, much could be done to improve outcomes for care leavers. Although legislation and policy designed to support care leavers as they make the transition to independence in adulthood have been introduced in some countries including Australia (Mendes, 2020; Stein & Munro, 2008), this has generally been poorly implemented (Strahl et al., 2020). Stronger, and more effective policies designed to bring the experiences of young people ageing out of care to a closer approximation of normative family life, allowing them to stay in foster homes until they are older, to return when plans fall through and to access continuing support as independent adults would reduce the vulnerability of this group and be likely to improve their long-term outcomes.

Implications for Adoption Policy and Practice

The findings indicate that adoption can provide greater stability, a stronger sense of belonging and better support for young people making the transition towards adulthood than long-term foster care usually provides. There is therefore a strong argument for making it more widely available to children in out-of-home care who cannot safely return home within a timeframe that is consonant with their developmental needs. However, the findings also have considerable implications for the recruitment and training of adoptive parents; for the support of adoptive and birth families over contact; and for post-adoption support to adoptive parents and children.

Recruitment of Adoptive Parents

Open adoption of children from out-of-home care is not the same as the closed adoptions of infants relinquished by single mothers that took place in the twentieth century, and adoptive parents now face very different challenges. Better understanding of the needs of adopted children and the detrimental impact of past policies has led to the development of much greater transparency in adoption practice: if open adoption plans are followed, the secrets and lies that characterised adoption in the past can no longer persist. The vast majority (87%) of the adoptees had post-adoption face-to-face contact with at least one birth parent, and almost all (93%) had contact with at least one birth family member. In the Find-a-Family programme, adoptive parents made the arrangements for contact and accompanied their adoptees to contact meetings. This meant that some level of communication between the parties involved was unavoidable and, as a result, some of the fantasies were dispelled: when they had to meet on a regular basis, it was harder for adoptive parents to cling to the myth that birth parents who had maltreated their children were monsters or for birth parents to believe that adoptive parents had stolen their children. Adoptees were also less likely to fantasise about returning to an idealised birth family when they saw them regularly and their problems were, sometimes painfully, exposed.

Some of the most successful adoptions appeared to be those in which the adoptive family included the children's relatives as honorary members of their own extended family. Although this was not always possible, or even desirable in some cases, it is noteworthy that the few adoptions in which contact was discouraged were markedly less successful in that, in interviews, these adoptees focused extensively on their past experiences and did not appear to have been able to move on. Concerns are sometimes raised that contact will undermine placements and increase the likelihood of adoptees returning to birth parents (Dodgson, 2014; Turkington & Taylor, 2009): this study found that the opposite was the case—it was those adoptees who did not have contact who were more likely to seek out birth family members and return to them (see also Grotevant et al., 2007).

Recruitment policies should reflect the reality of open adoption. Prospective adoptive parents need to be able to relate to birth family members without hostility and to understand their situation. There is no evidence from this study that adoptive parents whose primary motivation was their own infertility were less able to do this than adoptive parents who were motivated by a desire to help a child.

Recruitment agencies also need to be aware that one of the consequences of open adoption from out-of-home care is that it brings the role of adoptive parents closer to that of foster carers and this should be a consideration in setting eligibility criteria. Prospective adopters may need to be able not only to empathise with birth parents but also to provide therapeutic parenting to children who have experienced early trauma (Staines et al., 2019). The Barnardos adoptive parents had all been dual registered as foster carers, and many of them fostered their adoptees for several years before adopting them. This may have been one of the factors that led to the success of the programme.

Contact

The study shows that it is possible to recruit adoptive parents who will support open adoption practice. It also shows that regular face-to-face contact with birth family members can be maintained: at follow-up, on average 18 years after placement, 56% of the adoptees were still seeing at least one member of their birth family. Just over two-thirds (69%) of both adoptive parents and adoptees thought that, in the long run, contact had been beneficial. However, 60% of adoptive parents had found contact problematic, and more than one in four (28%) adult adoptees thought they had never benefitted from it. It should also be noted that adoptees who had no post-adoption contact with birth fathers were significantly less likely to have mental health problems in adulthood.

Data from the interviews raise a number of issues concerning contact that underlie these mixed findings and indicate where practice improvements might be made.[1] Almost all respondents (88%) thought that

---

[1] Interviewees tended not to distinguish between contact pre and post the adoption order; these findings therefore apply to all contact after the child had been permanently placed.

Barnardos should continue their policy of asking adoptive parents to accompany children to contact sessions, mainly to ensure that the child was safe and was not being manipulated by birth parents trying to undermine the placement. This is an important feature of the Barnardos programme both for adoptees and for children in foster care; and there is much to be learnt from it. Although adding to the burden placed on adoptive parents, it was much appreciated by the adoptees and is likely to be more beneficial than the common practice of arranging for children in care to be taken to meet parents in contact centres by volunteers who do not know them, their foster carers or their birth parents (see Humphreys & Kiraly, 2011).

It was also evident that practitioners should be clear about the purpose of contact, particularly where children are obviously frightened by birth parents; where they make it clear that they do not want to spend time with adults who have hurt them in the past; where relatives are abusive towards the adoptee; and where they arrive at contact sessions under the influence of alcohol or drugs. These are the types of situations in which there is a risk that face-to-face contact will re-traumatise the child and where careful consideration might be given to questioning its value at that particular time. It is evident from the interviews that 'agency' or the opportunity to make their own decisions about contact was valued by the adoptees. They had their own views about how contact should be tailored to the needs of each individual child (see also Neil et al., 2015).

Ask the children how much they want to see birth family. (Response to open-ended survey question from young man aged 18 months when permanently placed, aged 11 at follow-up)

Sometimes you need to look at the child to pick up on what they are feeling to try to limit the birth family contact. (Young woman, aged 7 when permanently placed, aged 35 when interviewed)

They should not be enforced. I found them traumatic as a child. (Young woman, aged 7 when permanently placed, aged 38 when interviewed)

I would have preferred to just see my dad and nan. (Young woman, aged 10 when permanently placed, aged 32 when interviewed)

In certain situations, face-to-face contact may not always be the most beneficial option. One adoptee thought that indirect contact would be more appropriate for children who had been seriously abused as he had been:

If they don't want to see them, and it affected them like it did me, kind of like figure something out to avoid that, that tension and stuff… I mean, for little kids, you could always do just scrapbooking and stuff like that. And make it creative. But then, at the same time, it's informing them about their life. And then with older ones, it's kind of similar process, like a similar approach,… and just like kind of show them something that shows them their past, and stuff like that. (Young man, aged 2 when permanently placed, aged 18 when interviewed)

Training

The evidence discussed above indicates that training for prospective adoptive parents as well as for child welfare professionals should include the factors that increase (or reduce) the likelihood that parents will abuse their children, the impact of abuse and neglect on children's subsequent development, the impact of secrecy and deception on children's sense of identity, and the rationale behind open adoption policy and practice.

Training also needs to cover therapeutic parenting skills within the context of the needs of children adopted from care. As we have seen, a high proportion of the adoptees had significant emotional and behavioural problems when first placed with their adoptive families; they also displayed a range of developmental delays including poor cognitive development. Adoptive parents needed to learn both how to better support their children themselves and also how to access self-help groups and specialist services where appropriate. In the words of one adoptive parent:

'These are damaged children and I realise now that placing them in a loving home is not enough, I feel that I may have been better equipped if I had attended some sort of counselling or self-help adoptive parents' group?

I believe that adoptive parents would benefit from training sessions in how to better manage/counsel a child who had been repeatedly let down by their birth family who did not show up for an arranged meeting, this I believe was a big factor in the low self-esteem of my daughter.' (Adoptive parent of young woman, aged 6 months when permanently placed)

Post-adoption Support

Finally, some of the key findings from the study add to the already extensive evidence base that demonstrates the enduring impact of abuse and neglect in early childhood (Brown et al., 2016; Felitti et al., 1998; Gerin et al., 2019; McCrory et al., 2017). They also provide further evidence of the persistent effects of early trauma even after those affected have spent many subsequent years in stable, loving homes (see, for instance, Selwyn et al., 2014; Sonuga-Barke et al., 2017). Adoption is intended to create a new family, and until relatively recently it was assumed that, after the order had been made, there would no longer be a need for specialist support; however there is now substantial evidence to show that adoptive families may need help at any stage in the child's development, and particularly in the teenage years (Adoption UK, 2020; Livingston Smith and Donaldson Adoption Institute, 2004; Selwyn, 2017). A recent survey of adoptive families in the UK found that 48% of those with older children were experiencing severe challenges and 42% of 16–25-year-old adoptees had been engaged with mental health services in the previous year (Adoption UK, 2020).

Barnardos assumed that the provision of specialist post-adoption support services would interfere with the process of normalising the new family, and adoptive parents who ran into difficulties were signposted to universal services within the community. However, it is clear from the interviews, and also from survey responses, that many adoptees and their families continued to require specialist support, particularly during adolescence, but also often into adulthood. The findings from the study add to the body of evidence indicating a need for post-adoption support services that can be accessed as and when required.

In my case, all helped ceased when the adoption went through. I had problems but had no one to turn to.... I think help is needed after adoption. I probably thought adoption would solve most of my child's problems, but it didn't. But I suppose that it is not Barnardo's responsibility for ongoing aftercare... although I do have a friend in my last caseworker. It is just hard as everything stops. Financially... keeping a teenager with ongoing medical and psychologic problems in a school with no financial support is very hard... (Adoptive parent of young woman, aged 9 when permanently placed)

Conclusion

A number of concerns underlie the reluctance to develop stronger policies to support adoption from care in Australia. These include concerns that children placed for adoption may have been inappropriately taken into care; that adoption disregards genetic and birth bonds; that legal ties with wider family members may be severed; and that adoptees are likely to suffer enduring identity problems. There are also concerns that adoptees may be subject to abuse in adoptive homes; that decisions to pursue adoption may not be focused on children's best interests; and that adoption may simply be a means of transferring and privatising the costs of out-of-home care, particularly when post-adoption support services are inaccessible or insufficient (Australian Federal Parliament House of Representatives Standing Committee on Social Policy and Legal Affairs, 2018; Cashmore, 2000). Similar concerns are also found in countries such as the UK and the USA, where adoption is well established as an integral part of the child protection system (DelBalzo, 2007; Ward and Smeeton, 2017), and in other countries where it is less common (Schrover, 2020). Such concerns must be acknowledged.

While inadequate assessment and poor decision-making undoubtedly lead to injustices in some individual cases, many of the findings from the study address these concerns. Almost all the adoptees had experienced significant levels of abuse or neglect before removals from birth families or were at high risk of maltreatment because of their siblings' experiences.

All adoptees had gone through rigorous legal processes in both the Children's Court and the Supreme Court. The birth parents of 24 children contested the adoptions in court, but there was no evidence that these parents had the capacity to meet their needs, and no evidence of inappropriate removal. Nor was there evidence that Aboriginal children were being targeted or affected by adoption policy. The Find-a-Family programme does not routinely take referrals for Aboriginal children, and only five (2%) of the full cohort were found to be of Aboriginal heritage post placement.

Legal decisions appear to have been made in accordance with the best interests of the child; evidence from the adoptees also makes it clear that almost all believed that adoption had been right for them. They valued the change in legal status because it brought security and made them full members of a new family. However, for most children, adoption did not sever links with family members—the open adoption policy was followed in almost all cases: 93% of the children had post-adoption contact with at least one birth family member and 56% were still seeing them when they were followed up, on average 18 years later. There is evidence that the open adoption policy also helped adoptees come to terms with their past and develop a stronger sense of identity.

Abuse can occur in any type of family and it is true that children who are vulnerable for other reasons are at greater risk. Abuse is also relatively common in out-of-home care (Royal Commission into Institutional Responses to Child Sexual Abuse, 2017). The study uncovered one instance of sexual abuse in an adoptive home which had been disclosed and led to the removal of the perpetrator, and one instance of emotional abuse that had not apparently been previously disclosed. As far as we know, about 2% (2/93) of the sample had been abused in their adoptive homes compared with 8% of the full cohort (16/210) who had made formal allegations of abuse while in foster or residential care.

While it is true that infertility was the primary motivation for the majority of the adoptive parents, there is no evidence to support the view that decisions to place for adoption were driven by adult interests. As we have seen, before the placement was made, there had been evidence of abuse likely to cause significant harm and a decision that the adoptees could not safely return home.

Although the study addresses many of the concerns that have been raised about adoption, it also raises some questions. The findings shed light on a number of areas where policy and practice might be strengthened, both in the field of adoption and in the wider range of child protection services. However, one criticism of policies designed to support adoption is that, in common with other child protection interventions, it is a 'sticking plaster' service, designed to mitigate the consequences of maltreatment rather than to address its causes. The high proportion of infants removed from birth parents within the first year of life in Australia, England, the USA and the Scandinavian countries has become a major concern (Backhaus et al., 2019; Broadhurst et al., 2018). One factor is likely to be an increase in poverty and reduction of family support services following the financial crash of 2008 (Thomas, 2018). Poor socioeconomic circumstances and inadequate family support services are among the stressors which underlie some of the parental factors such as mental health problems, substance misuse and domestic abuse which compromise parenting capacity, place infants at risk of significant harm and lead to their removal (Backhaus et al., 2019). Policies to support adoption from care have been criticised on the grounds that they can be a means of avoiding the need to address the systematic reasons why abuse and neglect occur and to support birth parents to provide safe and nurturing homes within an appropriate timeframe (Australian Federal Parliament House of Representatives Standing Committee on Social Policy and Legal Affairs, 2018).

However, while there is an obvious need to provide better support for parents and introduce stronger policies to prevent the occurrence of maltreatment, children still need to be protected from harm. There is now a wide body of evidence showing the extent to which abuse and neglect compromise children's long-term life chances (summarised in Brown & Ward, 2013); as long as child maltreatment remains prevalent, there will be a need for child protection interventions. This study adds to the body of evidence that shows that, where children cannot safely remain with or return to their birth families, adoption offers opportunities for recovery-to-normal development. Policies that aim to place these children for adoption are based on evidence that indicates this will offer them a better chance of stability, stronger long-term commitment, a higher level of support through the transition to adulthood and a greater chance of becoming part of a family for life than foster care is currently able to offer either in Australia or in many other countries. The evidence presented in this book suggests that for most of the Barnardos adoptees, this proved to be the case.

Key Points

- Summary findings from the research study indicate the extreme vulnerability of the adoptees at entry to their adoptive homes and the developmental recovery most achieved after placement. Adoptees were more vulnerable than care leavers, but more achieved successful functioning in adulthood. In comparison with long-term foster care, adoption appears to have provided children with greater stability, a stronger sense of security and belonging and more support as they made the transition to adulthood. The commitment of adoptive parents acted as a powerful protective factor, enhancing resilience and mitigating some of the consequences of early adversity.
- Most of the adoptees had experienced significant abuse and neglect before separation from birth parents. Greater focus in child protection policy on carefully targeted family support that addressed parents' difficulties might have prevented abuse from occurring and enabled some adoptees to remain with birth families.
- Early experiences of trauma had an enduring impact on the adoptees' wellbeing. There is a need for long-term support for children who are struggling with the sequelae of abuse, wherever they are living. For adoptive families this needs to be reflected in robust post-adoption support services, available for families to call upon at their discretion.
- The findings indicate a need for more robust assessments of parental capacity to change and more timely decision-making where children cannot remain safely with birth parents.
- Open adoption of children from care has brought the role of adoptive parents closer to that of foster carers. This needs to be reflected in recruitment and training policy and practice.
- Although most adoptees and adoptive parents thought that post-adoption contact had been beneficial in the long run, it had often been

problematic, and 28% of adoptees thought they had not benefitted. Contact needs to be carefully managed and tailored to the needs of each child.

- Policies that required adoptive parents to organise and be present during contact sessions were valued, as were opportunities for older adoptees to make their own decisions about contact arrangements.
- Policies designed to strengthen families and reduce the prevalence of abuse are clearly necessary; however, the study adds to the body of evidence that shows the benefits of adoption from care for children who have suffered or are likely to suffer significant harm and who cannot safely live with birth families.

References

Adoption UK. (2020). *Adoption barometer: A stocktake of adoption in the UK*. Adoption UK. https://www.adoptionuk.org/Handlers/Download.ashx?IDMF=c79a0e7d-1899-4b0f-ab96-783b4f678c9a. Accessed 2 Oct 2020

Australian Federal Parliament House of Representatives Standing Committee on Social Policy and Legal Affairs. (2018). *Breaking barriers: A national adoption framework for Australian children – Inquiry into local adoption*. Australian Government.

Backhaus, S., Ott, E., & Ward, H. (2019). *International network on infants, toddlers and child protection: Report of inaugural meeting*. Oxford University.

Biehal, N., Ellison, S., Baker, C., & Sinclair, I. (2010). *Belonging and permanence: Outcomes in long-term foster care and adoption*. BAAF.

Blakey, J. M., Leathers, S. J., Lawler, M., Washington, T., Natschke, C., Strand, T., & Walton, Q. (2012). A review of how states are addressing placement stability. *Children and Youth Services Review, 34*(2), 369–378.

Broadhurst, K., Alrouh, B., Mason, C., Ward, H., Holmes, L., Ryan, M., & Bowyer, S. (2018). *Born into care: Newborn babies subject to care proceedings in England*. The Nuffield Family Justice Observatory: Nuffield Foundation.

Brown, R., & Ward, H. (2013). *Decision-making within a child's timeframe, Report to Department for Education*. Childhood Wellbeing Research Centre.

Brown, R., Ward, H., Blackmore, J., Thomas, C., & Hyde-Dryden, G. (2016). *Eight-year-olds identified in infancy as at risk of harm: Report of a prospective longitudinal study. RR543.* Department for Education. https://assets.publishing.service.gov.uk/government/uploads/system/uploads/attachment_data/file/534376/Eight-year-olds_identified_in_infancy_as_at_risk_of_harm.pdf. Accessed 20 Oct 2020

Cashmore, J. (2000). What the research tells us: Permanency planning, adoption and foster care. *Children Australia, 25*(4), 17–23.

Cashmore, J., & Paxman, M. (2007). *Wards leaving care: Four to five years on.* University of New South Wales.

Davies, C., & Ward, H. (2012). *Safeguarding children across services.* Jessica Kingsley Publishers.

DelBalzo, J. (2007). *Unlearning adoption: A guide to family preservation and protection.* Book Surge Publishing USA: booksurge.com.

Delfabbro, P., King, D., & Barber, J. (2005). Children in foster care – Five years on. *Children Australia, 35*(1), 22–30.

Dodgson, L. (2014, November 11). Post-adoption contact: all change or more of the same? *Family Law Week.* https://www.familylawweek.co.uk/site.aspx?i=ed136606. Accessed 18 Dec 2020.

Felitti, V. J., Anda, R. F., Nordenberg, D., Williamson, D. F., Spitz, A. M., Edwards, V., Koss, M. P., & Marks, J. S. (1998). Relationship of childhood abuse and household dysfunction to many of the leading causes of death in adults. The adverse childhood experiences (ACE) study. *American Journal of Preventive Medicine, 14*(4), 245–258.

Gerin, M. I., Hanson, E., Viding, E., & McCrory, E. J. (2019). A review of childhood maltreatment, latent vulnerability and the brain: Implications for clinical practice and prevention. *Adoption and Fostering, 43*(3), 310–328.

Grotevant, H. D., Wrobel, G. M., Von Korff, L., Skinner, B., Newell, J., Friese, S., & McRoy, R. G. (2007). Many faces of openness in adoption: Perspectives of adopted adolescents and their parents. *Adoption Quarterly, 10*(3–4), 79–101.

Holtan, A., Handegard, B., Thornblad, R., & Vis, S. (2013). Placement disruption in long-term kinship and non-kinship foster care (2013). *Children and Youth Services Review, 35,* 1087–1094.

Humphreys, C., & Kiraly, M. (2011). High-frequency family contact: A road to nowhere for infants. *Child & Family Social Work, 16,* 1–11.

Livingston Smith and Donaldson Adoption Institute. (2004). *Facilitating adoptions from care*. BAAF.

McCrory, E. J., Gerin, M. I., & Viding, E. (2017). Annual research review: Childhood maltreatment, latent vulnerability and the shift to preventative psychiatry – the contribution of functional brain imaging. *Journal of Child Psychology and Psychiatry, 58*(4), 338–357.

Mendes, P. (2020). *Happier 21st? Victoria's out-of-home care comes of age*. Lens Monash University. https://lens.monash.edu/2020/12/03/1381837/victorias-out-of-home-care-comes-of-age. Accessed 17 Dec 2020.

Neil, E. (2003). Understanding other people's perspectives: Tasks for adopters in open adoption. *Adoption Quarterly, 6*(3), 3–30.

Neil, E., Beek, M., & Ward, E. (2015). *Contact after adoption: A longitudinal study of post adoption contact arrangements*. Coram BAAF.

Palacios, J., Brodzinsky, D., Grotevant, H., Johnson, D., Juffer, F., Martinez-Morah, L., Muhamedrahimove, R., Selwyn, J., Simmonds, J., & Tarren-Sweeney, M. (2019). Adoption in the service of child protection: An international interdisciplinary perspective. *Psychology, Public Policy, and Law, 25*(2), 57–72.

Parker, R. (1999). *Adoption now: Messages from research*. Wiley.

Royal Commission into Institutional Responses to Child Sexual Abuse. (2017). *Final report*. Commonwealth of Australia. https://www.childabuseroyalcommission.gov.au/sites/default/files/final_report_-_preface_and_executive_summary.pdf. Accessed 14 Jan 2021.

Rutter, M., Beckett, C., Castle, J., Colvert, E., Kreppner, J., Mehta, M., Stevens, S., & Sonuga-Barke, E. (2007). Effects of profound early institutional deprivation: An overview of findings from a UK longitudinal study of Romanian adoptees. *European Journal of Developmental Psychology, 4*(3), 332–350.

Schrover, M. (2020, April). Parenting, citizenship and belonging in Dutch adoption debates 1900–1995. *Identities*. https://doi.org/10.1080/1070289X.2020.1757252.

Selwyn, J. (2017). The adoption of looked after maltreated children in England: Challenges, opportunities and outcomes. *Developing Practice: The Child, Youth and Family Work Journal, 47*(2017), 50–63.

Selwyn, J., Sturgess, W., Quinton, D., & Baxter, C. (2006). *Costs and outcomes of non-infant adoption*. BAAF.

Selwyn, J., Wijedasa, D., & Meakings, S. (2014). *Beyond the adoption order: Challenges, interventions and adoption disruptions, RR 336*. Department for Education.

Sonuga-Barke, E., Kennedy, M., Kumsta, R., Knights, N., Golm, D., Rutter, M., Maughan, B., Schlotz, W., & Kreppner, J. (2017). Child-to-adult neuro-developmental and mental health trajectories after early life deprivation: The young adult follow-up of the longitudinal English and Romanian adoptees study. Lancet, 389, 1539–1548.

Staines, J., Golding, K., & Selwyn, J. (2019). Nurturing attachments parenting program: The relationship between adopters' parental reflective functioning and perception of their children's difficulties. Developmental Child Welfare, 1(2), 143–158.

Stein, M., & Munro, E. (2008). Young people's transitions from care to adulthood: International research and practice. Jessica Kingsley.

Strahl, B., van Breda, A., Mann-Feder, V., & Schroer, W. (2020). A multi-national comparison of care-leaving policy and legislation. Journal of International and Comparative Social Policy, 2020, 1–16.

Thomas, C. (2013). Adoption for looked after children: Messages from research. BAAF.

Thomas, C. (2018). The care crisis review: Factors contributing to national increases in numbers of looked after children and applications for care orders. Family Rights Group.

Triseliotis, J. (2002). Long-term foster care or adoption? The evidence examined. Child & Family Social Work, 7, 23–33.

Turkington, S., & Taylor, B. J. (2009). Post-adoption face-to-face contact with birth parents: Prospective adopters' views. Child Care in Practice, 15(1), 21–38.

Vinnerljung, B., Sallnäs, M., & Berlin, M. (2014). Placement breakdowns in long-term foster care – A regional Swedish study. Child & Family Social Work, 22(1), 15–25.

Ward, H. (2009). Patterns of instability: Moves within the English care system: Their reasons, contexts and consequences. Children and Youth Services Review, 31, 1113–1118.

Ward, H., Brown, R., Blackmore, J., Hyde-Dryden, G., & Thomas, C. (2019). Identifying parents who show capacity to make and sustain positive changes when infants are at risk of significant harm. Developing Practice, 54, 47–61.

Ward, H., Brown, R., & Hyde-Dryden, G. (2014). Assessing parental capacity to change when children are on the edge of care: an overview of current research evidence. RR369. Centre for Child and Family Research, Loughborough

University and Department for Education. https://assets.publishing. service.gov.uk/government/uploads/system/uploads/attachment_data/ file/330332/RR369_Assessing_parental_capacity_to_change_Final.pdf. Accessed 30 Dec 2020.

Ward, J., & Smeeton, J. (2017). The end of non-consensual adoption: Promoting the wellbeing of children in care. *Practice, 29*(1), 55–73.

Wulczyn, F., & Chen, L. (2017). *Placement changes among children and young people in out-of-home care. Pathways of Care longitudinal study: Outcomes of children and young people in out-of-home care. Research Report 8.* NSW Department of Family and Community Services.

Appendices

Appendix 1: Methodology

Aims and Objectives

The overall aim of the study was to explore the value of open adoption as a route to permanence for abused and neglected children in out-of-home care who cannot safely return to their birth families.

There were four broad research questions:

- What have been the life outcomes of those children and young people who were adopted from care?
- What contributed to their positive or negative life trajectories?
- How has open adoption been experienced by adoptive parents and adoptees in New South Wales?
- What are the views of young people who have been adopted about the importance of adoption to them?

© The Author(s) 2022
H. Ward et al., *Outcomes of Open Adoption from Care*,
https://doi.org/10.1007/978-3-030-76429-6

Sample

The initial sample was the full cohort of 210 children who were adopted through Find-a-Family between 1987 and 2013, their birth parents and their adoptive parents. Figure A1.1 shows the subsamples of adoptees and their adoptive parents at subsequent stages of data collection.

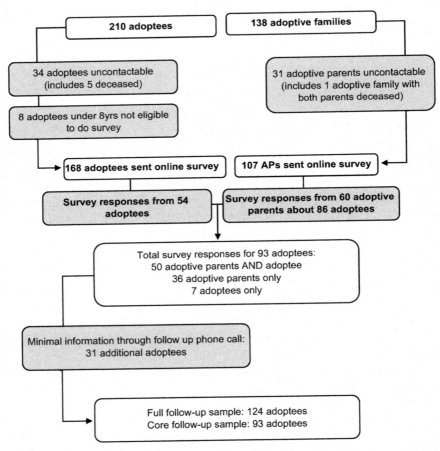

Fig. A1.1 Flowchart showing subsamples at different stages of data collection

Stage One: Baseline Data on Full Cohort

Baseline data on the full cohort of 210 adoptees, their birth parents and their adoptive parents were collected from documents on hard copy files and the Barnardos electronic case management system (LACES) at the time the adoption order was made. The children had been placed with 138 adoptive families and data concerning their adoptive parents were also obtained from application forms and electronic and hard copy files.

Data items were collected on two spreadsheets. The first covered demographic information about the adoptees, their birth parents and their adoptive parents; data from birth parents about factors related to the court's decision to place the child permanently away from home, such as age at time of adoptee's birth, substance use, disability, mental health issues, domestic abuse, incarceration, welfare history; and data from adoptive parents about education and employment history, economic status and motivation to adopt. The second spreadsheet mapped the children's pathways through the adoption process from first entry to care to placement with the adoptive family. The data included information about children's experiences of abuse and neglect prior to separation, age at first entry to care, age at entry to the permanency programme, age at adoption, nature of adoption application (consented, contested or not contested),[1] contact with birth family members, sibling status and evidence of behavioural problems and/or special needs at permanent placement.

Data retrieval was undertaken by social work students from the Universities of Sydney, New South Wales, Boston and Newcastle, and their work was checked for completeness and accuracy by a senior practitioner with knowledge of the adoptions. During the analysis, some data items were identified as missing and a supplementary search of the files was undertaken by paid independent social workers. This process also allowed for checking the accuracy of the initial data. The data were collected on Excel spreadsheets and imported to an SPSS database for analysis.

---

[1] 'Consented' adoption is an adoption application where all required consents to the adoption have been obtained; a 'contested' adoption is an application that is opposed in Court by a parent or other party to the adoption; a 'not contested' adoption is an application where all required consents have not been obtained but where the application is not opposed in Court.

Stage Two: Follow-Up Survey

Attempts were made to locate all 210 adoptees, together with their adoptive parents. (It was not possible to trace and follow up birth parents within the budget and timeframe.) Potential participants were contacted through a variety of channels. Some of the adoptees or their families were still known to Barnardos or still lived at the same address; other potential participants were located through Facebook searches. An advertisement was also placed in the RSVP column of the *Sydney Morning Herald* but only produced one response.

Two adoptive parents (in one household) and five adoptees were known to have died; a further 29 adoptees and 30 adoptive parents could not be contacted. In 2016, all other adoptees and their adoptive parents were invited to participate in an online survey, providing information about their current situation, adoption experiences and outcomes. Eight adoptees were considered too young (under eight years old) to participate, although their adoptive parents were invited to do so.

Four questionnaires were designed for completion by adoptees. These included age-specific questions for adoptees aged 8–11, 12–13, 14–17 and 18 years and over, together with a core group of about 20 questions that were asked of adoptees of all ages. Core questions covered issues such as contact with birth family members, life story work, views on adoption and contact. Age-specific questions covered issues such as educational progress, employment, relationships with partners and accommodation.

Adult adoptees were also asked to respond to the following series of questions, designed to explore their experiences of parenting after they had entered their adoptive homes:

Do your adoptive parents:

- help if you've got a problem?
- listen to you?
- praise you for doing well?
- do things with you that are just for fun?
- help you feel part of the family?
- spend time just talking to you?
- give you cards and presents?

Responses were then combined into a composite variable reflecting adoptees' views concerning whether they had experienced sensitive parenting.

Younger children were invited to complete questionnaires with the help of their adoptive parents and were not asked questions that touched on potentially sensitive areas such as their sense of security within the adoptive family or their relationship with their adoptive parents.

In addition to the questionnaire, adoptees were asked to complete a standardised measure of wellbeing (the Australian Child Wellbeing Project (ACWP, 2014) materials for 8- to 17-year-olds), and the WHOQOL-BREF (World Health Organisation Brief Quality of Life Assessment) for adoptees aged 18 and over (WHO, 1996). The ACWP measure was selected because it was created to explore profiles of different groups of Australian children and young people in terms of their wellbeing, with a particular focus on those who may experience disadvantage, including children in out-of-home care, and it was thought that these might provide useful comparisons with the Barnardos adoptees. The WHOQOL-BREF is an internationally recognised scale which is widely used to measure physical, mental and social wellbeing of adults. It was selected both because Australian population norms are available and because it had previously been utilised in an Australian study of adoption outcomes (Kenny et al., 2012) that offers some comparisons with the current study (see below). Completion of these measures was patchy, and the data from the ACWP were not considered sufficiently robust for analysis.

Two questionnaires were designed for completion by adoptive parents. These included age-specific questions relating to those whose adopted children were aged 4 to 17 or 18 and over, together with a core group of about 60 questions that were asked of all adoptive parents. Core questions covered issues such as changes to household composition after placement; adoptees' developmental progress; behavioural issues; continuing support for adoptees who had left home; contact with birth family members; impact of adoption on relationships with partner and birth children; experiences of post-adoption support; views on adoption and contact. About a third of all questions were designed to provide data on key outcome variables, such as the adoptees' current domiciles or their educational qualifications, that duplicated data collected from adoptees and could be utilised to fill in the gaps where responses from adoptees were missing or incomplete.

In addition to the questionnaire, parents of adoptees aged under 18 were asked to complete the Child Behaviour Checklist (CBCL) (Achenbach and Rescorla 2001), a standardised measure that is widely used to assess socio-emotional development in pre-school and school-aged children and young people. Australian norms are available for both the CBCL and the Strengths and Difficulties Questionnaire (SDQ) (Lehmann et al., 2014). However, the CBCL was selected because it had been used in two studies that might offer comparisons with the current study: the NSW Pathways of Care Longitudinal Study (POCLS) of children and young people who entered care on final orders in 2010–2011 (Paxman et al., 2014), and Fernandez's study of a cohort of children from the Find-a-Family programme (Fernandez, 2008, 2009).

The different instruments completed by the participants are detailed in Table A1.1.

Survey materials were piloted with six adoptive parents and ten adoptees. Minor adjustments were made to the final questionnaires to reflect the comments made by the pilot group. The survey was completed online using Survey Monkey. To ensure confidentiality, all participants were asked to respond using an anonymised research number.

Table A1.1 Online questionnaires administered

Age of adoptees	Instruments completed by adoptees	Instruments completed by adoptive parent (Primary carer)
4–7 years	N/A	Questionnaire E CBCL*
8–11 years	Questionnaire A ACWP** (Year 4)	Questionnaire E CBCL
12–13 years	Questionnaire B ACWP (Year 6)	Questionnaire E CBCL
14–17 years	Questionnaire C ACWP (Year 8)	Questionnaire E CBCL
18 years and older	Questionnaire D WHOQOL_BREF*** (Year 8)	Questionnaire F

*Australian Child Wellbeing Project (www.australianchildwellbeing.com.au)
**Child Behaviour Checklist (www.aseba.org)
***World Health Organisation Quality of Life (www.who.int/substance_abuse/research_tools/en/english_whoqol.pdf)

The Stage Two Follow-Up Sample

The survey yielded responses from 54 of the 210 (26%) adoptees (37 aged 18+ and 17 aged under 18). Adoptive parents were invited to complete a separate survey questionnaire for each child who had been placed with them. They provided information on their experiences of adopting 86/210 adoptees (41%). These data overlap on a number of variables so that, overall, we have responses concerning 93/210 (44%) adoptees and 86/128 (67%) adoptive parents; these form the **core follow-up sample**.

In an attempt to follow up non-participants, a number of phone calls were made and interviews held with Barnardos key workers. In the course of this exercise, some minimum outcome data were collected on a further 31 adoptees. This was not collected systematically and most has not been included in the main analysis. However, some objectively verifiable data items, such as whether the adoptee was still alive or whether they were still living with adoptive parents at the time of the survey could, in our opinion, be legitimately added to data on the same items collected through the surveys. Taken together, these minimal outcome data are available for 124 (60%) adoptees.

Potential Bias of Core Follow-Up Sample

There are 93 adoptees in the core follow-up sample, 46 young women and 47 young men; 33 were aged under 18 at the time the survey was completed in 2016 and 60 were aged 18 and over. For 7 young people, data are available from the adoptee alone; for 39 from the adoptive parent alone and for 47, from both the adoptee and the adoptive parent.

These 93 adoptees in the core follow-up sample were compared on a number of key variables with the 117 adoptees for whom there were no follow-up data, in order to ascertain whether there was any significant sample bias. Detailed analysis of potential bias is presented in Appendix 2. The two groups showed very similar profiles in terms of age, gender, type of abuse experienced while living with birth parents; number of adverse childhood experiences; and total number of placements before their permanent placement. Before being placed with their adoptive parents, the 117

Table A1.2 Comparisons between Stage One only group and core follow-up sample

	Stage One only (N = 117)					Stage Two (N = 93)				
	Mean	Std. Deviation	Range	Min	Max	Mean	Std. Deviation	Range	Min	Max
Age at first notification of maltreatment	14.4*	23.6	140	-6	134	24.1*	36.3	160	-6	154
Age at first separation	28.6	29.4	141	0	141	36.07	39.4	155	0	155
Age (months) at permanent placement	57.1	38.7	159	1	160	60.5	45.6	169	3	172

*significant to $p < 0.05$

adoptees who were not followed up (Stage One only group) had slightly more failed restoration attempts (m = 0.43, sd = 0.62) than those in the core follow-up sample (m = 0.33, sd = 0.63); the Stage One only group also showed a slightly higher prevalence of behavioural problems (52% vs 44%). However, neither of these differences reached statistical significance.

The only statistically significant difference between the two groups was that, at the time of first notification of maltreatment, the core follow-up sample were, on average, 9.7 months older (m = 24.1, sd = 36.6) than the adoptees in the Stage One only group (m = 14.4, sd = 23.6) (see Table A1.2).[2] This difference may also be reflected in findings that the follow-up sample were slightly older (m = 36.7, sd = 39.4) when first separated from birth parents than those in Stage One only (m = 28.6, sd = 29.4) and also when they were placed with their adoptive parents (follow-up sample m = 60.5, sd = 45.6, Stage One only m = 57.1, sd = 38.7), although these differences were not statistically significant. Length of exposure to abuse and neglect has been identified as having a significant impact on outcomes for children placed away from home (Rousseau et al., 2015). Both groups displayed a wide range of vulnerability factors. However, our vulnerability ratings (Chap. 3) showed no statistically significant differences between the follow-up sample and those who were not followed up.

---

[2] $t = 2.214$; $df = 144.8$; $p = 0.028$.

Stage Three: Interviews with Adoptees and Adoptive Parents

The purpose of the interviews was to explore how open adoption had been experienced by both adoptive parents and adult adoptees. Resources were not available at this time to explore how it was experienced by birth family members. The aim was to interview about 20 adult adoptees and 20 adoptive parents.

The interviews were semi-structured, using schedules designed to produce complementary responses from adoptive parents and adoptees. Questions covered expectations of adoption; relationships within the adoptive family; how contact was experienced by adoptee and adoptive parent; relationships with birth family members; transparency and open communication within the adoptive family; and transitions to adulthood. The interview schedules also included Cantril's ladder of life scale (Cantril, 1965). Before the interview, adoptees were also asked to complete Brodzinsky's Adoption Communication Openness Scale (Brodzinsky, 2006) and adoptive parents were asked to complete a version of the same scale in which minor adaptations had been made to the wording to make it appropriate to them. While this scale has not yet been formally validated, it has proved valuable in identifying how communicative openness is experienced by adoptees.

Interview Selection

Figure A1.2 outlines the process of selection of interview participants
Seventy-two respondents who completed the survey for adult adoptees, or their adoptive parents, expressed a willingness to be interviewed. These included 21 dyads, where both adoptee and their adoptive parent agreed to be interviewed, and 30 cases in which either the adoptee (5) or the adoptive parent (25) offered to participate; in other words, there was the potential to explore further how open adoption was experienced by 51 adult adoptees and/or their adoptive parents. Twenty-nine (57%) of these adult adoptees were young women and 22 (43%) were young men: within this population, there were also nine sibling groups, two families of three siblings and seven of two siblings who had been placed together.

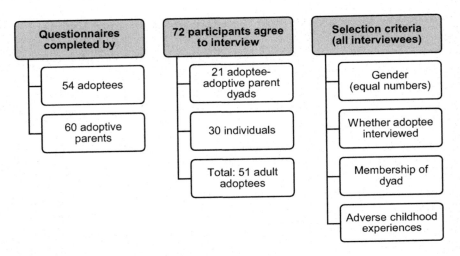

Fig. A1.2 Interview selection process

Fewer than one in four (12: 24%) were still living with their adoptive parents: the average age of these adult adoptees was 31 and many had left home as part of a normative transition to adulthood. Before being placed for adoption, the potential interview group had experienced substantial adversity: 30 (71%) had experienced four or more adverse childhood experiences and 27 (63%) had had three or more out-of-home placements since entering care.

The initial plan was to interview all those groups where both the adoptee and an adoptive parent had indicated their willingness to take part (22 dyads: 22 adoptees including two sibling pairs and 20 adoptive parents), on the grounds that these would give complementary, and sometimes contradictory, perspectives on the same situation. However, this group was significantly skewed towards young women (14: 63%). We therefore decided to aim for a quota sample of equal numbers of young men and young women and adoptive parents, matched for vulnerability according to numbers of adverse childhood experiences (ACEs) (see Felitti et al., 1998). Selection was based first on gender; second, on whether the adoptee (rather than the adoptive parent alone) was willing to be interviewed; third, on membership of a dyad and fourth, on matched number of adverse childhood experiences.

Table A1.3 Interview sample (*N* = 24)

ACEs	Male	Female
1	3	1
2	1	1
3	1	0
4	2	3
5	3	2
6	2	1
7	1	3
8	0	0
Total	13	11

Eleven young men had agreed to be interviewed: eight of them were members of a dyad, their adoptive parents having also agreed to participate, and three were lone volunteers. This group was then matched by ACEs with 11 young women and their adoptive parents, all of whom were members of dyads, yielding a potential sample of 22 adoptees and 19 adoptive parents. Contact was made to arrange interview appointments and 6 young men and 11 young women and their adoptive parents were interviewed. A further three young men were interviewed without the participation of their adoptive parents. Four adoptive parents of young men who did not participate were also interviewed. Altogether 20 adoptees and 21 adoptive parents (15 of whom were adoptive mothers) were interviewed: the interviews focused on 24 adult adoptees.

Table A1.3 gives details of the 24 adoptees who formed the focus of the interviews (the **interview sample**), showing the extent of their vulnerability as demonstrated by the number of ACEs they had encountered.

Interview Process

The interviews were undertaken face to face, except for one via Skype where distances proved excessive. All dyads were interviewed separately. Interviewees were given the choice of whether they preferred to be interviewed by the manager of the adoption programme at the time of the adoption, another Barnardos employee or an external interviewer who had no relationship with Barnardos. There were practical reasons why Barnardos staff were involved in conducting the interviews—and undoubtedly, this involvement encouraged some participants to come forward; on the other hand, the option of offering a choice of an external interviewer was introduced in order to mitigate the risk of bias.

Ethical Procedures

Formal ethical approval for all stages of the study was given by Loughborough University, UK. Before completing questionnaires or agreeing to be interviewed, all participants were made fully aware of the purpose of the study and the subjects to be covered and asked to give formal, informed consent. They were also informed that they could decide not to answer certain questions, stop completing the questionnaire or end the interview at any time, and have their contribution deleted from the database if they so wished, with no repercussions for withdrawal. Because the interviews touched on subjects that could be distressing, interviewers were ready to give information and/or to assist in referring participants to appropriate local services if required. The limits of confidentiality if abuse was disclosed were also clarified.

Analysis

Quantitative data were analysed using SPSS v22. A range of statistical methods were used to make cross-sectional and longitudinal comparisons between groups of children with different characteristics and experiences. Standardised measures were scored according to the accompanying guidance.

Interviews were recorded and transcribed by an external agency. The data were then analysed thematically at Loughborough University, UK, and Oxford University, UK. Both transcription and analysis were undertaken without involvement from Barnardos, in order to guard against potential bias. Qualitative analysis initially followed the structure of the interviews, which had been based on key themes. Further analysis, designed to reveal additional, unanticipated themes, followed the five key recognised stages of: familiarisation with the data, coding, developing and applying an analytical framework, charting and interpretation (Gale et al., 2013).

Appendix 2: Technical Notes on Stage One and Stage Two Sample Comparison

The sample was split into two groups based on whether or not data were available for Stage One only (117 adoptees: not followed up) or for both Stages One and Two (93 adoptees: core follow-up sample).

Gender Characteristics of Sample

Although the gender split was relatively even, there were slightly more boys than girls in both groups (Stage One only group: 63 (54%) males to 54 (46%) females; core follow-up sample 47 (50.5%) males to 46 (49.5%) females). Although there was a higher proportion of boys in the Stage One only group, the difference was not statistically significant (χ^2 = 0.227, df = 1, p = 0.63).

Types of Abuse

Table A2.1 shows the differences between the two groups in the types of abuse they had experienced. Although a higher proportion of adoptees in the core follow-up sample had been physically abused (41% vs 29%), the difference was not statistically significant. There were no significant differences between the two groups in other types of abuse experienced or in the proportion who had experienced polyvictimsation (all four types of abuse).

Table A2.1 Types of abuse experienced: Stage One only (N = 117) and core follow-up (N = 93) samples

Abuse type	Stage One only (N = 117)		Core follow-up sample (N = 93)		
	n	%	n	%	X^2
Neglect	91	78	73	78	X^2 = 0.016; df = 1; p = 0.901
Physical abuse	34	29	38	41	X^2 = 3.202; df = 1; p = 0.074
Emotional abuse	83	71	68	73	X^2 = 0.122; df = 1; p= 0.727
Sexual abuse	24	21	23	25	X^2 = 0.531; df = 1; p = 0.466
Polyvictimisation	11	9	12	13	X^2 = 0.815; df = 2; p = 0.665

Table A2.2 Adverse childhood experiences: Stage One only (N = 117) and core follow-up (N = 93) samples

	Samples	N	Mean	Std. Deviation	Independent samples t-test
Number of ACES	Stage One only group	117	4.47	1.83	t = 0.497; df = 208; p = 0.62
	Core follow-up sample	93	4.34	1.82	

Total Number of Adverse Childhood Experiences

Table A2.2 shows the differences between the two groups in the mean number of adverse childhood experiences (ACEs) encountered before entering the Find-a-Family programme. No significant differences were found (p = 0.62).

Behavioural Problems

Table A2.3 shows the differences between the two groups in the prevalence of behavioural problems identified at entry to their adoptive homes. No significant differences were found (p = 0.246).

Table A2.3 Identified behaviour problems: Stage One only (N = 117) and core follow-up (N = 93) samples

	Stage One only (N = 117)		Core follow-up sample (N = 93)		
	n	%	n	%	X²
Behavioural problems	61	52	41	44	X² = 1.34; df = 1; p = 0.246

Age (Months) at First Notification

The children in the core follow-up sample were nearly ten months older than those in the Stage One only group when abuse or neglect was first identified and children's services notified (Table A2.4). The difference is statistically significant at the p < 0.05 level: p = 0.028.

Age (Months) of First Separation

The children in the core follow-up sample were on average 7.5 months older than those in the Stage One only group when they were first separated from their birth parents (see Table A2.4). However, this difference was not statistically significant (p = 0.131).

Age at Permanent Placement

However, although the core follow-up sample were 7.5 months older at notification, they were only 3.4 months older than the Stage One only group when they reached their adoptive homes (Table A2.4). This age difference was not significant (p = 0.567).

Table A2.4 Mean ages at first notification, first separation and permanent placement: Stage One only (N = 117) and core follow-up (N = 93) samples

	Samples	N	Mean	Std. Deviation	Independent samples t-test
Age (months) at first notification	Stage One only group	117	14.35	23.60	t = -2.214; df = 145; p = 0.028
	Core follow-up sample	93	24.12	36.33	
Age (months) at first separation	Stage One only group	117	28.60	29.39	t = -1.570; df = 164; p = 0.131
	Core follow-up sample	93	36.07	39.37	
Age (months) at permanent placement	Stage One only group	117	57.06	38.379	t = -0.574; df = 181; p = 0.567
	Core follow-up sample	93	60.46	45.579	

Number of Restoration Attempts and Care Placements

Before they entered their adoptive homes, a third (32%) of the adoptees had experienced a failed attempt at reunification with their birth families. There had been slightly more attempts to reunite children in the Stage One only group (mean = 0.43 vs mean = 0.33) (Table A2.5), but the difference is not significant (p = 0.280).

Both groups of adoptees had experienced an average of about three placements in out-of-home care before entering their adoptive homes; however, the Stage One only group had experienced slightly more (mean = 3.556 vs 3.075) (Table A2.5). The difference is not significant (p = 0.331).

Table A2.5 Restoration attempts and placements in care: Stage One only (*N* = 117) and core follow-up (*N* = 93) samples

	Samples	*n*	Mean	Std. Deviation	Independent samples t-test
Restoration attempts	Stage One only group	117	0.43	0.620	t = 1.082; df = 208; p = 0.280
	Core follow-up sample	93	0.33	0.63	
Placements in care	Stage One only group	117	3.556	3.998	t = 0.975; df = 208; p = 0.331
	Core follow-up sample	93	3.075	2,875	

Table A2.6 Mean ages at follow-up: Stage One only (*N* = 117) and core follow-up (*N* = 93) samples

	Samples	*N*	Mean	Std. Deviation	Independent samples t-test
Age at follow-up	Stage One only group	117	22.60	9.371	t = -0.612; df = 183.5; p = 0.541
	Core follow-up sample	93	23.46	10.760	

Age at Follow-Up

There was less than one month's difference in the average ages of the two groups (Table A2.6). At the end of October 2016, the cut-off point for the follow-up survey, their mean ages were 22.6 vs 23.5; the difference is not significant (*p* = 0.541).

Appendix 3: Studies Identifying Risk Factor Thresholds

Vulnerability factor	Risk factor thresholds	Supporting evidence
Abuse type: number present	Extreme: All 4 High: Two or three factors Low: One or less	Finkelhor et al. (2011)
Abuse type: Sexual abuse (others types absent, one other, or two other)	Extreme: SA plus other types of abuse High: SA alone Low: No SA	Nalavany et al. (2008) Smith, S.L. & Howard, J.A. (1991)
Age at first separation: older than 3 yrs when into care (no gender differences)	Extreme: 48 months or more High:24-47 months Low: 0-23 months	Zeanah et al. (2011) Selwyn, J., Meakings S. & Wijedasa, D. (2015)
Time between first notification of abuse and first separation from birth parents	Extreme: more than 32 months: High 16-31 months: Low 0-15 months	Rousseau, D. et al (2015) Selwyn, J., Frazer, L. & Quinton, D. (2006)
Time between first separation and permanence placement	Extreme: 48 months or more High: 24-47 months Low: 23 months or less	Selwyn, J., Meakings S. & Wijedasa, D. (2015)
Age at permanence placement	Extreme: 4th birthday (48 months) or older High:12-47 months Low: 0-11 months	Selwyn, J., Meakings S. & Wijedasa, D. (2015)
Time between placement and adoption order	Extreme: 24 months and more High: 12-23 months Low: 0-11 months	Selwyn, J., Meakings S. & Wijedasa, D. (2015)
Placement moves prior to adoption: two or moves more likely to experience a disruption to adoption	Extreme: Six or more placements High: 3-5 placements Low: 0-2 placements	Selwyn, J., Meakings S. & Wijedasa, D. (2015)
Behaviour problems	Extreme: Care +2+ High: Care +1 or Care+2 Low: Care	Osborn & Delfabbro (2006) White (2016)
ACEs	Extreme: 8 or more High: 4-7 Low: 0-3	Felitti et al. (1998) Dube et al. (2003)
Failed reunifications	Extreme: 4 or more High: 1-3 Low: 0	Wade et al. (2011 Farmer et al. (2011)

References

Achenbach, T. M., & Rescorla, L. A. (2001). *Manual for the ASEBA school-age forms and profiles.* University of Vermont, Research Center for Children, Youth, and Families.

Australian Child Wellbeing Project. (2014). http://www.australianchildwellbeing.com.au/acwp-database. Accessed 6 Oct 2020.

Brodzinsky, D. (2006). Family structural openness and communication openness as predictors in the adjustment of adopted children. *Adoption Quarterly, 9*(4), 1–18.

Cantril, H. (1965). *The pattern of human concerns.* Rutgers University Press.

Dube, S. R., Felitti, V. J., Dong, M., Chapman, D. P., Giles, W. H., & Anda, R. F. (2003). Childhood abuse, neglect and household dysfunction and the risk of illicit drug use: The adverse childhood experience (ACE) study. *Pediatrics, 111*(3), 564–572.

Farmer, E., Sturgess, W., O'Neill, T., & Wijedasa, D. (2011). *Achieving successful returns from care: What makes reunification work?* BAAF.

Felitti, V. J., Anda, R. F., Nordenberg, D., Williamson, D. F., Spitz, A. M., Edwards, V., Koss, M. P., & Marks, J. S. (1998). Relationship of childhood abuse and household dysfunction to many of the leading causes of death in adults. The adverse childhood experiences (ACE) study. *American Journal of Preventive Medicine, 14*(4), 245–258.

Fernandez, E. (2008). Unravelling emotional, behavioural and educational outcomes in a longitudinal study of children in foster-care. *British Journal of Social Work, 38*, 1283–1301.

Fernandez, E. (2009). Children's wellbeing in care: Evidence from a longitudinal study of outcomes. *Children and Youth Services Review, 31*, 1092–1100.

Finkelhor, D., Turner, H., Hamby, S., & Ormrod, R. (2011). Polyvictimization: Children's exposure to multiple types of violence, crime and abuse.. *US Department of Justice Juvenile Justice Bulleti* . https://www.ncjrs.gov/pdffiles1/ojjdp/235504.pdf. Accessed 28 Nov 2020.

Gale, N. K., Heath, G., Cameron, E., Rashid, S., & Redwood, S. (2013). Using the framework method for the analysis of qualitative data in multi-disciplinary health research. *BMC Medical Research Methodology, 13*, 117.

Kenny, P., Higgins, D., Soloff, C., & Sweid, R. (2012). *Past adoption experiences: National research study on the service response to past adoption practices. Research report no. 21.* Australian Institute of Family Studies.

Lehmann, S., Heiervang, E.R., Havik, T., & Havik, O. (2014). Screening foster children for mental disorders: Properties of the strengths and difficulties questionnaire. *PLoS ONE, 9*, 7: e102134. https://doi.org/10.1371/journal. pone.0102134.

Nalavany, B. A., Ryan, S. D., Howard, J. A., & Smith, S. L. (2008). Pre-adoptive child sexual abuse as a predictor of moves in care, adoption disruptions, and inconsistent adoptive parent commitment. *Child Abuse and Neglect, 3*(12), 1084–1088.

Osborn, A., & Delfabbro, P. H. (2006). Research article 4: An analysis of the social background and placement history of children with multiple and complex needs in Australian out-of-home care. *Communities, Children and Families Australia, 1*(1), 33–42.

Paxman, M., Tully, L., Burke, S., & Watson, J. (2014). Pathways of care: Longitudinal study on children and young people in out-of-home care in New South Wales. *Family Matters, 94*, 1–18.

Rousseau, D., Roze, M., Duverger, P., Fanello, S., & Tanguy, M. (2015). *Étude sure le devenir à long terme des jeunes enfants placès à la Pouponnière Sociale Saint Exupéry entre 1994 et 2001*. Rapport Rechereche St-Ex 2013–2014. Unite de Psychologie de l'Enfant et de l'Adolescent.

Selwyn, J., Frazer, L., & Quinton, D. (2006). Paved with good intentions: The pathway to adoption and the costs of delay. *British Journal of Social Work, 36*, 561–576.

Selwyn, J., Meakings, S., & Wijedasa, D. (2015). *Beyond the adoption order: Challenges, interventions and adoption disruptions*. BAAF.

Smith, S. L., & Howard, J. A. (1994). The impact of previous sexual abuse on children's adjustment in adoptive placement. *Social Work, 39*(5), 491–501.

Wade, J., Biehal, N., Farrelly, N., & Sinclair, I. (2011). *Caring for abused and neglected children: Making the right decisions for reunification or long-term care*. Jessica Kingsley Publishers.

White, K. R. (2016). Placement discontinuity for older children and adolescents who exit foster care through adoption or guardianship: A systematic review. *Child and Adolescent Social Work Journal, 33*, 377–394.

WHO. (1996). WHOQUOL-BREF. https://www.who.int/mental_health/media/en/76.pdf. Accessed 6 Oct 2020.

Zeanah, C. H., Gunnar, M. R., McCall, R. B., Kreppner, J. M., & Fox, N. A. (2011). Sensitive periods. *Monographs of the Society for Research in Child Development, 76*(4), 147–162.

Index[1]

---

[1] Note: Page numbers followed by 'n' refer to notes.

© The Author(s) 2022

H. Ward et al., *Outcomes of Open Adoption from Care*,

https://doi.org/10.1007/978-3-030-76429-6